ABBY EICHORN

Dear Trauma

Reclaiming My Identity After Domestic Abuse

First published by Abigail Eichorn 2026

Copyright © 2026 by Abigail Eichorn

All rights reserved. No part of this publication may be reproduced, stored, or transmitted in any form or by any means, electronic, mechanical, photocopying, recording, scanning, or otherwise without written permission from the publisher. It is illegal to copy this book, post it to a website, or distribute it by any other means without permission.

Abigail Eichorn asserts the moral right to be identified as the author of this work.

Abigail Eichorn has no responsibility for the persistence or accuracy of URLs for external or third-party Internet Websites referred to in this publication and does not guarantee that any content on such Websites is, or will remain, accurate or appropriate.

Designations used by companies to distinguish their products are often claimed as trademarks. All brand names and product names used in this book and on its cover are trade names, service marks, trademarks, and registered trademarks of their respective owners. The publishers and the book are not associated with any product or vendor mentioned in this book. None of the companies referenced within the book have endorsed the book.

First edition

ISBN: 979-8-9937491-3-6

Editing by Jennia Herold D'Lima
Editing by Kate Davis Jones
Editing by Brooks Becker
Cover art by Danna Mathias Steele

This book was professionally typeset on Reedsy.
Find out more at reedsy.com

For Roan

There is no agony like bearing an untold story inside you.

> Zora Neale Hurston, Dust Tracks on a Road

Contents

Preface		iii
1	A Letter to Myself	1
2	My First Letter to Clay	14
3	Gunfights are Lost in Milliseconds	22
4	In the Beginning	36
5	Letter to Clay's Law Enforcement Brothers	41
6	The Cycle of Financial Trauma	54
7	Letter To My Parents	64
8	Little Girl Gone	86
9	Dear Trauma	95
10	For the Love of Travel	113
11	Letter to Kim	122
12	Letter to Colonel Pritt	127
13	The First Time	134
14	Letter to Passersby	139
15	Sitting in the Muck	155
16	Letters to Clay	164
17	Italy	169
18	A Mother's Plea	179
19	Learning to Snowboard and Other Life Lessons	190
20	Letter to My Best Friends	204
21	Clay's Eulogy	221
22	Letter to Clay's Friends	228
23	Finding Humility in Costa Rica	236
24	Memories	245
25	Letter to Hunter	257
Notes		265

Preface

Trauma can create an agonizing story that sits inside you and generates turmoil, not just in your mind, but in a way that is felt to the core. It twists at your organs, sits heavy in your stomach and weighs on your heart. The best thing a person can do is to get their story out so that it no longer haunts their every action, every dream. And if you are one of the lucky ones, you'll get it out on your terms and not your trauma's terms, so that you have the chance to heal with some grace.

I have been struggling with getting my own story on paper and out of my body for years. The memories inside of me, the details of that horrible night and all the horrible nights before it, the sometimes uncontrollable, heaving sobs, the unending sadness and desperation casting a gray haze over my every waking moment, it all spun circles of anxiety in my mind. There were nights I couldn't sleep, or worse, when I would wake up screaming from nightmares, flailing my arms in defense, tears rolling down my face. There were days I couldn't force myself to eat or would burst randomly into tears in public places, abandoning my errands in embarrassment to make a quick escape. All my fear and grief would phase in and out, alternating between the anger and guilt. It seemed like everyone else had been given the opportunity to tell their accounts of the "facts." I needed to get my story out of my head and I needed to be heard.

After years of agony, I stumbled upon a quote from Zora Neale Hurston on a small card of paper included in a book subscription, and it hit me at my core. My untold story was killing me. I taped that card to my bathroom mirror, right in front of my face, and let it haunt me every morning until I could get the story out of my mind, onto paper, and finally find some peace.

I have a truth too, and unlike so many of those who think they have the facts about what happened, I was there. For most of this story, there were only three of us who lived the experiences, and only two of us are still living. My anguish comes from the race to tell my story, so that when that third voice is finally found, when he becomes old enough to start questioning his memories, he will know that there was more than one side of things.

This story is my memoir. It is my first memoir—I will have many more; my life is only just beginning. The recollections in these pages are just that—recollections based on my memories. Many of those memories have been damaged by the trauma and have only resurfaced from years of intensive therapy and meditation, but they are as I remember them. The story is told as my recovery has unfolded; time may be compressed or not flow chronologically in some instances. Trauma is a spiral that moves both up and down, sometimes coming full circle only to break again and continue falling back into its original pattern. The chapters ahead reflect that journey.

1

A Letter to Myself

February 16, 2019

Hey Pretty Girl,

    To be real, though, you're probably not looking very pretty right now if you're reading this letter. You don't have to wash your face yet, but in a few minutes you will, and you'll be happy that you bought dozens of face masks to help with the puffiness. But right now, just cry. Because you miss him and that's okay. He was your pillar for many years; you wouldn't be who you are today if it had not been for the ten years that you had with Clay. And you know what? He loved you too, he just didn't know how to show you, but he loved you so much.

    So, cry. Grieving is normal, and mourning has to happen if you are ever going to heal from this. It is the price you pay to have loved so hard. Be sad, be angry. But then, when you're done, I need you to be grateful for the life you still have. Because as much as he loved you when he was sober, he still hurt you when he drank. And Abby, he tried to kill you. He put a gun to your head, and if you hadn't been such an over-confident badass and fought for this life that you have now, he would have pulled that trigger. Clay would have killed you if you would have let him. But you didn't. And the life you have now is hard, but it is blessed. You are going to save lives and inspire millions with your story. *In this moment, it sucks so bad but close your eyes for just one minute and envision the difference you will make in all those young lives. And breathe. Just breathe. Write it down. Breathe some more. You're going to be just fine. Now, go wash your face.*

A letter to you, from you.
Because I love you the most,
Abby

* * *

"I just need a notebook." This was my first request to my mom when I woke up the next morning. My head was pounding so hard I couldn't open my eyes, my face was puffy and swollen from the continuous sobbing, my brain still in a fog. I had been hoping I would wake up and find it had all been an awful nightmare. But it wasn't. And I wasn't anywhere ready to start healing. But I needed to start writing it down. All these emotions in my body were screaming at me, pouring out in uncontrollable tears and leaving my head spinning in confusion. The fear and hurt came first, followed by a grief that rattled my body in a way that I had never been shaken before, throwing me to the ground, pinning me to the bed, unable to breathe. These emotions would cycle quickly, triggered by every passing thought about the night before and the ten years leading up to it.

I started listing the things I needed to do, the insurance companies that needed to be contacted, the people I needed to call, the things I would need to prioritize replacing. I would have to follow up with the detective working on my case. I wrote all the things I wanted to say to him, to Clay, but never would be able to. I started a list of mantras to help me begin processing what had just happened.

"Mantra: Start with washing your face."

"To do: Pro bono family attorneys?"

"Mantra: Don't let the bastards get you down."
"Need: straightener, blow dryer, dog food..."
"To Do: Victims advocacy, insurance, doctor—wrist, Rebecca at 2..."
"Mantra: Get out of your head."
"Need: folder, running shoes, panties..."
"To Do: get property back from PD, new debit card, call Pastor..."
"Mantra: You can't think about it that way."

As my husband, and for years as my best friend, Clay had repeated this last mantra to me over and over again. I could hear it in his voice for days after he was gone. I was trying to follow this advice, to "not think about it that way," to think about it in any other way that I could make sense of it all. Trying desperately not to think about the fear he must have been feeling in those final seconds of his life, or worse, wondering if he had any conscious thought left at all when his finger had pulled that trigger. Trying not to think about my destroyed home, covered in his blood and tear gas. Trying not to think about never seeing him again, that Hunter would never see him again.

For the past ten years, when things had gotten hard and life wasn't going the way I wanted, Clay would say things like, "Don't let the bastards get you down" and "Can't suck blood out of a turnip." He mostly meant it to be encouraging, but we had both been raised to push down our emotions and face the world head on with a tough exterior. In our different ways, we knew we were expected to "just get over it" and to pretend like nothing bad was happening. Our feelings and our disappointments were not to be expressed; there was no feeling sorry for ourselves, and you were lucky to get what you got, "blessed," and it was far better to pretend like the evil in the world didn't exist in yours. You were expected to sweep the really bad stuff under the rug and give Christian grace by making excuses for others. You put a smile on your face, turned the other cheek, and then charged forward like nothing was wrong. For generations, on both sides, this was the way it was.

This night, though, as with many nights over the next several years, I was faced with a small dilemma: I couldn't stop sobbing long enough to wash my face and I couldn't "not think about it that way." I didn't feel like I should be grateful just to be alive. Mantras weren't working; the positive self-talk wasn't getting me anywhere. I couldn't hold up the tough exterior I had been forcing myself to wear anymore.

I had dragged myself off the couch long enough to force feed myself dinner. I pulled myself off social media, which had increasingly become an escape from my reality, as I doom scrolled through other people's perfectly curated lives. I had fought with all the will I had left in my exhausted body just to stay out of bed for even just a few moments longer and stumbled into the bathroom. There I stood, doubled over the sink, the countertop the only thing holding my heavy body up, pools of black tears from my mascara splashing into the sink, loud uncontrollable sobs echoing off the bathroom walls and saliva stringing from my open mouth as I gasped for breath, my body shaking violently, convulsing.

I mean, this was some real ugly crying and unfortunately, it was not new. I had been prone to this type of crying for months. Once it started, I couldn't get it to stop, and I didn't know who to ask for help. Who would still be around to help me pull myself back together after all these months?

I felt as if I had worn out the understanding of even my closest group of girlfriends, and that I could no longer go to them for comfort after all this time. I don't know if this was true. But I had just returned from my second trip abroad, had checked some truly amazing experiences off my bucket list, and taken some leaps of huge success at work. I worried I was the envy of my married friends whose time and income was spent supporting their families while my social media accounts were filled with elaborate trips and great adventures. Little did they know that I envied them. They were living the life I wanted so desperately to have back but felt I had failed at entirely. And how could they understand why I was still crying about this, about the loss of a man who had tried so hard to take my life from me? No, I couldn't go to them, not anymore.

I thought I had met someone I could move on with, that I could finally break my ties to Clay and escape the chaos with someone who was good for me. I felt that was part of the reason this had happened. Clay had found out I was seeing someone new, and it had triggered his drinking, and his rage. And now, the new guy I was seeing was nowhere to be found.

Even my own mother had become engulfed in her grief. The loss of her son-in-law and consequentially losing touch with her grandson had overwhelmed her capacity to regulate her own emotions. She barely seemed to have noticed my near-death, or how losing Clay and losing custody of our son could have been as earth-shattering to me, since, after all, it had been my idea to get the divorce. If I called her in these moments, the roles would inherently reverse and I would be the one consoling her.

The loneliness I felt radiated off the walls back at me with every grief-stricken scream that escaped from my body. When this crying started, I didn't know how to make it stop. Usually, I would end up exhausted in a heap of unconsciousness on the floor, curled up with my arms wrapped tightly around my knees, shivering from the fatigue of having cried so hard. I would wake up the next day in a grief hangover, my head pounding, face puffy, dehydrated, contacts fuzzy from the salty tears caked to them, but at least the crying would have stopped. My biggest fear was that the time would come when I wouldn't wake up at all. That one day, the grief and the guilt would just be too strong, and I would succumb to the statistics. I would fall victim to the end that everyone expected, that I might experience a fate similar to Clay's.

I lived, clouded in this terror, that I would eventually give in to all the guilt that I didn't deserve, the blame that should have never been mine, the grief that I couldn't control. So, I wrote myself this letter. I filled a basket with expensive chocolates, fancy teas, and a gross number of face masks. I made a list to remind myself of all the things I could do to bring a little peace and love to myself when I couldn't seem to pull it back together. I had to teach myself how to comfort myself and sit peacefully in my own company. To find some self-compassion despite not being able to look at myself in the mirror anymore. I felt so alone in these moments, but I had to refuse to let this beat me; to keep from turning it all back on its head. I had to see God do good with what the devil had meant for evil. I had to live.

* * *

July 14, 2018: Day one of this nightmare. Or so I thought. Years of therapy have shown me that I had been living in a nightmare for over a decade.

That night had just been the peak of the entire journey. But how do we know we're living in a nightmare when everyone else around us acts like our experiences are normal? That life was the only one I had ever known and had been the journey of many of the women before me who had raised me. It was even beyond the original expectations set for me by my upbringing, and so it felt stable, safe, comfortable. Then it was all taken away abruptly that night, spinning me into a world of confusion and self-discovery, grief and desperation, and also, dare I say, hope?

But I thought this kind of sobbing would be over by now. That I would have surely pulled myself together and had started to accept this new normal. Six months, I had read in my first book on grief, *Option B* by Sheryl Sandberg, six months until the acute grief would subside. I had grasped onto those words, intentionally reading them out of context. I convinced myself it meant that as long as I could get through those first few months, the pain would subside. I thought I was doing everything right—the therapy, the exercise, the meditation. I had done the research, read about grief recovery, and I looked forward to meeting my six-month mark so I could feel recovered from my trauma and ready for the self-actualization. I had also read that it would be about six months until the post-traumatic stress disorder might kick in, but in this case, I ignored that paragraph completely. I only wanted to know what it was going to take to start healing. *Let's keep this positive,* I thought, *not realistic.*

The first three months were the slowest days and weeks of my life. I kept track of each day because they crawled by so slowly that I felt as if time was dragging through molasses. The hours felt like days and the days felt like weeks, but I would look at the calendar and realize I was only a month into my nightmare, then only two months, and then I would realize that the nightmare was not something I was ever going to wake up from. I would be counting these days for the rest of my life. Somehow, though, I thought by the end of that January, I might be okay. Well, I suppose I had figured out that I would probably be okay; I just thought I wouldn't still be trying to convince myself of it.

* * *

When Clay and I talked about his death, it wasn't in these terms. I never thought my life might also be in danger. When we would talk about him dying, we'd typically be in a screaming match. I would be crying angry tears, and he would be in denial. It may sound odd that this was even a topic of conversation, but Clay had come so close to dying so many times that I knew one day I would be living through the horror of losing him. But it didn't matter how many times he would wake up the next morning without a single recollection of the night before. He had survived the night, or the drive, or the blackout, and he was still alive the next day. So, in his mind, he would always wake up the next day, asking me to sweep the whole incident under the rug, to stop thinking about it that way and forget it had ever happened, just like he had been doing his entire life, just like the example his mother and father had set for him. And he knew I would always be there when he did, just like I had been our entire relationship.

I would scream and cry about how sick I was of living through this but when the fighting would stop, I would be quick to forgive him and keep up our façade of a happy family. It was just the three of us—Clay, his young son, Hunter, and me, and to try to protect us, I would stop "thinking about it that way." In my mind, though, I knew. I lived with a sick foreboding that the day would come that he would start drinking and never wake up.

One day, I feared, I would passionately but ineffectively argue with him, he would get angry-drunk at me for the last time. He would get into his truck and speed off, killing himself, or worse, someone else. Or he might take off on his beloved Harley Davidson, like he had done so many times before. In the dark, he would make a poor judgment call and be thrown from the bike.

My most frantic arguments came after the times he took his gun with him in the truck, or when I woke up in the middle of the night and found him blacked-out drunk but awake, staring with a familiar blank, miserable look at the silver pistol, the five-inch Kimber 1911 that he had carried on duty for years. When he sobered up the next day, he would ask that we didn't talk about it; he would reassure me that he was going to stay alive and that I had no reason to be worried or angry. No matter what happened, he promised, he would watch his son grow up to be a man.

Many nights, I stayed up and watched the front door, listened for the sound of his truck and wondered if he would come home, hoping he would make it back alive but not sure what repercussions waited for me if he did. Most of these nights, I stayed up with him, risking his anger to sit and watch that gun with him, to be sure it stayed there, lying on the table between us. I would be too terrified to close my eyes and fall asleep because of what I thought he might do to himself, but never for fear of what might happen to me.

Those nights, if I could sit quietly for long enough, he would start crying and telling stories about his childhood. He felt bitterness toward his father for the abuse he had endured as a young boy, and he would writhe with fear at the thought of abusing his own son. He would tell stories of his law enforcement days and the horrors he went through to cover up mistakes at the sheriff's behest, the deaths that went unreported when a case didn't go the way that they thought it should have, the times they took justice into their own hands, and the guilt he felt from being their hired gun.

One night, he came home angry at me for something I can't remember. He went into an all-night rage about whatever it was he thought I had done wrong, calling me a bitch; I couldn't sleep with his angry yelling and insults waking me up every couple of hours. The next morning, when he was sober again, he explained sheepishly that he had been called out earlier the day. The subject of their call: a man, broken down from addiction, had stood off with police for hours, while Clay kept his sniper sight trained on him. The standoff only ended when the man took his own life in front of them all.

Some nights, I left him, sick of the fighting, unwilling to endure another all-night bender of sloppy, drunken anger. I would drive to a local hotel room so I could get some sleep and try to maintain a little stability in my life until he sobered up.

* * *

So why then, six months later, was I still choking on my tears multiple times a week? Doubled over the sink, unable to catch my breath, asking myself, "What would Clay be saying if he were standing here next to me?" I knew he would be telling me to pull it together. He would be telling me that I was the strongest woman he had ever known. He would say, "Ab, you saved your life. You didn't let me take you. You are such a badass, and you are overcoming everything I put you through. Now wash your face and don't let the bastards get you down." That was his favorite piece of advice, no matter what I needed to hear in my moments of distress, and I could still hear his voice in my head saying it.

Still, I cried, because like many strong, independent, and very capable women, I loved a man who had demons. I cried because there is more to domestic violence than the stereotypes of drunken, mean men and weak, sad women who do not love themselves, as I had been taught growing up. I cried because I was deeply and passionately in love with a man who loved me back just as much but had never learned how to demonstrate that love.

Clay was a man who had been betrayed by his family, by his law enforcement brothers, and who had sacrificed his own sanity for what he thought was service to others but then could not live with himself afterward. I cried because I had been raised to believe this was all something I could handle, that this was normal in relationships and I had been the one failing. But I couldn't control it, and I wasn't supposed to have ever taken that responsibility onto my shoulders to try.

Even when Clay was sober, he was not particularly affectionate. Regardless of whether he was trying to apologize or win me back after an argument, he was too practical to bring me flowers or buy me pretty gifts, too sensible for cuddling. But in those final months, something changed, and it was like he was trying to tell me the end was coming. He would lay his head on my chest, hold me all night, and look at me with those sad, soft eyes filled with so much emotion. He had been my best friend, and he is the person I can attribute so much of my strength and success to, even if most of the time it was in spite of him and his constant challenging and discouragement of my dreams.

When his demons came out, as they so often did, he did not know how to hate anyone more than he hated me. I was the only person who had never left him or let him down. I had been there through all of it and never let him fall. After all this time, I can now admit to enabling him at times, many times. But he knew that when he woke up the next morning, I *would* still be there, until one day I wasn't anymore. My guilt comes from knowing that was what finally broke him.

* * *

Nights like this, when I am begging God to let me fall asleep at 6 p.m. because I can't stand the silence of the loneliness around me and the depression screaming inside my head, I question my decision to leave. I question every decision I made to love myself more than I had been and to live the life I knew I was meant to live. Was I right to have followed my own dreams and let him fall without being there to catch him?

Knowing now that I would lose Clay so violently, that our son would be taken from me, that I would be single and alone and without the family I sacrificed so much of myself to have, I wonder, would I ever go back to the way my life was before I had said "enough"?

In the years following these nights, I have learned through this ugly and heartbreaking process that the "what ifs" will not do anyone any good. No amount of questioning what could have been can change my truth. Wondering what I could have done differently only leads to more heartache and doubt. It only slows my recovery, and it can't bring them back to me, no matter what my answer is to any of those questions.

But fortunately, part of having survived such an experience, of still being around to make these mistakes, is that if I want to sit in the "what if" and "should have been," then I get to do so without judging myself. So, I sit here on my darkest days and I ask myself, "When Clay gave me my ultimatum, to choose my freedom or to choose him, and I chose myself, would I take it back? Would I go back and sacrifice this person that I get to be now so that he could still have the life he was living with me in it and I could keep him, keep Hunter?" The answer, every time and without hesitation, is no. I still would have chosen my freedom.

The survivor's guilt is strong, and it eats away at my resolve when I think of having my own life to live to the fullest, that I continue to enjoy the activities he and I loved doing together and that I'm experiencing things he would have never wanted to try. The guilt I feel for his death, especially when I think of one day falling in love again, of having another family, remains persistent in the back of my mind, nagging, even after all this time.

The grief and trauma sometimes cripples my hopes and dreams. The anguish of losing my best friend in such an awful way, before he could see his son grow up, before he could say goodbye to his mother, wreaks havoc in my body and mind and causes unimaginable depression. The trauma of knowing our last minutes together were of him hating me so violently that I had to defend my life against his attempts to take me with him is the theme of constant nightmares.

But would I go back? Would I undo all of this to return to a home where his demons and drinking ruled his life and mine? To a time when I could not hope to have career ambitions or plans for a bigger family, living constantly with his fear of change and insecurity? Would I sacrifice all the hopes and dreams I had felt, now so within reach, to raise a little boy whose biological parents underestimated the selflessness and sacrifice it takes to be an intentional parent? If I knew that I could have Clay alive and Hunter back home with me and could shield them both from all this evil and cruelty, would I change my final decision to choose me?

No. I wouldn't. Because once you have experienced the peace that comes with giving up the illusion of control; when you finally choose to love yourself most, knowing that nobody else but you can, you walk away with enough strength to overcome the guilt, the grief, and the depression. It doesn't make it go away, you still have a tendency to want to control things, thinking, *knowing*, the good you could do in someone's life if they would just "let" you fix them. But when you feel this love and compassion for yourself, you start to step away from who you ever "thought" you should be, and you begin to find out who you are really meant to be, and that you don't have to live your life for someone else.

The joy of loving yourself first, that ever-elusive concept of self-love, is real, and it really does overcome all things. Even the most heartbreaking, darkest, most traumatic events of your life can be overcome by a mindset that can change post-traumatic suffering to post-traumatic growth. It is not easy, and for most of us, it is probably not even something that can be accomplished without community, resources, and a helluva therapist. But it can be done. I am doing it. I am a living, breathing example that you really do control your own responses, and what you allow others to take from your life. I don't know how long this journey will take me or what is waiting on the other side of it. All I know is that I chose to love me and so I can continue to move forward with faith. I would give anything in the world to have my best friend back, but his choices were not mine. All I did was choose me, because in my life, I get to do that. If I hadn't, nobody else would have.

2

My First Letter to Clay

July 16, 2018

I love you, Clay. I love you so much I can't stand it.
Always,
Abby

* * *

When I was sixteen years old, I dated my first alcoholic, though I didn't know that he was at the time. He was nineteen, and I thought drinking was just something people our age did. It was still "cool" to get wasted, so I didn't think anything of it when there were beer bottles in the shower or when he stood me up because he was at the bar.

Plus, my mother loved him. Austin had a farm boy, Southern-like charm, and gave the impression of being a very hard worker with his rough-neck attitude. She believed he would be able to provide for me, likely in farm and construction jobs, which was a very good life where we were from.

I had never seen my mother coddle a person like she did Austin when he came to our house in the middle of the night to get doctored after bar fights. She would stay up late to make all his favorite foods and desserts, sending him home with homemade fudge and pies. She had stopped cooking dinner for us kids as soon as we had learned to use a microwave, but she absolutely fawned over him like a 1950s housewife.

One night, after waiting several hours at his house for him to show up from the bar for our double date that we had now missed, I called my mom to come pick me up. A friend had dropped me off earlier in the day, and I was sick of waiting around. She showed up the same time he finally did, drunk and glassy-eyed as he stumbled into the house. As I stormed out to the car, I overheard her say to him, "You're going to have to choose. You're going to have to decide whether she is more important to you, or the drinking is." He chose the drinking. I had given him everything I had, had slept with him, abandoned friends and school to spend time with him, following my mother's lead had cooked for him. I had tried to earn his love, to be more appealing to him than the bars and the hunting trips and the other girls I knew he was with when he wasn't answering my calls. My mom had done everything she knew how to make him love our family.

That following Christmas, my grandma, knowing only the parts of the story she had been told by my disappointed mother, exclaimed to me in front of the whole family that if I had treated Austin better, maybe he would have stuck around and chosen me instead. This crushed my self-esteem and left me confused, not knowing what else I could have possibly given up to have been worthy enough to be picked over the alcohol. Nobody ever sat me down and told me that Austin's demons were his and his alone. Not once was I told that the whole time it was I who had deserved to be treated better. Nobody ever told me that I was good enough.

My next "long-term" (which was about a year) boyfriend was Drew. Everyone expected him to be my knight in shining armor. He was older, established in the Marine Corps, owned his own home, and, best of all, played drums at his church for the worship team. It didn't matter to my parents that he was a twenty-six-year-old man dating their seventeen-year-old daughter.

Once I was eighteen, the next expected step was for me and Drew to marry. I told my mother, Drew, adult friends, mentors, really anybody who would listen, "But I don't know if I want to settle down right away. I think I want to go to college and do some traveling first." I had no idea what either of those things even meant. The only travel I had ever done was sitting in the back-middle seat of my parents' Buick LeSabre, visiting my oldest sister in Texas, or the annual family caravan to Branson, Missouri, for my grandparents' anniversary, a whole four-hour drive.

Everybody knew I was notorious for letting my car run out of gas only miles from my closest gas station. On top of that, it was a family joke how pretty-but-naïve I was, so there had never been any talk about how I would get to, pay for, or even begin the process of going to college. Besides, how could I afford any of it if I wasn't going to be "married and taken care of"? They wanted me to believe the world was a dangerous place and I should be grateful for the safety of my small town and the cards I had been dealt.

I made the choice anyway. I chose college and travel instead of jumping straight into marriage. Despite all the red flags in my relationship—visible to me only in hindsight—no one in my family or church supported this choice. Mom, disappointed in me for "acting out" against this supposedly really great guy, kicked me out of the house for it. I was barely eighteen. She wanted to show me "how hard life can be without someone to take care of you." When that didn't force me back into Drew's arms, she arranged a meeting with our pastor.

"Poor Drew," I was told by this older, white man of God. Poor Drew and the way that I had been treating him; he didn't deserve this. I was shamed for what I had "done." For breaking his heart and leading him on. He told me I was too young and immature to move out of my parents' home, and I needed to ground myself better in my relationship with God before going out on my own. And that meant finding marriage because my mother was certainly not going to have me otherwise. By passing on this marriage I had sinned against God and given up the best thing that would have ever happened to me.

Less than a year later, I was homeless and had just struggled through my first year of junior college, sleeping in my car and on couches. That summer, torrential rains flooded the entire state border of Kansas and Missouri, covering almost 75 percent of my hometown with an unexpected one-hundred-year flood. Not having found steady work and still not sure where I was going to live or what I was doing with my life, I had volunteered in the response efforts, and by chance, luck, and way more confidence than I had reason for, I ended up coordinating hundreds of volunteers for over two months as they came pouring into town to muck out and rebuild our community. As I walked through the high school gym where the entire local, state and federal effort was being housed, I looked over at another volunteer in passing and said, "If I could actually get paid to do this work, this is what I would do forever!"

Not long after making this statement, still not sure that this could even be a real job, I joined AmeriCorps and was off to St. Louis, Missouri, a whole five hours away from home, to go live in the big city and "travel." I had still traveled so little that I went into my college bookstore and declared I would need some reading to keep my mind sharp while I took this short sabbatical and "traveled abroad." This was a big deal. While serving in AmeriCorps, I made it all over the state of Missouri and once to Montana. I may have even crossed over the Arkansas line when responding to ice storms.

When my first-year term of service was coming to an end, I had to figure out where I wanted to go next. Earlier that year, our team had driven through Wyoming on our way to Montana for a conservation trip supporting the U.S. Forest Service. There were beautiful large mountains like nothing I had ever seen. And while driving with these mountain views, I saw a cowboy chasing horses through a pasture.

Feeling more accomplished than I had the year prior, I could now move to Wyoming and maybe shift my focus to finding a cowboy to marry.

After all, I was still very broke, and while I didn't know it at the time, I was fully embedded in the expectations that had been laid before me my entire life: in order to be financially secure and be comfortable, I would have to find a husband. A cowboy in Wyoming sounded like a proficiently romantic way of going about this.

When planning how I would get across the country and to the wild west to find my future husband, I never thought to reference a map. And since I hadn't been driving or paying attention on the drive to Montana, or in any of my elementary school geography classes, apparently, I only realized that Wyoming was not in the Great Lakes (Wisconsin) area after I had accepted a job smack-dab in the north-central part of the state, right in the center of the Big Horn Basin.

Completely lost in the world and still so, so naïve, I had no idea what I had just signed up for. I was a little more experienced after AmeriCorps, especially after a handful of pretentious young adults made me recognize how much of a country bumpkin I was. That experience had only shown me how much more I had to learn about the world around me. It lit a fire in my mind for learning what there was outside of what I had been raised to know and believe, but I still had a long way to go to break the cycle that had been holding back the women in my family for decades.

I had only planned on staying in Wyoming for the cowboy search for one year, and then I would go to Oregon for college if unsuccessful. I had no reason for choosing Oregon except I had heard about the forests

MY FIRST LETTER TO CLAY

and waterfalls, the beaches and beauty and it sounded like another place I needed to experience in this new life of travel.

But those plans changed when I met Clay.

I was volunteering for his sheriff's department's search and rescue team as a part of my new AmeriCorps work in Wyoming. I had strolled into the office that cold December morning to take care of some paperwork from a recent search, and as I walked by, one of the deputies on the team gave Clay a nudge and told him he should introduce himself. The other deputy told him later I might be dating someone, but he'd seen the kid and he had a mohawk and had concluded that he didn't stand a chance as a long-term boyfriend (true). I remember having barely put any effort into my appearance that day, wearing sweatpants and a hoodie, my hair in a sloppy ponytail, prepared to make the long, three-hour drive to the closest airport so I could fly home for Christmas later that day. I certainly hadn't come dressed to impress, especially not my future husband.

He followed me into the small office where I sat, then reached out his hand to me in way of introduction. "Hi. I'm Clay Caldwell. Bryce said I should come say hi," he said somewhat awkwardly. "He said you are in search and rescue with him," he added quickly in response to the questioning look on my face.

All business, because I wasn't catching on to the purpose of the introduction, I shook his hand firmly in return. "Hey, yeah, I've been on the team since August. I just moved to the area." Then I added, "I'm Abby."

After another awkward pause, neither of us sure where to take the conversation, Clay promptly turned around and walked out of the office. I sat down and continued my work, not thinking anything more about it. Driving out of the parking lot about fifteen minutes later, I passed in front of Clay's patrol vehicle and gave a lazy wave and smile. He followed me home.

He hated it when I told this part of the story because doing this had been so far opposite of his reserved, risk-averse and somewhat shy personality. It really wasn't as creepy as it sounds. I only lived maybe four blocks away from the department, and when I finally noticed him back there, I thought he was pulling me over since I tend to be a not-so-stellar driver. So when I looked in my rearview mirror and saw him pulling up behind me, I stayed put, both hands on the steering wheel. As he walked toward me, I slowly hand-cranked down the window of my 1998 Sunfire and looked at him expectantly.

Instead of the lecture I was expecting, he handed me a slip of paper with his name and number on it, and mumbled quietly with a nonchalant shrug, "If you want to go to lunch sometime, you should give me a call," and then hurried off as fast as he had after that first handshake before I could muster a response.

Because I had been dating the guy with the mohawk, it took me four months to call Clay and take him up on that lunch. But that spring, Mohawk Guy and I broke up, and he went back to his wildland firefighting, or trail building, or to join the circus, whatever it was he was doing for the summer that couldn't involve me. I gave it a few weeks of young, naïve breakup grief and then called Clay. Having been raised to believe that I should be afraid to be alone and still only genuinely finding my identity in the attention I could get from others, I didn't think I had any time to waste.

The first thing I noticed when I sat down across from him, at our small table in the only restaurant in town that didn't also serve as a pool hall, was his kind, warm, brown eyes. He had soft crow's feet around his eyes, which would seem to indicate that he had spent a lot of time smiling, yet when I looked again, I could tell there was sadness there. He always seemed to squint slightly, his brow furrowed, concern on his face; he was reserved even when he was trying to enjoy himself. His smile was ornery but sweet though it constantly seemed a little hesitant. He had never worn braces, but his mouth opened into a perfect smile when he did enjoy a laugh. He was thirty-eight when we first met, and other than a few grays over the years, he never really seemed to age. Those eyes bore into me, the sadness reflected when he asked why it had taken so long to call him. I was honest with him but already regretted waiting to call.

He apparently forgave the delay in scheduling our lunch date because he followed up my response with, "Well, there are two things you're going to need to know about me: I have a three-year-old son, and I am a huge, huge Pittsburgh Steelers fan." I had already heard around town that he had a son, and one thing I knew about myself was that I'm prone to dig single fathers, so that wasn't a problem. But I had no idea what sport the Steelers played. I tentatively asked if they were a baseball team. He put his head in his hands for a moment, light-heartedly but clearly disappointed by the question. He informed me they had just won their sixth Super Bowl only the month before, beating the Arizona Cardinals. Fortunately, he must have also forgiven me for not knowing this, because he continued with our date.

Almost immediately, I regretted losing those first four months with him. One of the pointless regrets I will always have is the time that we each wasted in those first months and throughout the ten short years that we had together with our senseless fighting.

3

Gunfights are Lost in Milliseconds

July 19: Four days after my world had fallen apart, my last few belongings were finally released from evidence and I could retrieve them from the police station. Somebody had kindly wiped the blood off my phone, but my tablet still had dark reddish-brown fingerprints smeared across the back. Even then, it hadn't occurred to me that the tablet had been left in the living room where the fight had happened, not in the bedroom where the rest of the blood would be found. Hours later, my mom and I were driving to dinner, finally hungry, I had requested noodles and we ventured off to find some. Suddenly it came back to me in a sudden and abrupt flashback as if I were reliving it all over again.

These flashbacks would come any time I felt safe enough to let my mind rest. As I rode around Golden, Colorado, watching people go about their evening as if everything were still so normal, I thought again about the bloody handprint on the tablet that I still hadn't had the stomach to clean off. Then it came to me. I had seen a matching mark on the front of the neon yellow T-shirt I had been wearing during the fight, up near my collar—more blood smeared in streaked lines, and fingerprints.

Suddenly I was back in that moment, running frantically into my neighbor's upstairs apartment, shotgun in hand and Axel, my obedient German Shepherd, following me in. I heard her frantically on the phone with the police as I rushed in, begging her to let me hide there as I slammed the door of the apartment shut and hurriedly locked it behind me. I heard fear in her voice as she cried out, "Oh my God, she's bleeding. Her face is bloody, she's bleeding all over!"

Only I hadn't been bleeding at all. "Oh my God. Oh my God." I kept repeating to myself, completely in a daze and still trying to understand what had just happened. Moments later, I had caught my breath and looked around me, realizing then where I was and feeling the pain in the side of my face, the inside of my left cheek torn up from taking hard punches. I asked if she had an ice pack and I took it into the bathroom with me to assess my injuries. I tried to peer inside my mouth to see the damage, there wasn't any blood. I ran my tongue around my teeth, nothing was missing nor did it feel loose. I splashed water onto my face, dried it with the non-bloody part of my T-shirt and applied the ice pack, then I asked for some ibuprofen for the swelling, staying eerily and uncannily calm.

"Oh. Gross." I was suddenly brought back to the present by the sound of my own voice.

"What's wrong?" Mom asked, surprised by the sudden exclamation breaking the silence.

"I think I might have nearly bitten Clay's fingers off. I remember now—when I was screaming, he put his hand down the back of my throat, trying to keep me from calling for help. I bit down hard to get his hand out. I wonder if that's where all this blood came from, his hand." I paused, the realization of the flashback sinking in.

"I feel really bad about that; he must have been hurting so bad." I put my head down between my knees from the regret, but my eyes were so tired of crying all I could do was sit there in dread.

"Abby, the reason why his fingers were in your mouth was because he was trying to keep you from screaming so he could kill you. You shouldn't care that you hurt him back."

"Yeah, I guess you're right," I said as I rolled my tongue around the inside of my mouth and along the front of my teeth, disgusted with myself, survivor's guilt flooding my emotions.

It took weeks to remember everything in bits and pieces in flashbacks. When I would think back to why I was now responding to the world in a certain way or when a new fear would present itself, I would suddenly remember certain scenes in full detail. The morning after it all happened, when I was first finding out the full level of my loss, hearing that Clay would not be coming out of that apartment alive, I knew I needed to get to Cheyenne, to Hunter. I needed to be there to tell him and hold him close.

My closest girlfriends all lived there too so I would have a place to stay and their love to keep me going until I figured things out. I didn't have anything to my name other than the pajamas I had left the house in, some borrowed flip flops from the neighbor, and my German shepherd, Axel, who had thankfully followed me out when I ran for my life. Everything else was contained in my apartment, which was now a crime scene, and likely completely destroyed.

A close friend, Emily, was on the phone with me as I paced outside the county kennel, waiting to get Axel back from where the police department had placed him the night before as a place for him to stay away from the chaos of the scene and the police department. "Abby, can you tell me what you need? Don't go to the store—come straight here. We're going to get you the things you need, but I need you to tell me what those are."

"If you can just get me a toothbrush, I think I can get everything else, but I just really want to brush my teeth." I literally could think of nothing else. I thought it was because I had been up all night and hadn't brushed my teeth since the night before. I was realizing now, four days later, that it was probably because somewhere in my mind, I knew that I had the remnants of Clay's flesh in my teeth. *I must have had so much blood in my mouth,* I thought. I never remembered tasting the blood. It took several days for my sense of taste to come back and over a month before I gained my full range of vocals again from the damage to the inside of my throat from him trying to stop my screaming.

* * *

Along with not remembering many of the details of what had happened, I also had never smelled any alcohol that night, although Clay was on at least his seventh bottle of whiskey in just a short number of days by the time he came through my apartment door. The bottle was there; I saw it in his left hand as he walked in. His face was in mine the whole fight. But when the officers asked if I had smelled alcohol, I had not. Still, I had moments of fear and discomfort the next time someone went in for a kiss after he had been drinking, and smelling it on him, I involuntarily pulled away. I would be brought back to that night for years after whenever I smelled hard liquor in the air or on someone's breath.

Some memories of that night burned into my brain in full detail almost right away. I felt unreasonably calm and level-headed almost the entire fight and afterward. As I sat in the apartment two floors above mine that Axel and I had escaped to, waiting patiently for Clay to surrender so I could go back home, the neighbor and I chatted about everything that led to that night and my relationship with the man just a few steps below us.

We talked a lot about Hunter and Clay, and I told her about our life together. It still hadn't crossed my mind that he had just tried to murder me. I instead thought with some sick relief that this would finally be his rock bottom and he would hopefully be forced to get the help he desperately needed. There was no way he could justify a way out of this one, and if nothing else, the courts would for sure require a full stint in rehab.

I may have only been sitting there on the floor of my neighbors' living room for thirty minutes or so, though it had felt like hours, when I heard a gunshot from my apartment below. I remembered then my hunting rifle I kept in the closet. It came to mind that it might have been his final shot, that he had given up the fight, and I curled up on the floor, trying to cry, but the tears wouldn't come. I wasn't ready to believe it was over. I was wrong, though; it hadn't been over yet. Speaking with the detectives about half an hour later, they told me the lights in the apartment were switching on and off, so they knew he was still alive in there. "No, that gunshot was external; it was meant for our guys," he told me. Without thinking, I sighed a deep, "Oh thank God," knowing there was a chance Clay would still come out of there alive.

For the next several hours, I cooperated with every call from what seemed like so many different officers, answered all their questions calmly, and gave them the information they needed to negotiate with Clay and get him out alive. I was so relieved it was still an option that I felt less worried about my own dire situation and what I had just survived, instead feeling hopeful and energized to help.

Every few minutes, a detective or negotiator would call the neighbor's phone. Mine was still in my apartment, apparently being used by Clay to negotiate his surrender. They would ask about Clay's past as a law enforcement officer, his experience as a sniper. They asked whether he was a narcissist, and I assumed they were assessing his skill set for the barricade and standoff with them.

"No," I said, "he genuinely is one of the best shots out of Wyoming; he's telling you the truth."

They asked what I thought might be topics they could talk to him about that could calm him down. I told them to talk to him about his son. He wouldn't want to leave Hunter behind. I put them in touch with his friend, Phil, who had been living with him and Hunter for the past few months; maybe he could help.

Once when they called, they asked, "If we walk into your garage and look east, what would we see through that wall?" In other words, if we shoot a can of pepper spray through that sheetrock, will it land in your bedroom?

"It would land in either the bathroom or the coat closet." I responded after they explained why they were asking. They tried it anyway, and everything in my bathroom was destroyed by a bright pink oil that would never wash off.

By the time the SWAT team evacuated us, leading us down the back stairs of the apartment complex and straight into an armored vehicle, I was starting to feel some of the physical pain that would plague me over the next several weeks. I followed these men, nervously observing their ballistic helmets and bulletproof vests set up on the outside of their uniform shirts, their rifles strapped across their chests. I was reminded of photos I had seen of Clay in the same equipment, geared up for his own operations on his department's joint county SWAT Team.

These men were different though. They were faceless to me; I didn't know what lay underneath their uniforms as they circled in formation around me to protect me from any stray bullets or even deliberate attempts on my life. I have never been easily intimidated, but I stared and felt an uneasy gratefulness that they were on my side. *But are they?* I wondered, having my own biases about law enforcement and concerned for the prejudice they may have about me as a victim of domestic violence.

Before jumping into the armored truck, I hesitated. I looked right into the face of the officer standing in front of me, ready to help me up the steep metal step, and said, "It is your priority to bring him out alive, right?" He sternly corrected me. "Our first priority is the safety of the civilians in the area." Well yes, okay, of course..."But are you going to try to get him out of there alive?" He looked straight back at me and reminded me of what I already knew deep down. "Ultimately, that is going to be up to him."

They evacuated us to a spot that was only far enough away so we were outside of the range a rifle could kill us—a Red Lobster parking lot up the street from the corner my apartment sat on. Then they separated Axel and me from all the other neighbors who had also been evacuated, taking everyone else to the police station to report their accounts of what had happened. I watched the neighbors from the next floor above my apartment walk away. I saw the same faces I had seen staring down at me coldly when I ran, terrified, out of my apartment through the outdoor walkway.

I have no idea how long our fight lasted, but as calm and collected as I had been in my mind while the fight was actually happening, I had also been screaming my head off the entire time. I had screamed a variety of things: "Somebody please help!" "He's trying to kill me!" "Somebody please call 911!" My front door had remained open the entire fight; I could see that out of the corner of my eye. And yet, as I sprinted out of my apartment, confused and not sure where to hide, I looked up at all of them standing on their balconies, watching and listening to the fight but not helping, smoking cigarettes and lazily hanging over their ledges to watch what was happening below. I wondered what they would tell of their accounts of the fight when they arrived at the police station for questioning. I wondered if any of them would have felt guilty if they had quietly watched me die that night.

* * *

Since that night, I have searched frantically for answers about how I survived against all odds. So many people shared opinions: it was from my "training," as if my very brief law enforcement career or youth martial arts might have had something to do with it. Someone else said it was simply because my will to live was so much stronger than his will to kill me. Still, I needed something more; I needed science to clear up my confusion, my survivor's guilt. My therapist helped me put some pieces together when she explained that though Clay was much larger, he was so intoxicated that his reactions would have been slower, his mind not thinking as clearly as mine was with all the adrenaline flowing. I still wasn't satisfied with that explanation. My nervous system's choice to fight, without any ounce of my own control, felt so animalistic that I was almost fearful of myself and my ability to do what I did.

I may never understand how I managed to keep my wits very consciously about me, first grabbing the gun in his hands as it came level with my face, then by keeping it gripped firmly in my hands, trapped between our bodies with Clay's entire 260 pounds on top of me on the couch. I was thinking clearly enough to know I could easily overcome his grip. He had always had weak wrists and my hands were strong; I could turn the gun on him and pull the trigger. But something inside of me couldn't do it. As quickly as the thought came into my mind, I knew it wasn't an option. There had to be another way.

Knowing now that I could have ended that fight right there and saved my life without a fight, guaranteeing my survival, I still don't think I could have done it. Speaking with my therapist later about why I couldn't have pulled that trigger even to save my own life, she told me, "There is a very big difference in knowing that somebody has died, finding a person dead, and watching a person die in front of you. If you had pulled that trigger, you would have had to watch Clay die right in front of you." Pulling the trigger may have saved my life in that moment, but the guilt would have eventually killed me. Instead of bringing myself to shoot a man I had loved for so long, I chose to gamble with my own life, hoping we might both have a chance to live.

So instead, I gripped the gun with every ounce of strength I had in me, and I pushed it out and above our heads, still lying vertical on the couch, with my arms and his locked straight above us. My face was pressed hard against Clay's chest while he tried to fight to gain control over the gun, so without being able to look up at it, I felt around with my fingers for the magazine release. I was remarkably familiar with this gun in particular, the Kimber 1911. Clay had practically raised me on the 1911 style pistol.

I had a Colt, he had a Kimber, and date nights would consist of visiting shooting ranges, speed reloading, and sometimes even building-clearance drills. Afterward, I would stand next to him, cleaning my own gun while he cleaned his. I could take a 1911 apart down to the springs, and I knew what I had to do. I dropped the magazine into the couch cushions. He pulled himself up to look into my face when he realized what had just happened, and I saw fury mixed with a familiar look of quiet and otherwise unexpressed awe.

One side of this response was from the drunk Clay, hell-bent on pulling that trigger and taking out decades of rage and hate on the only person he had ever been able to count on to take it. The other response came from the scared and skeptical man I had known all those years, questioning my every capability, and then surprised and impressed every time I showed him that, for the past decade of our relationship, I had been growing up and paying attention to his life lessons. That was the look of silent admiration and awe I got from him every time he saw that I had become the very capable woman he had wanted me to be those first years we were together.

But the drunk Clay couldn't let me beat him. He pulled back his fist and started swinging at my face. I wouldn't remember this part in much detail for days. But in my right hand, I continued to hold the gun with everything I had, my arm still stretched out above my head, and with my left, I bent my elbow to pull my forearm across my face. I took turns blocking swings from Clay's fist and then reaching up to pull back the gun's slide as hard as I could, trying to release the last round seated there in the chamber. When I wasn't yanking on the slide, I threw the safety back on before blocking another hit, knowing that Clay had safeties on both sides of this gun and exactly where I would find them.

* * *

When the SWAT team finally arrived, they asked, "Which one of you is the victim?" I reluctantly raised my hand. *I guess that is me,* I thought. After we had gotten into the armored truck, another officer asked, "Is the victim in here?" He wanted reassurance that their mission of getting "the victim" to safety was in play. Everybody looked at me, and I felt the judgment on their faces from the commotion that I felt partially responsible for. I again identified myself quietly, not wanting to be associated with myself in that moment. I was already assuming blame for the chaos we were all living through.

We parked at the staging area with all the other officers, the incident command post where the ambulance was waiting for me. All the responders were rushing over, calling into the crowd, "Is the victim here?" "Where is the victim?" The word cut like a sharp knife, like they were screaming it harshly at us. Their top priority was to get "the victim" to safety, to be sure my life was saved along with everyone else's, but the word was ringing painfully in my ears, and I just wanted it to stop. As I would learn later from many of them, there isn't typically a live victim around when these things happen, so maybe more than anything, the first responders needed to see my face, know I was okay, feel the relief that this time, at least this one time, they had succeeded in getting the victim out alive.

I could tell everyone was mostly worried about my well-being and my safety from the relief shown on their faces and the concern in their voices, but the term "victim" felt so impersonal, like an attack on everything I was trying to be for myself. With every mention of the word, I would cringe, wishing they could come up with a different term to identify me by. It felt like I was swallowing a rock every time I heard it. "You're the victim?" There it was again, the rock now landing hard in the pit of my stomach. I could feel the disassociation from who I was as a person. My identity had been boiled down to just one phrase: "the victim." It was sobering. No pun intended.

* * *

In all seriousness, though, I have struggled with the identity of having been a victim of domestic violence for years since this incident. I certainly didn't feel like a victim in that moment; hadn't I just won that fight? Even afterward, I tried correcting a friend, who in return explained, "No, Abby, you were a victim of that attack. It was something very horrible that was perpetrated on you without your control or consent. It happened *to you*. You were a victim." I look back on not only this conversation but the many incidents when Clay picked on me, tore me down, and even, much to my lasting shame, hurt me physically.

Our whole relationship I had avoided associating with the label "a victim of domestic violence," and so for much of the time after that night, I didn't either. True to form, even my closest friends would say, "We don't know how this happened to you; you're such a strong woman." I didn't fit the "mold" that we all saw in the movies, and honestly, neither did Clay as an abuser. Neither of us met the stereotype of what they taught us in sex-ed during the 90s. There were no bruises in hidden places, no controlling of my time and social life, and Clay was closer to my own family than I was. I didn't check the boxes listed in the pamphlets and I didn't know how to identify as a victim while also holding onto my identity of being a strong and capable woman, so I just couldn't accept it.

This is such a difficult part of my identity to come to terms with even now after years of therapy. In writing this chapter, I researched, "How often are women killed in relationships," and I found these shocking statistics:

- Nearly twenty people per minute (more than 10 million annually) are physically abused by their partner in the United States.[1]
- Slightly more than 2 in 5 (42.0% or 52 million) women report being physically abused by an intimate partner in their lifetime.[2]
- The presence of a gun in a domestic violence situation increases the risk of homicide by 500 percent.[3]
- An estimated 10 murder suicides occur each week in the United States, killing nearly 1,200 Americans each year. In nearly two-thirds of these an intimate partner of the shooter is among the victims.[4]
- Of all murder-suicides involving an intimate partner, 95 percent were female victims.[5]

I continued my research and learned that femicide, defined as the murder of women specifically, can almost be predicted by research when we combine previous physical violence in a relationship with the female then leaving the home, moving away from the place where the abuse was occurring. In a study by the American Journal of Public Health, I found that 79 percent of women murdered by their partners were physically abused by their partners prior to their death and that the separation of that woman, like when I left Clay to move to Denver, increased her chances of femicide by five times what they were originally.[6] You combine those stats with the one above about the firearm and it's no wonder I was surrounded by first responders just wanting to get their eyes on my living body. To say I was lucky to be alive is a drastic understatement.

Even with all these statistics, my very first emotional response to this data was, "Yeah, but I wasn't *really* abused." Still. Today. The well-therapied, logical, healing side of my brain screams to reason with me: "Dude (I call myself dude sometimes), yes. You were abused." Clay didn't beat me violently like you see in the movies; it was mostly emotional, in the form of controlling my life out of his own fear and addiction. But he did shove me into the wall sometimes, he would throw a full laundry basket at me in his fury that I wasn't folding it and putting it away after he washed it. He was constantly tossing my things around the room carelessly when I would ask him not to, and the thing that made me the most angry? He would say demeaning, awful things to me while poking me hard in the chest. These hard pokes would come with the full force of his arm and set me back, leaving fingerprint-sized bruises on my collarbone and the front of my sternum.

I hate admitting this, but coming to terms with it has allowed me to understand the danger I was really in and to begin healing from it. I never told my parents this was happening, would never have admitted it to friends, and have never even admitted most of this to my therapists. Because then I would *maybe* have had to admit that I was a victim and was staying with a man who was abusing me. In my mind it was "only poking;" it wasn't a punch or a kick to the ribs, it wasn't a mark on my face, it wasn't something I had been warned about when taking my self-defense classes. It didn't seem like stereotypical domestic violence like I had learned about in school, so what was I even admitting to? That Clay was a jerk and I was living with it? Throughout our relationship, confusion about what I was experiencing often filled my mind, but I didn't have nearly enough self-confidence to do anything about it anyway. It had never occurred to me that maybe I should be considered a "victim" of domestic violence. It certainly never occurred to me that I could have one day become a femicide statistic.

A very important note here from the author: the research conducted in this chapter is a very high-level summary of the articles I discovered and does not even begin to touch on other very important data regarding domestic violence; including the rates of femicide for women of color. Reported in the National Intimate Partner and Sexual Violence Survey: more than half of non-Hispanic American Indian or Alaska Native women (57.7%), more than half of non-Hispanic black women (53.6%), two-fifths of Hispanic women (42.1%), and almost two-thirds of non-Hispanic multiracial women (63.8%), reported having experienced intimate partner and sexual violence.[7]

4

In the Beginning

It would be only a few weeks after my first lunch with Clay when I met Hunter, something that only seemed strange looking back years later. But Hunter's mother was not around, and a single father's income doesn't provide for babysitters and date nights, so there was little we could do together that didn't involve him toddling along.

His father had brought him into the sheriff's office knowing I would be there for the final evening of a training course I had been taking. During a break, I wandered into the next room to find him sitting there with his daddy, annoyed to not be at home playing. He had his favorite Spider-man ball cap on, and his plastic six-shooter strapped to his shorts, an item that would be a staple of his everyday outfit until kindergarten started a few years later.

I excitedly knelt to his level and in a higher pitch voice than I intended, introduced myself and asked how he was doing. He had a deep scowl on his little face, a look that became characteristic of both him and his daddy far too often. He looked straight ahead, staring past me with that infamous glare, pretending not to notice me. His father laughed nervously, but Hunter was unwavering in his clear displeasure at being there. I tried to engage him in conversation but to no avail.

Many of our follow-up visits went the same way, with me trying to connect with him, and him clinging closely to his father and acting as if I didn't even exist. It was awesome. Not until I started spending time with him one-on-one while his dad went to work did he start to warm up to me.

Soon after this, and still very early in our relationship, I began coming over to Clay's house to watch Hunter for him while he worked and gradually the little boy started to let me into his life. Clay's ex-mother-in-law, who lived about thirty-five minutes away, would require Clay to provide her with a full tank of gas, steak dinner, and payment to come "babysit" Hunter while he worked and she remained reluctant at that. Appalled that a grandmother would put such a price on spending time with her grandson, I offered to watch him for free to help Clay out. In exchange for some DirecTV and free range of the fridge, I didn't mind watching him to spite the old lady who couldn't voluntarily come see her only grandson.

And just like that, we suddenly became a family. It really happened that casually for us. There was never an argument about how we would raise Hunter or debates on our expectations for him. For example, Clay hadn't weaned him from his bedtime bottle yet, and so we worked together to shift to a sippy and then to put him to bed without milk at all. He was also still in diapers. Clay was doing his best as a first-time single dad and could only do what he knew how with a baby at home and no reference on a timeline for any of these things. We went shopping together to create a "toy bag" that Hunter could pull a small surprise from each time he used the potty; he was out of diapers in a week.

The first time I went grocery shopping for the three of us as a family, Clay was aghast at the amount of money it would cost to buy fresh fruits and vegetables versus the canned goods he had been purchasing prior, and then they became a regular part of our meals. Hunter's birthmother did not take him for full weekends yet, considering him to be too much work at that little age, so it was just the three of us the majority of the time, and it was perfect. Except when it wasn't, when Clay would try to mask a lifetime of hurt and trauma with alcohol, which turned him into a completely different person.

I don't know if he ever healed from his divorce, but he would act tough about his supposedly cold marriage whenever I asked him about it. Looking back, I see he was so much more brokenhearted than he ever admitted, and our relationship had come along far too soon after the paperwork had been finalized.

The story Clay gave me, though, was that Kim had given him an ultimatum—marry her or break up with her—so he gave her the credit card, told her to buy a ring, and they went to Vegas to elope. They were married for five years, and from what he had said, they wanted to have a baby together. But after Hunter was born, things changed. Kim suffered terribly from postpartum depression. She was unable to produce breast milk for her son, and that caused her even more depression and led to her distancing herself from both of them.

When they came home from the hospital, Kim laid her newborn down on the couch and walked away, not even noticing when Hunter fell off the edge and began crying. He went for two days without his first meal, waiting for his mother, until Clay, frustrated and hurting for his son, drove into town and bought some formula against his wife's wishes.

A year later, Kim began an affair with a fellow highway patrolman and left Clay the year after that. He told Kim she could have the house and the vehicles, but he was taking Hunter. She didn't hesitate to agree. She gave Clay the impression that trying to raise a baby alone would be too hard, especially while focusing on her career and her new relationship.

Clay, who had initially left his job in law enforcement to support his wife's career, took his son and moved back to Clinton, asking for his job back. He had been the department's only sniper instructor, the school resource officer, and an all-around quality community police officer, and his department was glad to have him back on the force. They allowed him to continue his career at the schools, scheduling him to work from eight to four so he could be home to raise his son.

Clay's story is not unusual, the burdens that come with a partner's abandonment are not only known by women. But he was already a well-established alcoholic when Kim divorced him. His traumatic experiences in law enforcement had him checking out, suffering from post-traumatic stress disorder (PTSD) and sleep deprivation.

Even worse, he had been beaten and belittled his entire childhood by his own father. As one of three children, Clay always seemed the one to take the brunt of his father's anger. His mother had stood by, absent and passive in her own way, and Clay was left feeling like a sacrificial lamb so that she and his two siblings had the security of an employed man in their lives. So Kim's abandonment hit him that much harder than it might have for other men.

Clay's father had also come from an abusive home with an alcoholic father who knocked him around and mistreated him. His mother had come from the same; her father was still alive and still just as mean. Coming from this long cycle of trauma, Clay already knew that alcoholism was in his blood, and he didn't expect it would be something that he would ever overcome.

Hell, with that many generations of alcoholism, he had never even known there was anything outside of the norm with this amount of drinking. The first year of our relationship was spent with him getting drunk and accusing me of wanting to leave him for someone else, taking out the hurt from what Kim and Tom had done to him until I would finally have enough and walk out.

Initially, that was our cycle—we would fight, and I would leave since I still had my own place. A day or so would go by and Clay would contact me, or maybe he would come by my work to bring me coffee or ask me to breakfast to talk. I would go for it every time. At twenty years old, I could barely afford my own coffee, and I was far from having the emotional maturity to recognize this was dependence forming—for both of us.

5

Letter to Clay's Law Enforcement Brothers

Once the responding officers had confirmed I was "the victim," they took me to an ambulance that had been waiting for me in the parking lot at the makeshift incident command post. I let the paramedics look me over, but I knew I didn't have any life-threatening injuries, at least not any that were physical. I had been sitting in that apartment for what felt like, and may have been, hours. I had already been applying my ice pack and had taken some Ibuprofen for the swelling, which common sense told me would be coming.

I took note for the paramedics of exactly how many milligrams I had taken and at what time. I had been icing my face, which I only knew initially was hurt because the neighbor screamed at the amount of blood on my mouth when I first walked in her door. I checked myself for a concussion several times, albeit awkwardly, walking into the dark bathroom and asking my neighbor to turn on the light quickly while I watched my pupils in the mirror expand to their normal size. I maintained that uncanny calm and took care of myself while we waited for Clay to surrender, for someone to come get me and let me back into my home. I wasn't going to die from my injuries; at least I knew that much.

I walked into the ambulance casually, described the measures I had already taken to check on my health while I was waiting, and followed their directions to assess all parts of my body. They asked me to move my jaw and check my teeth with my tongue to see if anything felt loose. It still hadn't occurred to me where all the blood might have come from, but I had washed it away while waiting. The inside of my cheek was raw and torn and my throat was sore, I assumed from the screaming.

Throughout the course of the night, I realized there was swelling and stiffening in my left forearm. And since I remained so oddly level-headed this whole time, I transferred the ice from my face to my arm, routinely testing the range of motion in my fingers and putting pressure on my wrist at all different angles. Feeling no additional pain, I did not think it could be broken. But I also had no idea why it hurt so badly. I explained the pain to the paramedics, showed the range of motion in my wrist and fingers, and told them I wasn't concerned. Maybe I had hit it hard on something when we were wrestling. Who knew?

I had a burning behind my left ear that I also could not identify the cause of. I didn't even know why I brought it up. It was so faint initially and I didn't have a concussion, so I wasn't worried about that either. I felt burning between my thighs as well. This I knew was because of the fight over the second gun.

***

Despite all my manic screaming during our fight, my mind was still. I was thinking clearly and processing what was going on, considering carefully what my next step should be. In the midst of everything, I had a thought from years ago, remembering one of the many women's self-defense classes I had taken, suddenly recalling that when bad things like this happen to women, not only are people less likely to put themselves in harm's way, or even in an uncomfortable position, to interfere with a fight, they are also unlikely to "believe" the screaming of others as an actual cry for help. Often people want to make the comfortable assumption that some girl is super drunk and doesn't want to go home. This is exactly what my neighbor from the third floor up had been thinking was happening up until this moment; she told me as we rehashed the chain of events leading to me sitting on her living room floor.

When I remembered this during the fight, I realized I needed to be much more specific about what was happening, so I started screaming, "Somebody call 911" over and over again. These words finally triggered action. Her boyfriend came downstairs to "check things out and let the dog out," and she picked up the phone to call 911. Not knowing how long I might have been able to keep control of the gun or if one of the blows to my head might have rendered me unconscious, these two actions very likely saved my life when I otherwise may not have survived.

I heard, and thanked God when I did, "Sir, you need to stop that. Please stop." I suddenly snapped out of my head, out of the methodical thought process, and back into the frantic moments of the fight. "He's going to kill me!" I screamed. "He's going to kill me and he has a gun! Please don't let him kill me! Please get the gun! It's here, I have it here! Please take it! Please don't let him kill me!" I couldn't stop screaming these things, hopefully more coherently than what I remember when I look back. When he finally gained control of the handgun that Clay and I had been wrestling for, Clay immediately went for the shotgun that had been lying across my lap.

I had grabbed the shotgun as a precaution earlier in the night. Axel had been growling at the door while I sat on the couch doing my homework. I was awake only by chance. Typically an early riser, I am usually in bed by that time of night. Thirty more minutes, I had told myself, hoping to finish one more assignment.

As a single female living alone, I don't know that you can ever be too careful. I'm known for my routine days, and I had no intention of ever becoming a victim of some weirdo watching me come and go and knowing when I would be home or out. When Axel growled, I went to my bedroom and grabbed the gun from next to my bed. I came back to the living room and realized my blinds were still open; safer to close those so nobody could see through. I had also been sitting with my back to my front door. Years of being surrounded by people with law enforcement experience and ways of thinking told me I should opt to face the door. Every one of these actions contributed to saving my life.

I sat back on the couch, put the gun between myself and the cushions, and put my laptop back on my lap only moments before I would watch the deadbolt, very slowly and without any sound, spin from locked to unlocked. That slow turn of the bolt still haunts me to this day as one of the longest moments of my life.

The shotgun never came into use. When I saw the door unlocking, I knew it was likely from the key that Clay held in his hand on the other side, even though I wasn't expecting him. But I also knew that perhaps it wasn't, and so I had lifted the shotgun momentarily so I would be ready for whoever it was. When I saw it was him, I lowered it again. Then I saw the large, brown whiskey bottle in one hand and watched him pull the handgun out of his pocket with the other without ever saying a word. It was too late to pick the shotgun back up. I know now that I could have never shot Clay anyway, even when my life depended on it.

While we had been fighting over his handgun, I was all too aware that the shotgun was still lying there between us. I always kept a round in the chamber because I never wanted to waste time trying to load it if I needed to use it. Now, all it would have taken was a pull of the trigger if he had gotten ahold of it.

So, while we both had hands on the smaller of the two guns, my legs were wrapping around the longer one like a figure-eight, the butt sitting on my hips and my thighs gripping around the back of the barrel, getting the tightest hold I could while shifting under his weight. Once the neighbor showed up and took control of the handgun, Clay lunged for the shotgun, shoving the good Samaritan out of the way and grabbing the middle of the barrel with both hands, standing now with the strength of all his weight behind his grip. The neighbor man stood there, dumbfounded, an empty handgun in his hands.

I tightened my thighs around the shotgun in a leg wrestle and held on for dear life, my brain trying to register my next steps. I realized then that without Clay lying across me, I could sit up, and I grabbed ahold of the gun with my hands, keeping my legs tightly in place, wrapping my whole body around it where I could. Then I went to work peeling his fingers off it, beginning at the thumbs where my mother had once taught me was the weakest point of a man's grip. Once I released the shotgun, I stood and immediately unloaded it as I had with the smaller gun, racking it loudly in the night air three times to drop the shells onto the floor so that even if he got the gun, he would have to fight me to get it reloaded.

* * *

The burning I now felt between my thighs as I sat in the back of the ambulance was from the broken blood vessels from the rubbing and extreme grip that my legs had had on the gun. I would find out the next day that the bruising on the inside of my legs had gone so deep that it had broken through the skin in several places, leaving it torn and shredded and bleeding. To this day, I have never complained once that the muscles in my thighs keep me from fitting back into a size six pair of jeans, the size I was wearing three years prior, before I had started exercising them regularly. I will never again fat shame the way my legs and butt fill out my pants. That strength saved my life.

I must have seemed far too calm and in control as I sat in the back of the ambulance, reflecting through the pain, still dulled from the adrenaline flowing through my body, because as I left the truck to go find Axel and head to the police station, one of the paramedics said, "Hey, have a great night!" I looked back at him, unsure of how to respond, and said, "I mean..." and then just trailed off as we both realized the ridiculousness of his statement. I gave him an uber fake, toothy smile, and said, "Yeah, you too."

* * *

That night I sat for eight or so hours in mostly silence with only my spinning mind to keep me company. I waited in fearful anticipation in my pajamas and borrowed flip flops, sitting in the police station breakroom at one of the many round, white plastic tables. The cold radiated up from the neutral floor tiles, the high ceiling and angled windows glared down at me from above. Maybe they were designed as an attempt to make the room more stylish, or to warm it and make it more welcoming by letting in natural light during the day, but to me they just made the room seem that much larger, making me feel even smaller.

There were two officers assigned to watch me and liaison with the negotiators and SWAT teams on the ground. Two, because they're trained to provide a female officer for victims of domestic violence. A thoughtful touch, but I have never been someone to blame all men in general for this whole mess.

They were both kind and empathetic, but there wasn't much to talk about once the paperwork was finished. I sat in the hard, plastic cafeteria chair, cold and feeling exposed with their eyes on me all night, with nothing else to do but stare at the clock in front of me while the hours passed by. Occasionally, one of their phones would ring and they would come to ask me more questions about my apartment's layout or details about Clay and his past. Every time the phone would ring, I would look up, hopeful that he had surrendered or that they had breached the apartment and were transporting him to the hospital to detoxify his blood of all the alcohol.

The detectives who called offered little information. They didn't know yet whose side I was on, and they pleaded with me not to call Clay and interfere with their negotiations, a request I was more than happy to comply with. Despite all of this, I was relieved every time they did call, because if they were still trying to get in, then Clay was alive.

Although they could not share information about the standoff, they did begin to fill me in on what I might be returning to. "You may want to start thinking about where else you're going to stay for a little while, you won't be able to return to this apartment." As if they were unsure that I really understood what they were saying, they went on, "we've been using a lot of gas and pepper spray and it's going to be all over in there."

Later, on another call, "It isn't just in the air. Your clothes, furniture, everything is probably lost at this point. You're going to need to buy all new things."

"We think Clay might be hiding in your vehicle in the garage, we're going to have to winch it out." A process which nearly totaled my 4Runner as it was forcibly towed out, dragging almost every panel across the walls of the small garage door opening.

To each of these updates I simply thanked them for letting me know, understanding that my only choice was acceptance; the damage was done and they were doing their best to get Clay out of the apartment. Besides that, I was already starting to understand that my things were just that, things. I had survived and if Clay could get out alive, did anything really matter beyond that?

A detective came into the room early in the morning and told me all this again. "I am so sorry that you're going through this," he showed genuine empathy but they wanted to manage my expectations of what I was going to find when I returned to the apartment. I don't know if "comforted" is the right word, but my fears of discrimination were lessened by his professionalism and concern, which was a vastly different experience than what I had with police officers in the past.

As this same detective stood in front of me explaining how my belongings had all been destroyed, he got a phone call. It was Kim. Earlier in the evening, the detectives called Clay's former law-enforcement agency to ask about his skill level and tactical experiences. Clay left their department three years prior after finally becoming what they called "a liability" for his drinking.

In vindication of their still-hurt feelings over his breakdown and the exposure it gave their office, they called Kim. They put her on alert so she could begin her clinch on Hunter's life, preparing her to capitalize on this moment of sudden parental control that she had forfeited over a decade prior. This was something Clay's former sheriff had threatened him with when he was leaving the force and even prior to that, when he wasn't getting his way with Clay's behavior. As if they hadn't done enough to let their brother down, they stuck this one last nail in Clay's coffin, setting his son up to lose even more than what he already was going to.

"How did you find out about this?" he asked her as he looked hesitantly at me and then walked away to finish the call.

* * *

At about six in the morning, the two officers who had been watching me all night went home and switched out their role with a SWAT member just coming off his shift at my apartment. Occasionally, while sitting in the waiting room, I took a break from staring at the wall and tried to lay my head down. I was exhausted from being up for so many hours straight, but I still could not sleep, not knowing how this night was going to end.

When I finally managed to close my eyes for more than a couple seconds, I was awakened harshly by the SWAT officer on his phone, debriefing in obnoxious detail how "crazy" his night had just been. He said things like, "Can you fucking believe it?!" "Nah, man, he was just some fucking drunk." "It's over. It was over at 3:42."

I sat up and stared at him in disbelief. He never even looked up to see me listening to him recounting my night right in front of me. He finally ended his phone call just as I was holding back the urge to throw up. I laid my head back down on the table, trying to cool my forehead on the plastic surface.

About an hour later, another officer walked in, and the same story commenced.

Didn't they realize that Clay was one of their own? That fifteen years ago, he had been in the same position this officer was? The man they called a "fucking drunk" had been driven to those depths by his work. Instead of getting him any kind of help and support, he'd been tossed aside, and now to the same men he once called his brothers he was just a "crazy" story to share.

I stood up, shoving my chair out behind me harder than I meant to. "I don't need to hear you debrief; I'll wait in the hall." I exclaimed to them both, as I turned to storm out of the room. He watched me for a moment, wide-eyed and looking shocked, as if surprised that I could even hear him. The other officer looked at me and then immediately broke eye contact and stared at his feet, apparently embarrassed; at least one of them seemed to know better.

I waited in the hall on a hard bench, too small to lay down on, for two more hours. When I walked back into the room where the SWAT rookie remained, he was still in the same chair, his head tipped back, asleep. I walked all the way up to the desk where he was sitting, and he didn't flinch. "Nice," I said. He still didn't open his eyes. I took a business card and a pen from the desk in front of him and wrote my mother's cell phone number on it—this would be the only access to a phone I would have for days—and I left it in front of him on the desk. As I neared the door to leave the room, from clear across the cafeteria I heard him call out, "Amy!"

I turned around to look at him without any emotion on my face. "Abby," I said. "I left you a number where you can reach me. I'm leaving."

He ran up to me. "Hey, I'm really sorry. It's just been a long night for me."

I stared back at him coldly, unblinking for a long second, then turned around and walked out.

I reached the top of the stairs to the entryway, lost, since I had been brought in through a back door the night before. "How do I get out of here and to the front of the building?" I asked the officer behind the counter.

"Um...are you, uh, being released?" he hesitantly asked me.

I realized I probably did look like they had just let me out of the overnight drunk tank. "I'm the victim from Kentucky Drive," I said, recognizing the ironic power that this statement would have with him.

"Oh!" he said, his face suddenly softening. "I'm so sorry. Out that door behind you and down the stairs."

As I left the police station, I had no idea that the third phase of my nightmare—losing Hunter—was just beginning.

* * *

A Letter to Clay's Law Enforcement Brothers

February 2, 2019

Dear Clay's brothers,

"Clay, Thanks for always having our back, brother. You'll be missed."

Remember that? The note written across the framed sketch of a sniper in his tactical gear, lying prone, watching the backs of his brothers while they worked. The gift that you gave him when he left your department the first time, it still hung on his bedroom wall that early morning as he sat there on my bed in Denver, surrounded by the SWAT team.

For years it was so much easier to hand him a beer and tell him to toughen up; to build him up with toxic masculinity. You hosted fight nights and got wasted, driving home after because as long as you were a part of the family, you were all untouchable. When he started to struggle, when he wasn't bouncing back and he was looking for an out, you shamed him and tormented him, you covered up his pain with excuses and by blaming me.

After Clay left the department the second time, when you hypocritically forced him out of the department for his drinking, he didn't go fishing anymore, didn't feel like camping. He rarely golfed. All the things you know he used to love so much he could no longer feel joy in. He stopped smiling and couldn't find enjoyment in life. He never again found his identity outside of the brotherhood of law enforcement, even when he did have the energy to try. He never recovered from the betrayal. After having been there for all of you, having your backs for so many years and sharing drink after drink after drink with you to cover up all the pain, he was left alone when he became too vulnerable.

When he tried to get sober, you discounted his efforts, intimidated him out of seeking help by threatening to take away his position in the school. He was terrified that someone might see him walking in and out of the therapist's office and asked to meet for his appointments in discreet locations. He brought me back to Wyoming with promises to get healthy and you punished him. He was your best officer, at everything he did, and you withheld his marksmanship awards and recognition to prove a point, to show him that he meant nothing to you if he wasn't going to play your game. You knew he was trying to get out, to break your cycle of toxicity, to escape the drinking and the violence, and you held him back; you called the departments he was trying to transfer to and you told them not to hire him, that he had a drinking problem.

Then, at your very next chance, you pushed him out of the family. You knew about his addiction all along and chose not to support him. Even in the final moments of this man's life, you still couldn't bring yourself to stand by him and forgive him for falling apart, for being the one to expose the culture and break from the pressure.

You knew years ago that he was losing control. I told you, remember? I told you I feared the day would come when Clay would hurt himself or someone else with his drinking. You drove me out of the department, out of town, just like you would do to him years later; in fear that if anyone admitted that Clay was falling, then you would lose your most loyal officer. But you lost him anyway, first to his alcoholism and PTSD. But His demons looked so similar to your own they scared you, and so you kept pushing him until he fell over the edge and we all lost him.

Like every one of you, Clay had been exposed to all the horrific trauma of the job. You were the ones who ordered him to do some of the worst acts of violence and then you covered it up. You knew what he was going through and you knew he was struggling long before it ever came to a head. Yet when it finally did, you labeled him a "liability" and exiled him from your brotherhood. The only liability was that he might have exposed all of you by exposing himself; by admitting to his alcoholism and trauma, you would have had to face it too.

In his final moments, you still couldn't let go of your own pride and "masculinity" to be there for him. Instead, you chose to twist the knife, to reach out and share your self-righteousness and gloat about his failures to his ex-wife, in turn reaching even lower than you ever had by hurting

LETTER TO CLAY'S LAW ENFORCEMENT BROTHERS

Hunter too, taking your last shot at a man who had exposed your agency and so many others for the toxic culture that it is. The man who finally snapped from your pressure, your shame, and your approach to being emotionless, unfeeling men. You betrayed him for revealing what you all really are— human.

Shame on all of you,
Abby

6

The Cycle of Financial Trauma

By the time Clay and I had moved in together the first time, I was twenty-one and tens of thousands of dollars in debt not only from the credit cards but from medical bills and the student loan money I had been using to feed and house myself for the first years of my adult life.

I had been raised to have what I wanted, as long as I whined loud enough for it. Everything had been purchased on credit cards. I didn't know how else to get it. The only money management advice I remember hearing from my parents was my dad occasionally saying to me, "Just because you have money doesn't mean you need to spend it." Other than that, if I complained enough while I was growing up, I eventually wore down one of my two parents, and I could have pretty much anything I wanted.

Every August, my mom took me to "the city," which really only meant the suburbs north of us, and we went shopping for school. Several hundred dollars would be charged to each of our family credit cards so I could get a whole new wardrobe. I filled my closet with clothes I liked but that were far behind the current style. Everything fit me oddly, hanging loose and baggy because she had a terrible fear of me growing out of anything before the end of the school year or my jeans fitting "too tight" and bringing the wrong kind of attention.

Out of style and incredibly unsure of myself, I was incessantly bullied in school for what I was wearing, which then led to me not wanting to wear it at all. I felt I was constantly trying to buy the right things to make others like me, and I was failing at it. And so the hundreds of dollars, plus interest, of outfits purchased would go unworn, hanging in my closet until the next August when we would go through the cycle all over again.

We were living well outside our means and when my dad lost his job of thirty-three years, our family lost our primary source of income. We had credit card debt in the tens of thousands, and zero reserves, which only caused more credit card debt as my family struggled to pay for groceries. I was spoiled and practically helpless, without any semblance of a work ethic. The loss was sudden, to say the least. One day there was an income to make minimum payments on the cards and put food on the table, and the next, my brother and I were being told not to snack in between meals because food was expensive, and we could not afford to replace it as quickly as we were eating it.

I had an after-school job, but I was making a very minimal income and it was spent as quickly as I earned it. I had a checking account that was constantly overdrawn, and I was living days short of paycheck to paycheck. So when my mom came to me, only weeks before school started, and informed me that I would be buying all my own school clothes that year, I was floored. First of all, there weren't even enough paychecks left before school started to get the wardrobe I was accustomed to, and second, I would not have known how to save for it even if she had given me some sort of advance notice. I didn't have a single idea how to keep money aside for something like this.

So when I turned eighteen, my first stop was at a rural corner gas station where I bought my first and only lottery tickets and my next stop was Maurice's (a twenty-something-style clothing store popular in the Midwest), where I promptly took out my first credit card and then immediately maxed it out on clothes, feeling accomplished and relieved to finally have all the outfits and shoes I had ever wanted.

My Maurice's and then subsequent Target credit cards would stay maxed out for several years after I first opened them. Even with zero income, these companies were happy to lend me thousands of dollars, and I would spend it on clothing, food for myself once my parents really had cut me off, and gas for my vehicle; but mostly, I spent it on clothing. I was striving so hard to figure out who I was going to be in the world and was trying to find value in my appearance and in what others thought of me.

When I turned twenty-one, my Pontiac Sunfire that I had been given when I turned fifteen had been run into the ground. The clutch was shot, brake pads bare, and I was forever getting stuck and stranded in the harsh Wyoming winter. I needed a new vehicle and had my mind set on a new Jeep Liberty even though it was far outside of my budget. Payments, insurance, and maintenance on a vehicle had never crossed my mind. I was living my life on credit cards I couldn't pay off, and somehow it never occurred to me that I might not be able to make a car payment.

Clay didn't know about my credit card debt at the time, or my complete lack of knowledge of money management, and trusted that I was responsible but just too young for a loan, so he cosigned for me. Within two months after bringing the Jeep home, I had shattered the windshield by following too closely behind a garbage truck and had to take out another credit card to pay for the replacement. Between that, the taxes and registration, and whatever other crap I bought, I had maxed it out to the tune of about $5000 in the following few months.

When Clay realized how desperately clueless I was about money, he set out to teach me everything I needed to know about managing a budget. The day he learned how much debt I was in, he sat me down and explained how not okay it was to live this way, that credit card debt was not the only way to have everything I wanted. He calmed me when my bills came in and exceeded my income, telling me, "They can't suck blood from a turnip. Give them what you can." And for the first several years, he sat down with me at every paycheck and worked with me through paying off all my debt little by little, at the same time teaching me to manage my money and live within my own means.

When I was living with him, he covered the food, house payment, and utilities while I worked to put every penny toward my credit card and medical debt. Even then, I had a lot to learn. I came home once from a day trip with friends with stupid things I had purchased, like a new cowboy hat, accessories for a hunting bow I didn't even use, and all the clothes and shoes I had wanted. He was understandably frustrated but negotiated with me on what I would return, then he wouldn't give in to my whining and complaining, making sure I really did go back to the store and return the random stuff I had never needed.

Money was a defining issue in our relationship, and our little family. Managing it, maintaining it, and trying to trust each other with it was a constant problem. Even as I developed more money management skills, Clay always saw me as that young woman who had gotten into all that credit card debt. No matter how much I learned, grew, and changed, he refused to acknowledge that growth. And so we fought, made up, and fought again about money. Despite all the turmoil, Clay was helping me to become a responsible adult and I needed that guidance. Plus, we were a family, and I was committed to remaining a family. I wanted Clay to commit to that, too.

Two years into our rocky relationship, I found a diamond in a pawn shop. It was big, and beautiful, and a great price, and I convinced Clay to buy it so we could have it put into a setting that would fit me. He agreed and told me he would hold it until we were "ready." There was never any real clarity to what "ready" meant, and the ring became a bargaining tool. He never proposed, but when I moved out after a big fight (I did that a few times) he gave me the ring to convince me to move back in with him.

It didn't last. I had thought his giving me the ring, and me moving back in, was a sign that we were "ready." But as I began to plan the wedding, we started to fight more and more. Even though I was working on a budget and DIY-ing as much as I could, the expenses still triggered him. Clay's drinking got worse. He got increasingly violent. One weekend, he took Hunter to visit his parents, leaving me behind. I packed my things and moved out again, and I left the ring behind.

I was twenty-two. I moved to neighboring Midtown, Wyoming for a nannying job and tried to rebuild my life. But even though Clay and I were technically broken up, we were still a family, and Hunter was still my son. My parents made that abundantly clear. My parents, particularly my mom, didn't approve of my "independent" choices, and when they came to visit me, they expected to see Clay and Hunter. That meant anytime my parents came to stay with me, Clay and Hunter did, too. Sometimes, my mom would even make plans with Clay before confirming them with me.

My parents weren't the only ones pressuring me to go back to Clay. I had started attending a church in my new town, and I was the odd one out. The women of the congregation made it clear that it was strange that I wasn't married. The younger women saw me as a cautionary tale, and the older women were always trying to set me up. No one in my life supported me disentangling my life from Clay's.

At Christmas, about six months after I had moved out, Clay invited me on a hunting trip with his family. After two days of hiking at high altitudes, in single degree temperatures, and through several feet of snow, I finally shot my first elk. And right afterward, Clay proposed. This time, he told me, he really "meant it."

That was the commitment I had been waiting for. And what else was

I supposed to do? Everyone around me had made it very clear I *should* go back to Clay. I started planning the wedding again, and the closer we got to the wedding date, the more his drinking and violence escalated. Just like it had the first time.

Despite the pressures from the congregation, my pastor had warned me that if Clay continued calling me names and treating me badly, he wouldn't feel comfortable officiating the wedding or even letting me hold it at the church. As much as I wanted to get married and have Clay commit to me, I understood there was truth in my pastor's words.

That spring, Clay called me crying, once again yelling at me for being a "psychotic bitch." He was drinking himself through a trauma response. He had been on a call earlier that day where a woman stabbed herself repeatedly in front of him. His taser had malfunctioned, and he was the only one on scene, so instead of taking her on with the knife, he could only stand there waiting, his gun pointed at her in case she decided to come after him, while she stabbed herself in the stomach again and again until his backup arrived.

I didn't know this part of the story until way later but I was sick of being called names and treated this way every other weekend. Despite the judgment and criticism from our friends and family for canceling what was now our second engagement and our wedding, I didn't want to spend the rest of my life this way. I called it off again.

* * *

A few weeks after the broken engagement, I was out with several friends, and we had been drinking. I let one of the guys stay over at my place, and we crashed together, on top of the covers and fully dressed, although the absurdity that I wouldn't have had the right to fuck him all night if I had wanted to was the most offensive thing about this entire situation. And still, it was my fault when Clay showed up at four the next morning, unlocking my door and walking right in, and then wrapping his hands around my friend's throat until he turned red and then purple, finally letting go but only after Clay left clear handprints around his throat.

What I really took the heat for was going to the police afterward. I was so broken down about what should and shouldn't be happening in my own life, and my own value, that I wasn't going to initially. Then Clay called my mother. He cried frantically to her about what I had done, how I had treated him, how I had been with that man in my bed, sinning. She called me, and later she would tell me it was because she was concerned for my safety. But that isn't what she said to me at the time. Instead, with judgment in her voice, so much "Christian" cynicism, she flatly said, "Clay called me and told me what you've done," making it clear she was disappointed in me for having put myself in such an inappropriate spot and having caused Clay so much hurt.

I couldn't listen anymore to the accusations that I shouldn't have the authority over my own body to make my own decisions with it. I could no longer take the blame for how Clay had been treating me all those years. I couldn't stand to think that I might have somehow been claimed for the rest of my life and would never have the right to move on with someone else or have a life free from Clay and his abuse. When I found out that she had shut down her store to take his call and had been there for him when I had never taken priority over her work even on my darkest days, it felt that much more crushing. Later, she explained to me why she did this, why she gave me the silent treatment for months and took Clay's side. She allowed me to stand all alone with the consequences of this decision because she knew that in the end, I would be fine. She didn't know that Clay would be fine, whether he could take the hard things that were happening to him. She knew I could.

I made the decision to go to the police. Then the real shit show started. The local police officers were professional about it but having already experienced the backlash of Wyoming law enforcement and their protective brotherhood, I knew better than to trust anyone. I never received a call from a victim's advocate, but I knew the woman I tried to seek help from in Clinton had been fired and chased from town for going against a cop, so I wasn't surprised when nobody else wanted to mingle. Clay lawyered up and was put on administrative leave, although his department still hadn't planned on firing him until he had broken the restraining order several times by calling and harassing me. Even then, they allowed him to take an early retirement gracefully. The day he lost his job, my mother called me, crying.

"How could you do this?! How could you threaten Clay's livelihood like this? You know that he might lose Hunter now, don't you? That Kim might come and take him from Clay and Hunter will never see his father again! How could you do this to them?" When Clay learned that I had called the police, he called my mom to tell her my actions would surely cause Kim to fight to have her son full time, which of course would mean my mother would never see her grandson again. His guilt trip and threats worked, and she was horrified that I would be so careless and selfish.

Several days later, she called me again, still criticizing me for what I was putting Hunter through and trying to convince me to make things right again.

"I ran into Detective Davidson today. I told him what had happened and asked if there is any way you could fix this and make it go away." She was almost optimistic and excited that she may have found a solution to the mess I had made.

"He said that all you need to do is call the police and tell them you lied about the entire thing and they'll drop all the charges! That poor boy was just in the wrong place at the wrong time, it didn't have to come to this."

Her spirits quickly dropped again when I refused to make this call.

I tried to explain to her that not only had I not lied and that by doing this, I would be sacrificing all my principles but also that "that boy" had been in the exact place he should have been because I had every right to have invited him to stay over. She didn't want to hear either of these things.

After this, she stopped calling. The silent treatment lasted about six months. All the way through my very first disaster deployment with the Red Cross to historical Colorado floods. I had no mother, no boyfriend, no friends even, to share my experiences with as everyone reveled in the fact that I could cause Clay so much pain.

Is it any surprise I went back to Clay when I came home from that deployment? I had been offered a full-time position with the Red Cross, and I needed to move across the state. I had no money from the six months I had been deployed as a volunteer, and I had no way to get my things to Cheyenne. I had no family, and my friends didn't understand why I needed to move for some job. Couldn't I just stay and work in hospitality my whole life so I could be with them?

I ended up apologizing so I could have help moving. And since I had been the one to come groveling back, Clay never needed to learn to take responsibility for his actions. As a part of the trade off, I called the county prosecutor to tell him I couldn't testify against Clay because I wouldn't be able to take time off from my new job and come back for court, which was partly true. When he tried to force it, without a victim's advocate to help me navigate any of this, I sided with Clay's attorney to have the charges dropped so I wouldn't risk my new position and my chance at a future. My mother finally started speaking to me again when I let Clay and Hunter move to Cheyenne with me and wrote Clay's resume and cover letter to get a new job. His family never forgave me. Clay never forgave my mother for calling and making me so mad that I would do such a thing. Nobody except for me ever took any responsibility for any of it.

***

When I was twenty-five, I finally gave into marrying Clay. I practically forced him into a ceremony after years of broken engagements and second thoughts and against the advice of those who knew us best, but at least in compliance with church teachings. A month after the wedding, I went home to visit my parents and attended my childhood church with them that Sunday. A deacon, a man I had looked up to and respected in my childhood, greeted me with a hug and a huge smile when I walked up to the door. He told me, "I am so happy for you, to see you finally settling down and finding some stability in your life." Twenty-five years old. Stable. Settled down. It was the seed I needed planted to realize this was nowhere I should be at twenty-five years old. If this was meant to be "it" for me, my life had plateaued way too early.

7

Letter To My Parents

May 13, 2019

Dear Mom and Dad,

    I once crossed paths with a person who said to me, "Can you accept that your parents were only doing the best that they knew how?" I don't have the slightest idea who that was now. It could have been a therapist, but I actually think it was more of an acquaintance. Somebody who left my life as quickly as they came, and why I was even talking to them about the challenges from my childhood in the first place, I haven't a clue. But that has stuck with me over many years. I often repeat it to myself when I see my peers having adjusted so well and so quickly to adulthood, leaving me jealous of the guidance and the support they received in that transition when I often felt so alone during mine.

    But then I think back on what little I know of your childhoods, of your own parents. And I see Dad's father sitting on his recliner with his newspaper, having worked hard bringing in the income all day, and so having done his part for his family, he sits, disengaged with the world and with his children. He doesn't hug and he doesn't play. In fact, "men don't hug" was something I recall him often telling my brother, even as a small boy. I imagine weekends were spent in the garden and around the property, but the time spent together on these days was because the kids were doing the outdoor chores, not because he was deliberately choosing to spend time with them.

And I look back and remember you rolling on the floor and wrestling with us as young children. You took us trick-or-treating, although I remember your reluctant attitude and frustration of being surrounded by noisy, hyper children. You tried, exasperatedly, to help me with my math homework while I pouted and slept at the table out of defiance.

I thought I needed a stricter hand; someone to hold me accountable for my poor choices instead of overlooking them to maintain the peace. I needed rules. On the other hand, some of the most empowering guidance I ever received came subtly from you, Dad. "You can't marry someone that you know now; it has to be someone you haven't met yet" (advice that you gave me when, in second grade, I was convinced I'd be marrying Jimmy Johnson), or "Don't tell your mom this, but I agree with you. You need to get out of this town. Let me check your oil and tire pressure before you go" (after I had stormed out the second time Mom had kicked me out, launching me back out into the world that kept spitting me back) and "I just don't want to see the military break your spirit." Dad, you were doing your best to overcome the example that had been set for you, and yet, for so many years as a young adult, I held your shortfalls against you instead of seeing how hard you were trying.

The little I know of Mom's childhood is that she was the oldest of five children and was responsible for raising and protecting all of them in a small Kansas farmhouse. Protecting them, as in, from their own mother and the hard world around them. We were raised with a loving, though grumpy grandmother, full of Christian legalism but affection for her grandchildren. My mom was raised with a hurting mother, who masked her childhood trauma with pills. Grandpa was gone all hours of the day, working to provide for his family. Meanwhile, Grandma had breakdown after breakdown, stemming from having lost her own mother at such a young age, forcing her to be the homemaker at twelve years old while her brother and daddy abused her physically and sexually. What chaos for you to grow up in, Mom, trying your best just to keep your little brothers and sisters safe and alive.

I find myself being angry and hurt by your judgment of me, your criticism of my choices. Even when I know that you had to raise five babies, including yourself, in such uncertainty and poverty. I know you were only trying to protect your own babies with the tools you were raised with—control and fear. When you grow up learning that your control over a situation is the only certainty that anyone around you has to rely on, of course you would irrationally fear losing that control. Especially when it happens to be your own daughter, exerting her own stubborn willpower to take it away from you so she can go out and navigate this terrifying world without you. I get it, I do.

But it's still hurtful. And I try to balance that hurt with the grace of knowing that I was the one who was born into your lives. I didn't have a blank slate of the world revolving around me when I came to earth. I entered into the drama of your lives together, combined with all your pasts and dreams and disappointments. And you were only doing your best to protect me from the experiences that were now driving your lives, from what happened to you when you went out into the world; or so I tell myself and do my best to believe with everything inside of me.

Sometimes, against my best efforts, the hurt is too strong and turns into anger. Anger because growing up, I only saw what I wanted to see in you, and it was good. I worked so hard to be just like you. I wanted to be the community organizer, the woman in town people came to when they wanted to get things done. The one who showed them all that a "housewife" could also be a boss and they should all step aside. And then I grew up and received all the criticism from you for being that person I wanted to be so much like. You never meant for me to be a free-willed feminist, someone who debated whether I wanted to have children or change my last name in marriage, someone who did exactly as she wanted and never let anyone bully her into a life of societal norms. Apparently, I had taken it too far.

The harder I worked to be independent and strong, the more it seemed you disapproved of who I was becoming. Yes, be strong, but not so strong that you upset others or stood out too much. As I got older, I learned that even your own battles were only within the confines of making sure everyone around you still liked you at the end of the day. I needed you to care less about what those other people thought.

I needed you to not care about what Clay thought of you. All those times you guilted me about "keeping you from Hunter" because I had broken up with Clay, for moving out and standing up for myself; every time you took his calls and stopped work to listen to his heartache and shamed me for my decisions. I needed you then.

I know you assumed I would be fine on my own, that I was going to be okay and he might not be, so you needed to pick his side and be there for him. But the truth was, I was lost. And the more my own mother, my own friends, his friends, everybody around me told me that standing up for myself in our relationship was wrong, and giving my life to him and Hunter was right, I walked right back into a dangerous situation that I should have never been in. Maybe you were right, and he wouldn't have been okay if you had chosen me over him. Maybe if he had lost his life earlier because he didn't have you and his family to support and enable his poor choices, then you would be the one filled with all this guilt over his loss. I wouldn't wish this feeling on anybody. I don't know what the right answer was in that case, lose him sooner by not enabling him or lose him later because we all did. But I know I needed you, and I didn't know how to be okay with all of it on my own.

Trying my best,
Abby

* * *

While I was sitting stunned and lost with my neighbor in her apartment, waiting for everything to end so I could go home, so I could know Clay was still alive, I realized I only had one phone number memorized. My mother's cell phone.

My parents had just been in Denver a few days before this on their way to Colorado Springs for my dad's bi-annual Navy reunion. When I called her to tell her where I was and what was happening with Clay two floors below me, they were only an hour and a half away. Before I was split from the rest of the crowd for questioning, I made one last phone call to her. I didn't know whether I would be home by the next morning or not, and not knowing whether I would even have a phone to reach her on, we agreed to meet in front of the police station at 9 a.m.

As I walked out of the building that morning, still confused about when I would get to go home, whether I even had a home to go back to, I wandered around the outside of the building for a little bit, lost in thought. I still had about fifteen minutes until nine and knowing that Denver was possibly the largest city they had ever driven in, it wasn't likely that they were going to make it on time.

I decided to circle around the building to get my bearings. Coming around to the backside, I suddenly realized where I was. I had been here before, many times before. This was the beautiful building with all the windows that backed right up to my morning running path. I had passed this building almost every morning for the past year, wondering what it was; possibly a conference center or theater of some sort, I had thought. Those tall windows I had always admired lined the high ceiling I had been looking up at all night.

Clay and I had run past here when he had joined me only weeks prior as he trained for the races we had coming up. I stood there for a moment watching people running and biking by, going about their normal, healthy routines, without a single thought to the tragedy that had been unfolding only a mile away all night long. I decided to start walking in the direction of Colorado Springs; maybe my parents would pass me on their way.

I hadn't made it very far before another police officer picked me up. He had been driving past me, going the opposite way, and promptly flipped around to pull up next to me. Even without having ever met me, he somehow knew by my disheveled look who I was and stopped to check on me. Perhaps the SWAT babysitter I just walked out on called him, or the officer from the front desk, unsure of whether they should send me out into the world, should they still need to ask me about the standoff.

He was kind enough though and offered to take me to the nearest coffee shop. He let me use his phone to call my parents and tell them where I would be. They were a little turned around anyway and happy to meet somewhere on the main route. He explained that the negotiators had lost contact with Clay a few hours earlier, but they were going to send some robot cameras into the apartment to locate him. Perhaps he had passed out, I reassured myself.

When we arrived at the coffee shop, my parents had already parked. I ran to them, hugging them both tight. It would be months before I would fully embrace how near I had come to losing my life, but the emotion of the night and the anxiety we were all feeling over Clay was not lost on me, and I felt comforted to have my mom and dad there with me.

After the officer said a few words to them and we made brief introductions, he left. Instead of staying for coffee, we drove a couple of blocks away, closer to the apartment. Next door to my regular grocery store was a breakfast and brunch restaurant I had been wanting to try. Naively expecting the whole ordeal to have a halfway okay ending, I thought I might be able to stomach some breakfast.

On the way there, the detective called to speak to me, asking whether we were still at the coffee shop. I told him where we had gone, and he asked that I wait for him before going inside. He let me know they were sending a team into the apartment to extract Clay. Based on camera images, they had reason to believe he was no longer a threat. It didn't occur to me what that might mean. Or perhaps it did and my brain wanted to refuse to understand, to remain in denial.

My parents went into the restaurant to reserve our seat since it was a busy Sunday morning. I stood outside with the officer while we waited for the radio traffic to let us know what this second-shift SWAT team found. I remained calm. Clay had been on the other side of these calls before. He had once responded to a woman who had cut her wrists in the bathtub. By the time he had gotten there, she was a stark white-blue color, floating in a tub of bloody-red water, and he wrote her off as dead while he waited on the ambulance and coroner.

To his surprise, the paramedics arrived on scene to find a pulse and were able to rush the woman into emergency care where they saved her life. I don't know what quality of life she was left with; I only knew the look of guilt and shame that Clay had on his face as he told me how he had almost watched this woman die instead of doing anything to help her.In my mind, this would happen to Clay. He would be passed out somewhere in the apartment, barely alive after the alcohol poisoning and the overwhelming amount of tear gas I had been told was in the air.

I questioned the competency of the officers checking on him. "They'll bring in a real paramedic before calling it, right? Someone with some emergency medical expertise is going to be there and determine whether he's dead? You aren't leaving this to your officers, are you?" The detective reassured me that these officers had some very legitimate combat medical experience. *Good*, I thought, *they'll know the difference.*

Then we got the call. It didn't come over the radio as I had been expecting. The detective walked away, answering his cell phone. After only a moment, he walked back to me, his head down, with a somber and regretful look on his face. "Abby, it's been confirmed. Clay has been found deceased. From self-inflicted blunt force."

I didn't know what that meant. Not just the blunt-force part, but I couldn't understand any of it. "No. No, Clay can't be gone. He can't really be dead. No...." All I could do was stare and deny the news.

"I'm going to go get your mom and dad," he said as he went into the restaurant.

They had to have known as soon as he walked in without me that the news I had received wasn't good. My mom came rushing out the door with her arms stretched out toward me, but I collapsed to the ground before she could reach me. I lay right there in the center of the shopping district, unable to control myself as I sobbed the hardest I ever had. Sobbing that wouldn't end for days, even weeks and months, as I grasped the news that this man I had known so intimately for so long was suddenly no longer going to be in my life anymore; that this friend who had been there for me in my own dark days, who had mentored me and taught me so much about life, who had been there for me so many times when my own family had let me down, had been hurting so bad, that he had died alone in my apartment in this tragic way.

I crawled to my feet and found a place in my father's arms only to collapse again at his feet as I screamed out in anguish. "Hunter's DADDY! Hunter doesn't have a daddy anymore! Oh my GOD!" And there I lay again, curled into a ball, uncontrollably shaking, unashamed as snot and tears poured down my face as the memories and the loss flooded over me, overwhelming me. Onlookers walked by, appearing stunned and staring at the dramatic scene, but I didn't care. I didn't have the ability to care about anything else other than losing my best friend and Hunter losing his father. I didn't know whether I would ever get off that sidewalk again; maybe I could just lie there until the pain went away. I believed I might never find the strength to get up and face life without him again.

I regained enough of my composure to stand again only to hear the words "blunt force" ring in my ears. Not wanting to accept that Clay could have left this world deliberately, my mind started filling in the blanks about what this could mean otherwise. Maybe he fell and hit his head? With that much alcohol in his system, he could have easily passed out while standing, right? Then I remembered, after having gained control of the shotgun the night before, a brief moment where Clay had lunged at the neighbor to try to get the handgun back. Somehow, they had ended up on the couch and Clay had the man wrapped in his legs with his arm wrapped around his throat in a choke hold so strong he could break the man's windpipe. I had driven the butt of the empty shotgun into the side of Clay's neck and collarbone, trying to hit a nerve or a pressure point, anything to get Clay to let go of the man's throat.

"Blunt force." I collapsed again in hysteria. What if I had caused Clay's death by giving him a concussion? What if the blunt force they thought was self-inflicted had been something I had caused and Clay had finally succumbed to the injuries? I sobbed even more, asking the officer if that's what they meant, if it was my fault he was dead. My mom had known instantly what the officer had meant by blunt force—that there was nothing I had done to cause this. Instead of telling me any more in that moment, though, she just held me, and the officer just looked on quietly, empathetically, while my mind continued searching for answers.

Eventually, I could stand long enough and could stop crying in long enough spurts that we could talk about what to do next. I wouldn't be seeing the apartment again for almost a week. The officer offered to put me in touch with victims' advocacy, but I was still bitter at the term "victim" being applied to me, especially knowing Clay was the one who had died that morning, not me. Plus I had no idea what they could even offer me at this point. Supposedly, they could give me a room for the night and spare clothes, but that wasn't my first priority. I needed to get to Hunter. Once I managed to get into contact with two of my best friends from Cheyenne, they went to work finding out where Hunter was, who had him, and whether I could see him. They made up the basement guestroom for me and bought me clothes and toiletries and we headed that direction.

We lived through one more nightmare while trying to get Axel back from the kennel, finally forcing him from them with my tears and hysterical cursing about what I had just been through. He was covered in his own pee, hungry, and scared. He had been transported to a county kennel since he could not wait with me at the police station. It turned out to be a filthy place with cold employees who stared blankly and without emotion at me as I begged for my dog back with tears running down my face. Even at the time, I noticed how young the lady was, to be judging me, making assumptions about why my dog had been brought in, demanding I return later in the day once she had filed the appropriate paperwork for his release. I wondered how she had become so hard and cold at such a young age, what her future was going to be like with her being so callous this early in life.

Before leaving Denver, I asked for a cup of coffee, knowing the withdrawals that would be waiting for me if I didn't at least try to drink some of it. I never even took a sip as the calls started pouring in and the crying continued, and we made our way north to Cheyenne, Wyoming.

* * *

On the long, tear-filled drive with my parents, Emily, one of my closest friends at the time called me to tell me that her long-time partner, Jack, and their good friend, Travis, both of whom were Kim's first and second-line supervisors, had been sitting with Kim all morning. They were waiting to get the news about Clay's death. Having been tipped off by Clay's former agency about what was unfolding in Denver, Kim had apparently been preparing herself for the news that she would suddenly have sole parental rights over their son.

She had so little to do with the decisions around raising Hunter that she didn't know who his pediatrician was, his teacher's name, or even what medications he was taking. She had only ever paid a portion of her child support, and some months, like in February, she would try to prorate the amount for the twenty-eight days instead of paying for the full thirty-one days of the longer months. She had never had to take a sick day with him, wouldn't have him over if he was grounded from gaming and television, and had never needed to buy him new clothes, since she would just keep the ones he was wearing when he showed up and send him home in pajamas or sweats that he had outgrown years prior, even if he was going to school first.

This was a constant area of frustration for me because it always felt like she was the fun one, only showing up when there was somewhere exciting to go. She would take Hunter to buy whatever toys, pets, or candy he wanted. Since she didn't have to feed and clothe him, she could afford to do all the things he wanted to do. One time, she even bought him a pair of birds just because he asked for them. He later told me he didn't even want the birds; he gave her his sad face and knew she would buy him whatever he wanted. So he tried it with the birds and got them just as he had asked.

Meanwhile, I would be the one frantically yelling at him to scarf down his snacks and change into his game uniform while we sped across town to his football games. Once there, sweating and mad at each other, Hunter choking down an apple with his cleats untied and my heart racing from the drive, she would suddenly show up with a smile and a bag of candy and convince him to sit on her lap right there in front of all his teammates and his coach. I watched from across the field, frustrated that she had been too busy to pick him up from school herself, making me look like the unorganized one just so she could sweep in and save the day in the moments that he disliked me the most.

Clay reminded me, often, that if she were any better of a mother, then I wouldn't have had the opportunity to be as involved in Hunter's life as I had been. At the time, I believed it, and it brought me some relief to know that at least he was in football, at least he was getting the clothes and nutrition he needed, at least I could give him a foundation of having a work ethic and showing kindness toward others. Although now I disagree, because had she chosen to be a responsible mother, Hunter could have been blessed by having two good moms instead of just one and he wouldn't have had to suffer from the other's mind games. He could have had the support and cheers from two moms on the sidelines instead of feeling the shame from one of them for the trouble of being there and the desperate encouragement from the other.

After weekends with her guilting him into not making her leave the house to take him to birthday parties or convincing him that his sports were terribly inconvenient for all of us, I would spend the next two weeks trying to re-boost his self-esteem. I would encourage him to take up his own space in the world and to fight for his right to be a kid after catching him in a lie that he thought was what his dad and I wanted to hear, instead of what he wanted for himself. I could have really used the help and support of a second mom to encourage him instead of one fighting me every step of the way to give him the childhood he deserved.

* * *

It had been less than three hours after finding out that Hunter and I would never see Clay again, on this drive to Cheyenne, that Emily told me, "Kim has decided you should stay away from Hunter right now."

"Wait?! What are you talking about? Who is going to tell him that his daddy has died? Who is going to hold him?" My heart sunk even lower than it had already been, now sitting deep in my stomach, making me nauseous in the back seat of the car.

I had seen how Kim handled, or rather, avoided, vulnerable conversations with her son. Kim's husband, Tom, had passed away only a couple of short years prior from kidney cancer. Even though we knew that Kim and Tom had abandoned their marriages and children to have their affair, they had eventually married each other, and Tom had been Hunter's stepfather for almost nine years. He had been the one who spent time with and raised Hunter when he had to go to his mom's house on the weekends; the one who threw the football with him and made sure he had a good breakfast and clean clothes.

Kim never even told us that Tom was sick; we found out through a mutual friend of ours who had received an agency email about the former patrolman's terminal condition. Kim later told us that she had not wanted us, or Hunter, to know, although she never explained why not.

When we offered our sympathies, we were met with indifference, but she did insist that she wanted to be the one to tell Hunter in her own time and asked that we not say anything to him. Months passed and Tom got sicker. Kim's sister texted Clay and kept him up to date, but Kim still insisted she would be the one to tell Hunter, and we respected her wishes. Tom was hospitalized from the illness and then moved into hospice, all in about a week and a half. Still no word.

One morning, we got a text from Kim. "Tom just died. Please let Hunter know." He was never even told his stepdad was sick, was never given the opportunity to say goodbye. He should have had months to prepare, and instead, was surprised that this man he had come to love had been taken so suddenly from him. Kim didn't list Hunter in Tom's obituary as a survivor. When Hunter went to the funeral and chose to speak in front of the mourners when given the opportunity, many of Tom and Kim's coworkers thought Tom had adopted a "little brother" of sorts through a program because they had no idea that Kim even had a child.

Understandably so, Clay had originally hated Tom, and Kim for that matter, for the affair; for taking his wife from him. He hated him even more for taking her from Hunter. But he had grown to appreciate how the man had cared for his son, took care of him, and spent time with him when he was with his mom. Knowing he had wished Tom dead at one point, he was overwhelmed with guilt over his passing. Clay spent the next several days drinking, trying to make his grief go away. Between Clay's intoxication and Kim's indifference, there was nobody else around to tell Hunter that his stepdad had died. So that evening, he and I skipped baseball practice and took off for the mountains for a hike.

I told him while we walked along the edge of the lake, and he cried. I held him for a while and then we hiked some more, talking about death and loss and his memories of Tom. I came home that night to Clay's rage for Hunter having missed ball practice and zero regard for the pain I had just saved him by sitting with his son through his first big loss so that he could continue avoiding it with his drinking.

* * *

Now, sitting in the back seat of the car, I was frantic. Kim couldn't possibly feel she was the best person to tell him his daddy had died. She had never been there for him through so much as an unscheduled day of school or a doctor's appointment. She had never had to force him to do chores or eat vegetables, she had never disciplined her son or told him no. Never in either of their lives had they had to experience a negative moment together, and she thought I didn't need to be there to tell him that his daddy was gone so unexpectedly? It turned out she didn't feel she should have to either. She just wouldn't tell him. In fact,

Clay had been gone for over three days before Hunter would hear the news. But he still wouldn't be allowed to see me or speak to me once he did.

* * *

The next morning, I woke up with the worst headache I had ever known.

I'd only been able to sleep at all because I had been awake for the past thirty-six hours. Even then, sleep only came to me after crying myself into unconsciousness, wrapped in my mother's arms and a quilt I had shared with Clay during our marriage. But the torrential migraine I felt when my eyes finally opened early the next morning hit me hard. I couldn't see straight and could barely lift my head from my pillow. Then the memories flooded back and reminded me why I was feeling all this pain, why I found myself in Juni's basement guestroom when I opened my eyes.

I hadn't had any water for over 36 hours, not since I sat waiting for news of Clay, refilling the miniature water bottle the officers had given me from the bathroom sink. I hadn't eaten since hours before that and it had been at least forty-eight hours since I had had a cup of coffee. After nearly a lifetime of drinking coffee, I was starting to suffer from some painful withdrawal symptoms Weeks later, after the dehydration, low blood sugar and caffeine withdrawals had passed, the burning pain behind my left ear remained. I would gradually discover through flashbacks over the next few days that I had been taking hard, heavy punches to the side of my head during my fight with Clay.

With all these factors compounding on top of my emotional turmoil, I called for my mom from the next room, the sound of my own voice calling out added a throbbing to the pain in my head. She came in, swollen-eyed herself, and sat with me, offering to get me anything I needed.

"Here, I have some ibuprofen in my purse. There's a glass of water here next to your bed. You should try to start drinking that. I'm sure Juni has made some coffee; I'll go see."

I knew all these things would probably help. I understood how important it was to get rehydrated, and I knew what happened to my head when I missed my daily caffeine fix. A few sips and a couple of pills probably would have made me feel better, but I couldn't bring myself to want the pain to go away just yet.

I sobbed back at her, "How can I think of feeling better right now when Clay will never get that chance? He can't feel better! He died because of his pain, and here I am, still alive! The least I can do is sit here in pain too. It's too unfair to think I could ever feel any better!" I cried until my eyes ran dry again and I couldn't pull any more tears from my body, expecting at the time this was all I would be doing for the rest of my life.

Later that day, I called the therapist Clay and I had shared, both as a couple and individually. I had regular appointments with her early in our marriage while working through my need for validation and mommy issues. He had been trying to overcome his drinking and anger about his past. Both of us worked desperately together to show love to one another despite the cycles of trauma that sometimes left us barely able to navigate the world around us. Rebecca was the most authentic and real person I had ever met. She had always been straight with me and so nonjudgmental with Clay while we processed our wounds from the past.

I took my mom to my appointment the next day. I rehashed what had happened during the fight, though I still did not register that I had lived through something so harrowing. Losing Clay was the most agonizing part, and it was all I could focus on. He had just been in to see Rebecca the previous Thursday morning. Only two days prior to getting in that truck and driving to Denver. I sat there, horrified, as I realized he had not asked for help in those final moments.

Rebecca, having specialized in trauma as a result of her own time in law enforcement and then subsequently from working with and supporting the law enforcement community through her work as a therapist, outlined the next steps that I could be expecting.

"The trauma is going to cause you to lose interest in things that you once loved."

As I heard these words, I was already in a very deep denial. I still wasn't eating, but I had had my coffee by now, and my mind was racing.

I am sure she said a lot of other things, valuable and important things. My mind in overdrive, I only remember hearing some of what she was telling me. She said I would need to move forward with a mantra, to tell myself, "I am okay. I am in control. I am safe." I repeated that to myself for months, often sitting on the floor of my apartment out of sight of the front door should someone enter and try again to take my life.

* * *

While I was staying with Juni, I had to tackle the seemingly insurmountable logistics of putting my life back together. That started with moving into a new apartment just a few units away, as mine had been destroyed that night.

There's a chance I never would've known any of the details of how Clay had died by suicide and would have been stuck wondering what "blunt force trauma" really meant. But the "bio-cleaning" crew that had come into my apartment to remove the evidence of his death had done a piss-poor job.

From day one and for months after, I found things covered in splatter and blood, which only solidified the flashbacks I had of his death, flashbacks of him wrapping his mouth around the barrel of the rifle and the pure explosion of everything inside of his head. I was forced to understanding how far his fluids had spewed by knowing where my items had laid, strewn around my room, inside of closets and hanging on the walls, as I discovered for myself that they had been ruined by the biohazard left behind from his death.

Moving from the destroyed apartment into my new place, I was fortunate to be surrounded by friends and family helping me to unpack and move the trash bags full of my belongings. Everything that had been kept was thrown haphazardly into these large, white bags—picture frames, candles, clothing—without much care and then piled up in one of the apartment's less-affected rooms. The idea was to only leave me with the items that were not covered in biohazard, tear gas, or pepper spray, which ended up limiting me to only those things that fit into plastic bags.

The furniture had been destroyed, soaking up all the hazardous materials from the night. The shoes lining the walls on my bedroom floor were covered in a pinkish-orange splatter, turning up in one of my white bags for me to sort through myself, and most of my clothes, those piled in my hamper and hanging where my closet doors had been left cracked open, were consumed the tear gas and splattered with blood. While I stayed at Juni's house during the big cleaning, the owner of the cleaning company called and asked me about certain items she felt I may want to keep or have destroyed.

"There's a painting of zebras over your bed. It's covered in blood and stuff; do you want me to try to clean it though? It looks important."

"What about the lingerie all over the top of the dresser? It still has tags on it, but it's pretty saturated."

At this, I broke down into more tears, sitting at Juni's kitchen bar, sobbing and choking on my guilt.

That new lingerie in the Victoria Secret bag sitting on the dresser had just been purchased earlier in the day. The image of Clay finding that bag in his drunken stupor and pulling it all out, knowing in his heart it wasn't bought for him, and then sitting down to blow his head off, flashed through my mind and crippled me into a ball of self-degradation. Why couldn't I have just loved him instead of leaving? If only I had been satisfied with that life and not always looking for more, he would still be alive.

Juni and her husband, Abe, came to Denver to help me sort through all the white trash bags. My mom was there, my best friend Jamie, and Brad, the guy I had just begun dating before all this unfolded. Abe had been a highway patrolman all his adult life, and Brad had been a combat medic. This was strategic and a grossly dissociative decision on my part. Somehow, I knew I would be needing their unique skill sets. And I was right. Searching through the white trash bags was hard enough, but finding the shoes initially flooded me with great relief, believing they had survived and wouldn't need replaced. Then as my mind rolled through the observation that they looked so filthy for some reason, and then the final sickening conclusion that they were covered in Clay's blood, I frantically passed them off to Brad who quickly repackaged them in the bags and removed them from my new apartment.

Even worse was the bag of donations I found among the rest of my belongings. Out on the patio where we had piled everything, so as not to track any tear gas into my new apartment, I ripped open another white trash bag. I immediately recognized the clothes in it were not even clothes I had planned on keeping. In fact, hadn't I already donated these? I thought hard about where these might have been left. They weren't in the closet; they had recently been pulled out and...my brain slowed down...I had stuffed them into a white trash bag. I had left that bag next to my dresser, next to where I kept the splattered shoes, near the lingerie that had been so saturated...I stopped tearing into the bag and folded it back onto itself to shield myself from the contents.

"Brad!" I called out. He must have heard the urgency in my voice because he came running onto the patio. "Take this," I told him. The bag had been wide open when I had last seen it. I hadn't been the one to tie it up.

Brad would never tell me what he found in it, though he and Abe were noticeably furious after this. They wanted to save me from any more distress. And they could have, except Brad shared his experience with my victim's advocate, who passed it along to the cleaning team, who called me a couple of weeks later to foolishly ask if I ever gave my dog rawhide. Confused, I stuttered over my answer but long story short, no, I don't.

"Well," she said, "I think what you all found in that plastic bag was a rawhide. We compared it to the other bioproducts we found at the scene, and it didn't match what we were seeing. So we think it was just a rawhide for your dog."

I don't buy my dog rawhide. I knew immediately why Abe and Brad had been so upset on my behalf. The bio cleaning crew had wiped down the outside of the bag, tied it up, and piled it with the rest of my things, with a large chunk of Clay's skull in it.

When I called Juni to tell her what I had learned and confirm my suspicion, she asked what I expected to happen when someone shot themselves point blank with an elk rifle.

I had shot my first elk with that rifle, on the same mountain ridge that Clay had proposed to me. It had been a birthday gift. After this the flashbacks increased in gruesome detail. In the end, my victim's advocate recommended to the bio cleaning crew that they not charge me beyond what my advocacy benefits were going to cover. They complied and never sent me a bill for the mess they left me to work through.

Although it didn't make the images go away, I tried to meditate through them, telling myself it wasn't Clay lying there bleeding all over the bedroom, waiting to be found; it was only his body. It was just the physical remnants of his life, the biological parts of him that were left.

Clay had been long gone before he even pulled that trigger. Arguably, from his recorded blood alcohol content, he was gone before he even entered my apartment that night. Even as I tried to convince myself of this, it didn't stop the fear I felt for him in those final moments, wondering if he cried in desperation, surrounded by snipers, SWAT teams and flashing lights; tear gas beginning to seep through the cracks under the door.

Under the very close supervision of my therapist, I finally sat down with the lead detective on my case and asked him to tell me the details of the scene from when he had found it. Where had Clay been sitting when they found him? Did they actually find the magazine and extra round from the gun in the couch, or had I been imagining it? Did he still have the fingers on his right hand or had they been bitten off in my efforts to continue screaming for help? I didn't want to hear any of these details, but without them, my mind wouldn't stop putting the pieces together on its own. The stories my mind made up about what happened that night after I ran from the apartment haunted me more than the parts I was present for, and I needed to know the truth so my imagination would stop trying to create one for me.

The brain is just like any other part of your body: when it becomes injured, you sometimes must open the wound back up to let it heal. Like you might need to open a flesh wound to treat an infection or reset a bone so it can heal back correctly, the brain is no different. I followed this meeting with a very intense therapy session, but after this, the flashbacks of Clay's death stopped. I was able to come to better terms with what had happened and to understand why the impact on my belongings had been so severe.

Now I know that Clay hadn't barricaded himself immediately after I escaped. In fact, he had left the apartment and run to his truck. He found that he was too drunk to drive away though, backing first into several vehicles and a carport before pulling forward into a neighbor's garage. He then abandoned his truck and ran back into the apartment to hide after seeing that more law enforcement were coming onto the scene.

I have to wonder, had Clay ever really planned on killing himself that night? Or was he too drunk to have even made a plan prior to leaving his home? After all our recent arguments, I imagine he was expecting to find me sitting with a man there on my couch instead of my homework when he walked in. Had he planned on only killing me and then walking away? Was he too drunk to even know what was going on? These are answers I will never have. I will never know if this was a planned murder-suicide or just a murder gone wrong. Maybe he had planned on shooting the man he expected to find there, and when he found me alone, was filled with too much rage and determination to let anyone go without feeling the hurt he had built up in the anticipation. On the other hand, when I look at the statistics for femicide, they all align to predict that this exact thing was going to happen and that I would die that night for all the decisions I had made to leave for the final time.

8

Little Girl Gone

At twenty-five, I had achieved everything I was told I should have by this age. I was married, I was a mother, I had a family and home of my own.

And yet, it wasn't enough. I sat in my garage after work every single day, crying silently over my failure to have a white-picket-fence type life and to make this relationship work. I would sit with tears rolling down my face while I thought of everything I had been expected to do with my life: look pretty, act dumb, get married, have children, maybe get a job, but if you're good enough, you'll never have to. Then I would look at how desperately I was fighting to do just that, and I would feel like an utter and total disappointment to everybody.

The worst part was, I wasn't even fighting against Clay to have success in these areas. Yes, we would fight, almost nightly. But our fights weren't about me falling short in my ability to be a great mom and devoted wife. In fact, we may have lived decades together in a mask of peace and happiness had I just given in to being content with our current situation. In a way, that may have been the easier road, to just give up and be what I had been raised to be: a submissive, respectful wife. Go to church, bring baked goods to the Sunday potluck, host baby showers, and serve my family. I could have chosen this route, and Clay would probably still be alive. But I might still have died. If not outwardly, certainly inwardly. And then I would be the one looking at my life in forty years, angry that everything I had given up was now gone, and so was the man I had given it up for.

I lived for years in this frantic nightmare. Coming home from work to desperately scream at Clay to get sober, begging him to take Hunter to baseball practice, to join us camping, for the love of God to just clean the kitchen so I could get thirty minutes of time with my schoolwork. But I wasn't fighting with him for the life that I had. I was fighting with me, for having given up so much of myself trying to make this life work. I was living with so much anxiety knowing that the dreams burning inside of me were dangling just barely outside of my reach. I was operating in survival mode, coming home every night and abandoning myself to keep Clay alive and Hunter sheltered. I would never truly achieve what my life was meant for if I continued down this path and I was terrified that eventually, I would lose it; I would lose myself.

I met with Rebecca sometimes weekly for almost the entire three years Clay and I were married, working so hard to learn how to love myself for who I truly was. I originally went for relationship support, knowing even just a few months into our marriage that nothing had improved with the exchanging of rings. Clay wasn't any more supportive of my ambitions, even after my career had kept us afloat financially for months before he found work again and even after that until his schedule stabilized. Getting married hadn't healed him from his addiction to alcohol and it hadn't stopped the fighting.

What I learned from therapy is that the problem didn't sit solely with Clay though. In fact, my anxiety was only partly due to his actions. After years of working on myself with the help of an amazing therapist, I finally came to the realization that my anxiety had grown out of a struggle to love myself for even my most basic qualities, let alone many of my desirable ones. I couldn't love myself for the past seven years of growth since Clay had met me, as a naïve and spoilt child, because he would never acknowledge that I had come so far. I couldn't be proud of my master's degree that I had worked tirelessly to achieve, the late nights spent after Cub Scouts, dinner, and nightly story time, sacrificing sleep and any thoughts of hobbies or fun, because instead of praise and approval, my family, friends, and coworkers had simultaneously shrugged off the accomplishment.

I wanted to do so much more. I wanted to grow my career, my family, my life's work to coach and inspire others, but without the permission and approval from those around me, I didn't think anything would ever be enough. I was a high-functioning achievement addict, with only extrinsic motivation to keep me going. And without the approval from others, I was on a hamster wheel of goal-reaching, trying with desperation to one day be "good enough." On the outside, I appeared to be one of those uber successful women who gracefully balanced being an engaged and devoted mother, wife, homemaker, and career woman. I was killing myself trying to be everything the "Proverbs 31 Woman" had taught me to be.

Sitting on my therapist's couch after years of internally drowning in inadequacy, she asked me to imagine my ten-year-old self: who I had been, how I dressed, at the happiest I had ever felt. Reaching deep into my memories, I saw her, my younger self, running barefoot around the yard pretending to solve crimes and leading her detective club with nobody but herself in membership. A tomboy and very socially awkward, in her too-long jean shorts, cut off just above the knees, frayed from the dull kitchen scissors used to make them. Rebecca asked me to imagine that little girl standing in front of me and to tell her how much I loved her and how proud I was of her.

After several moments of bringing her image to mind, I finally saw her standing in front of me, in her sloppy, dishwater-blonde ponytail and her large blue eyes, smiling up expectantly at her older persona. Even with that very vivid image of my younger, most true self standing in front of me, counting on me to say those words, I couldn't bring myself to do it. I couldn't tell her I loved her. Instead, I surprised myself by getting frustrated with that young me, angry even, fighting back the hot tears of pride and refusing to say it because I couldn't mean it. I didn't know how to love myself anymore, and I didn't know at what age I had stopped feeling good enough even for myself, but I couldn't bring myself to even look at her anymore, ashamed.

My entire life, I had been unknowingly fighting to find this girl again while trying to lose her at the same time. It seemed like every time I felt the pull to seek her out again, I was pissing people off, and finding my way in life was suddenly so much more challenging. I would choose that girl over who my mother wanted me to be, and it would be months before I would hear from my mom again. I would choose that girl over who the church raised me to be, and I would be met with judgment and prayers and more women's Bible studies; I could hear the "tsk, tsk..." when I talked too much of my love for my career.

I was once referred to a holiday romance movie when I was excitedly sharing that I was applying for a job in Denver. It was a dream job opportunity but one that would either force my husband and son to move to support me or cause us to separate, living apart and possibly divorcing. "You know, there was this really great movie I watched the other day about a woman and her dog! She thought she would choose her career in the big city too but then fell in love and chose to get married in the small town she was from! You should watch it." But every time I tried to give that little girl up and settle for the small-town life and give up on my dreams of moving to the big city, I found darkness, depression, and a profound amount of fear that I was missing out on so, so much more for myself.

I could look back on my entire life up to this point and see that every time I sought that little girl out, I lost everyone around me, but I found myself in ways that were transformative and pivotal. After the storm of disappointment from others, the path would clear, and my way would be made smooth and my life would be ultimately inspired and intentional again. All I had to do was reach my hand out to that little girl, take that first step toward her, and I could leave the fear and anxiety of my life behind and build one for myself that I loved and deserved.

* * *

The dreams of traveling, of exploring other opportunities in the world, still tugged at my heart. Deep down, I felt there was more to life than this servitude I felt trapped in, and I wanted to believe there was more out there for me. Working in my state emergency management job, I worked with federal teams coming to the state to help with our small disasters. They all told their glorious stories of travel like those I had always wanted for myself. They told their war stories of arriving in a state hit by a hurricane, and while the whole rest of the country was looking right, at another disaster-impacted state, they would go left to the new incident. They would have limited resources and none of the media hype, and would set up their response, weathering storm-surge waters and wading through flooded streets, and save the day, along with thousands of people, from the chaos of flooding and catastrophic hurricane winds. I listened to these stories and thought maybe I had missed all those experiences for myself, that I was no longer in a "position" to chase those dreams I once had.

Going home after being in the field with these teams, I was filled once again with anxiety about having missed out on my big opportunities, to save lives and travel, helping in all the hardest-hit places. I knew deep in my heart that this was still a big part of my own personal legend, but I had no idea how to get back to it. From where I was standing, I felt my chance to hunker down during hurricanes and drive along city streets covered in sand from a storm felt so out of reach after the life choices I had made to "settle down," to be a mom and a wife.

I asked Clay with hope in my heart, "Maybe I could still do something like this? Maybe I could still fulfill my career passion of being on those teams and responding to those events?"

He would look at me like I had lost my mind. "Thank God you have me," he said. "To keep your feet on the ground and your head out of the clouds."

At the time, I was convinced that I should be grateful to him for keeping me grounded, reasonable. But the small voice in the back of my mind would wonder, "Wait, why not?" I was in my twenties and in the early stages of my career and my life. Why couldn't I grow into this person I knew I was meant to be and why couldn't Clay support it? He was aware that I would literally dream of these exciting aspirations at night, that I lived and breathed emergency management and he knew of my passion for helping people on a national level. I wanted him to support it and couldn't understand why it sounded so out of reach to him. All I needed was one word from him and I could be off, fulfilling who I was meant to be in the world. Yet every time I brought it up and asked him to look at potential job locations with me so we could pick a place we would both like, he would give me a flat "no."

"Of course you're past that point in your life. We aren't moving Hunter and shaking up his entire life. He'll hate us for it!" His own trauma of moving all over as a child was reflected in his fears. I was afraid too, panicked even, that eventually my opportunities really would pass me by.

Every time I did get the opportunity to travel, whether across the country for training or to another town within the state to meet with local officials, Clay was triggered and drank heavily while I was gone. He blamed it on feeling too much pressure not to drink when I was home, so this was his opportunity to let loose a little. Except me being home had never once stopped him from drinking either, and this was not about just grabbing a six-pack so he could polish it off without judgment. These were full-blown benders that would sometimes last for days.

I never knew what kind of disaster I would come home to. Whether Hunter had made Cub Scouts or baseball practice while I had been gone or had even been picked up from school some days. Or if anyone had been cooking for dinner or if they had ordered out every single meal while I went without, eating side salads to save my per diem for the tight family budget. I didn't know whether or not any of them would still be alive or if they might have both died in a drunk driving accident.

Returning home from these trips, I would be overcome with the feeling of my lost dreams, anxious all over again with a sinking feeling of dread. I wouldn't sleep at night and was constantly on edge during the day. Had I really missed my opportunity to find my destiny and be who I was meant to be? Could I not have a family and a career that I loved at the same time?

And what about all the well-adjusted adults I knew who had moved all over as children contributing much of their resilience and open-mindedness to their experiences? Could this possibly be right, that I had peaked in AmeriCorps and my life was now committed to the expectations of motherhood and answering to a husband for the rest of my life? Was there nothing else? If my heart is telling me to follow my dreams, and I continue to ignore it, will it eventually stop speaking to me?

Early in my career with the state, I went to Maryland for training at the Emergency Management Institute (EMI) for the first time. I was thrilled to finally travel for work, to have the chance to learn and train in my field and explore a new place. Having barely met my travel goals after AmeriCorps, it felt like such a magical opportunity. I had never been to the Mid-Atlantic, but I had always believed that I would love it deeply.

At the time, EMI was my field's academic mecca, and I would be networking with other professionals for an entire week. Not only am I a terrible nerd when it comes to emergency management academics, but I knew so few people like me that I was elated to go and meet others who I could connect with.

I flew out a day early, ran an all-women's 5k in Baltimore the next morning, and toured the entire Inner Harbor, eating all the crab cakes I could find, and then wrapped the day up at a baseball game at Camden Yards. I could travel! And I could explore! It was a small feat, but this was the most freedom I had had in years, and the idea of following two of my dreams in one week had me on an absolute high.

Several weeks after returning home and still riding on the high of my big trip, I went to the end of the driveway to check the mail and found correspondence from the county court system with Clay's name on it. It was the official summons for the DUI he had gotten while I was away. He had gone to a bar, got wasted, and forgot to turn on his headlights for the drive home. He called the nanny to come and get him from jail the next morning and neither of them had told me anything about it. Clay had hired an attorney and began a legal battle and meanwhile I had been living in foolish ignorance.

My fear about traveling away from home and leaving them on their own had been fully realized. The anxiety doubled after that and whenever I left home, even on short trips, I would fret the entire trip, desperately trying to control everything from afar. Nightmares would haunt me and I would wake up with a dreadful feeling that things at home were not okay, and maybe my travel was the cause.

After we divorced, I felt like I could finally start to travel on my own terms. When I had told Clay of my plan to travel abroad for the first time, he had been discouraging, to say the least. Telling me there was no reason to leave the country, that I would not be safe going alone, wouldn't be able to afford to go anyway. At the time I was also saving money to take him to Pittsburgh to see a live Steelers game at Heinz Stadium the coming fall, and maybe I wouldn't have been able to afford both. It didn't occur to me that I was still sacrificing my dreams and goals for him or how unfair it was that he accepted this trip but didn't encourage me to do my own traveling. Instead, I always felt guilty for enjoying new destinations without him and Hunter there with me to share in the experience.

Clay had been so limited in his upbringing, his childhood spent in small towns, on ranches and reservations, that he had never known just how accessible and enlightening travel could be. His family had raised him to be fearful, to think small when it came to the world and the people around him instead of to wonder what he could learn from them. Travel was unknown, expensive, and unnecessary.

9

Dear Trauma

November 6, 2018

Dear Trauma,
    Fuck you.
    Sincerely,
    Abby

A week after Clay's death, I felt pulled to be in a house of God for comfort.

I had spent the past seven days trying to find the energy and purpose to live. I would eat and hydrate just enough to function and compartmentalized everything else into neat boxes, sealed up tight until I had the capacity to reopen them and face what was inside. My first priority had to be finding a new home, to get a roof over my head and reestablish some stability as a place to start my recovery.

That first Sunday, though, I needed a break from it all and I just wanted to be in church. I didn't know if I would get through the full service, or whether I would sob the entire time and leave embarrassed. But I wanted the nostalgic, childlike feeling of being at the feet of my Father, something I had not subscribed to for a very long time. I felt a tugging on my heart, a yearning, maybe even a regression to my own innocent upbringing, and I knew there was nowhere else I should be that morning.

I showered and got dressed, putting on makeup for the first time in days, and my mother and I went to church. In the years leading up to this week, I had grown to be so angry and bitter toward the church from my earlier experiences, blaming this community for the limited beliefs I had in myself. Yet, I had still been attending on and off for the past year anyway. Clay and I had wanted somewhere to take Hunter when they visited, and I needed some sense of community and closeness with God, even if I didn't know that I was even doing it right anymore in my struggle for independence from the legalism of it all.

As I stood there surrounded by people, waiting to see how my emotions were going to hold up, I found myself wanting to reach out and grasp those around me, looking for someone to hold me close. This wasn't like the small-town congregation I had grown up with; people didn't hug their church pew neighbors as a general practice so, it wasn't going to happen organically, but I wished it would. I wanted to be hugged so badly. I had kept such a cold persona when attending this church in the past, not making any attempts at building friendships or connections. Now, in my time of desperate need for others, I wished desperately that I had done things differently, that I had hugged more people.

The worship music began and the voices of the crowd around me rose up together in song. I braced for the breakdown. Instead, something else happened that I struggle to explain in words. A peace and calm I had never known flooded my body. It *washed* over me.

I felt the weight of it, thick and warm like honey pouring over me, starting at the top of my head and flowing down to cover my face and the back of my neck, over my shoulders and down my body like an ocean of stability and reassurance that I desperately needed. It filled my body, as it flowed, with such calmness and I immediately knew that in the end, when all of this was finally over and I had reached the other side, it was all going to be okay.

Clay was still gone; that couldn't be undone. But my son, my life, the end of the story, somehow, it was all going to be right in the end. I had so much peace come over me that I didn't cry at all during the service. I went back week after week, the words of the songs and the sermons seeming to be designed for what I was going through. I worshiped and felt, without a doubt, that Hunter would one day be standing next to me again, worshiping with me, that he was going to survive this. God was moving the mountains I couldn't do anything about; He had control over the areas I had none over. I just needed to focus on healing myself and let Him work.

* * *

Before Clay's death, I underestimated the power of depression. I thought I could overcome it with mindset and exercise, that I could fight through it like I might have with a cold. The first time I tried, and failed, to flip the bird to trauma was only about two weeks after I lost Clay. I wasn't even close to returning to work yet and my mom had gone back home just four days prior. I wasn't even sleeping through the night yet, waking at every sound. The only thing that had kept me going, kept me fed and hydrated after being left on my own, was knowing I had my next Spartan race coming up in a few days.

Clay and I were signed up to run it together. We had just completed his first race about three weeks before his death. He was so proud of his accomplishment that he went home and signed up for the next two events to achieve what is called a Spartan Trifecta, all three races of different lengths completed in one year. I was already signed up, as these races had become an annual tradition for my closest friends and me. It never crossed my mind that I wouldn't still run in the next two races now that he was gone. It occurred to me that it could be therapeutic even. I knew it wouldn't be easy, but I was surrounded by my girls, and they would get me through.

Little did I know how heavy trauma can really weigh. I packed my bags and drove to Colorado Springs for the race. Since I was normally the one to make the race-eve plans, nothing had been arranged, and I was left getting dinner and spending time alone that night, left with my thoughts to keep me company. "No bad vibes on race weekends." I repeated to myself a mantra I had used many times before.

Running in the race the next morning was terribly emotional and so much more difficult than I thought it would be. I was unable to remain in the moment and focus on what I was doing, and my body forced its way through the race purely from muscle memory. My closest girlfriends were right there next to me the whole time, talking me through it, carrying me across obstacles and encouraging me to keep going. I knew it was my first step to getting myself back, but Rebecca had been right—the joy was gone.

Two weeks after this, I ran the third and longest of the races with the same group of girls on Saturday and then tacked on a spontaneous fourth race the following day so a friend would not have to complete her trifecta alone. After running my third Spartan race since Clay's death, she and I had our traditional burgers and beer in downtown Estes Park before going our separate ways. I wandered around the hosting mountain town for a few hours, aimlessly and without seeing anything, the world a blur. Not finding the same feeling of elation I was accustomed to after a weekend of racing, I finally gave up and drove home.

Even though I had accomplished this significant goal with my physical body, I quickly understood that I had not beaten the trauma. I had not magically overcome it like I was expecting to, transitioning from the adrenaline high of the survival mode into an endorphin high from the race, thinking that would somehow end all the pain. Instead, I walked in the door of my new apartment, laid all four medals haphazardly onto the kitchen counter where they remained for days, and curled up into a ball on the floor and cried. I never once felt elated, couldn't accept the congratulations coming from friends, and couldn't muster giving even the smallest damn for my accomplishment. My body was in such great shape that I had mindlessly completed three obstacle course races in two weeks...My body was in such great shape that I had fought off my best friend's attempt to murder me.

These races had only provided milestones along the way to just surviving. I was jumping from one life event to the next, trying not to stay in the moment, trying not to think about anything other than what I needed to do to stay alive so that I could make it through the next event, the next reunion and the next holiday, without Clay and Hunter.

* * *

I was still recovering, both physically and emotionally, from finishing my races for the year, when I was faced with my next big obstacle. Only a month and a half after losing Clay and Hunter, I would be celebrating my golden birthday, my thirtieth birthday.

Up until now in my career, my coworkers had loomed over me in age and often treated me as their own daughter or granddaughter when relating to me as a peer, which made it hard for them to take me seriously. I have had bosses pat me on the head and tug on my ponytail, and coworkers compare me, to my face, to their own adult children still living at home in the basement, wondering how they could possibly respect anyone as young as me.

I had been waiting impatiently for years to turn thirty, hoping to be taken a little more seriously in my profession. This felt like a milestone age, when I could finally transition into adulthood, and from now on whenever someone would look at me and say, "What are you, like twenty-something?" I could finally say, "Uh no, I'm thirty, thank you very much." For several years, I had been looking forward to thirty being the year I would finally be exactly who I was meant to be in every possible way.

As the day loomed closer, I slowly realized that it could never be the celebration I had wanted it to be. Only forty-five days after losing Clay, I was still learning how to make it through a single day without hearing his voice. Had he been alive, we likely would have celebrated much like we did my twenty-first birthday—with him buying me dinner and forgetting to get a card. It would have been low key and undramatic because he wasn't overly sentimental and still had a terrible phobia of spoiling me, knowing just how entitled and helpless I had been when we first met.

I hoped I would at least have a great girls' night planned and would still party my little heart away in observance of my passage into adulthood, but even that didn't sound like a good idea anymore. Seeing people and trying to force myself to feel joy and happiness did not appeal to me. I didn't want to stay home and mope either though—I knew I would be terribly disappointed if I looked back and realized I spent my thirtieth birthday in bed. On top of that, I am somewhat cursed with a Labor Day weekend birthday, every year competing with family plans and camping trips, and everyone had already made their plans for the three days off.

I had to act. Not just to save my birthday but to save the entire year ahead of me; I had to face the work deployments, anniversaries, and memories without completely losing myself in the pain. If I was going to have anything good at all to look back on at the end of all this, I had to start anticipating these worst days. I needed to make a plan for how I was going to intentionally get out of bed each day and live my life again.

My biggest fear around the battle with depression and this anticipation of hard days was the accompanying suicide risks. Some call it the Werther effect, or copycat suicides. This terrifying concept is found in studies by Harvard Medical,[8] University College London,[9] and the American Journal of Psychiatry[10] and it was telling me that my rates of also dying by suicide during this time were significantly increased, in some cases up to 65 percent. Even scarier still, the rate of dying by suicide increases to three times that for children who have lost a parent to suicide,[11] especially those without the love and support system to get through their loss. Unfortunately, because of who I am as a person, I had already researched these statistics early in my trauma recovery and I was terrified by what I found.

I was fearful for Hunter and myself when I thought of our increased rates of depression, PTSD, and all that we were about to live through. I also knew that helping Hunter was outside of my control right then. His biological mother and Clay's family had made sure of this by refusing to allow me to contact him. I had immediately started a fight for custody but it was fruitless, as one attorney explained to me, because no judge in Wyoming was going to go against a biological mother or a law enforcement officer when it came to a custody battle, and Kim had both on me.

All I could do was fight to keep myself alive. Killing myself would only justify to Hunter's bio-mom and Clay's family that I wouldn't have been fit to take him anyway. They were punishing me for Clay's death, blaming me for failing to keep him stable. If I died now, they would consider it an admission of guilt. They would have won in their game of vindication and it would have left Hunter without my truth and my support when he was finally old enough to choose it for himself.

Sometimes, on my darkest days, lying on my floor and drowning in my feelings of guilt, this was the only thought that kept me alive; I had to stay healthy and just get through the next year. I had to stay alive and be there for Hunter, even if it would take years more until I really could be. To do that, I had to start taking care of myself. I wasn't going to be able to let myself go, abandon all my hobbies and my health, succumb to any excuses for why it was okay and normal to lose myself in my trauma. I knew if I let that happen, then when the time came to fight for my life again and again over the course of the next year, eventually I might not feel like I had anything left to fight for.

So, I spontaneously got on an airplane to meet a friend in Birmingham, Alabama, just to get away from my apartment and out of my head. Finding myself lying again in bed, but now in a random hotel room and on my thirtieth birthday, I looked around the room for something to write on. Taking the small notepad left there on the desk, along with the ballpoint pen with the hotel logo along the side, I curled back up in bed and I wrote down a list. I made a list of everything I could think of that I almost never got to do in this life, and all the things I loved so dearly but would have missed out on ever doing again had I died that night. I reached out to my network on social media, still not opening up to anybody outside of my immediate circle about what had happened and asked for some ideas.

Suggestions came pouring in from others who were inspired by my plan. I took a few that sounded just ridiculous enough, a couple I hadn't really thought of, and one or two that I felt a little guilt-tripped into adding (like the mission trip I had zero plans of following through with). I didn't worry about whether I could afford to do all these things; I didn't care that I didn't even know how to go about some of them or if I would fail along the way to find the resources to accomplish them. Some of the items on the list were so outside of my comfort zone that I don't even know why I added them. And many, I would find, were not reasonable to expect of myself with the battle going on in my mind.

One thing I know about myself, is if I write something down, or even worse, share it with the world, I am going to do everything in my power to get it done and prove that I was successful. I had already learned through therapy and self-reflection that I have this whole achievement complex and a small desperation for affirmation from others. In this case, though, I chose to use it to my advantage and it saved me. Because to accomplish the items on this list like I just said I was going to, I had to start getting out of bed in the morning. I was going to have to start eating healthy again and taking care of my body, going for runs and getting to the gym. I had to start budgeting very, very carefully and stop all the retail therapy. Whether it was even realistic to think of accomplishing these goals was never a question. I just dove in headfirst, ready to fight with everything I had; not just to survive the next twelve months, but to come out of them having grown from the trauma with a hell of a story to tell and never having to regret missing another experience.

* * *

August 30, 2018

My Thirty in Thirty Goals

1. Pay off the 4Runner
2. Travel Alone Abroad
3. Run the Spartan Ultra
4. Attend Yoga on the Rocks
5. Place in a 5k
6. Go Out in a Little Black Dress
7. Read a Real Book (not audio!)
8. Overnight Kayak Trip
9. Climb Two 14'ers
10. Run a Sprint Triathlon
11. Visit a New National Park

12. Get a Tattoo
13. 30 Days of Random Acts of Kindness
14. Go to a Cattle Branding
15. Go on a Mission Trip
16. Complete the Rough Draft of My Book
17. Go Snowboarding
18. Go White Water Rafting
19. Learn a New Language
20. See a Concert at Red Rocks
21. Go Paddle Boarding
22. Give a Motivational Speech
23. Write in a Yoga/Meditation Journal Weekly
24. Learn a New Skill
25. Go to a Play
26. Visit a Museum
27. Begin Volunteering Somewhere
28. Take a Leap of Faith
29. Find a Mentor
30. Complete My List While Maintaining all A's in school

Writing out my Thirty in Thirty goals on my birthday was one of the best choices I made for my recovery. My mission to check every item off this list was the only reason I got out of bed some days. For the first several weeks before I created it, the only thing I might have accomplished all day was brushing my teeth; sometimes taking a shower felt like success. Other days, I would spend all morning pulling myself together to go for a run, only to come home and crawl back into bed once more. Eventually, though, these small accomplishments toward reaching my Thirty in Thirty became the only reason I was able to look at myself in the mirror and take my next step, my next breath, and face the world in front of me.

It would have been so easy to bury my emotions down deep and fall into autopilot mode. I had walked away from everything I originally thought I had to live for. I had been divorced before the age of thirty, left my son with an unhealthy father and a mother who couldn't show interest in his life, and then, subsequently been blamed for the death of my ex-husband and punished with the loss of said son. All this to follow my own dreams. Although extreme, I was a cautionary tale from the viewpoint of my uber-religious upbringing; this is what happens as a result of individualism and feminism. Couldn't I have just been a martyr-wife like I was supposed to be? Would Clay still be alive if I had? Why did I have to challenge the system and inconvenience everyone with my choices?

The facile option would have been to succumb to the darkness around me and quit working toward so many of the life goals I had set for myself. Nobody would have blamed me; from the tones in their voices and with the frequency that they needed to hear from me, I could tell they were all expecting it. After traumatic experiences and the intense grief that comes with losing a close loved one, people often lose their jobs, fall into financial ruin, and disconnect from their friends and loved ones. In fact, every time I spoke to my family, it seemed like they were concerned I might give up on life at any moment. I could hear it in their tone.

"I haven't heard from you today, I'm worried,"

"Have you seen your therapist today? You don't sound like you're doing okay,"

"Oh, you're crying uncontrollably again. Do you have somewhere to go to get out of the house and be around people?"

It was well-meaning, but it got irritating, listening to their weary concern and what felt like judgment. They were worried, but not about whether I was going to be okay, more so with whether I *wasn't* going to be okay. And while there were many bleak days where I may not have been, their questions felt discouraging, as if they doubted my ability to survive when instead I really needed encouragement that I would make it through.

The horror that loomed during my First Year hung over my head like a storm cloud, ready to suck me up into the sky at any moment. I was surprised to find it wouldn't be the first Christmas or even the first birthdays missed that would be the most challenging. Instead, it would be the first camping-weather weekend of the year that would be the hardest; the start of baseball season, and the reminder that I would never see Clay standing on the patio grilling for us again. The first-year anniversary of the memories we would never make again caused the fresh waves of grief to wash over me and made those days feel like they lasted the longest.

I found that helping others through their own grief helped me significantly. I joined a grief support group through my church and met women who had lost their partners after sometimes forty and fifty years of marriage. Their lives had been so intertwined with their spouses' after all those years that they struggled to redefine and find themselves after their losses. They never expected to be in this position, to need to search for their lost identities. After so much time with another person, they no longer enjoyed any of their own hobbies or knew what to do with their free time. Some of the women had never needed to manage their own finances, didn't know which bills to pay, or how to care for their homes because they simply had not needed to in decades. They were grieving of course, but many of them also had feelings of suppressed anger mixed in with their pain.

Many of the widows were resentful toward their husbands for breaking their promises. After all, they had vowed to always be there for them. The women hadn't planned on outliving their husbands; they were supposed to go first so that the lives they had given up to be wives and mothers would never have to be anything else than just that— a sacrifice of themselves so they could forever be taken care of; that was the agreement. I watched as these women cycled through their emotions each week and as they came to the awareness of these feelings, and the confusion and guilt that bubbled up from the complexity of their loss.

I loved on them so hard. Many of them became my close friends as I coached them in self-care, something they had never made time or space for while raising their families and serving their husbands. I taught them to set boundaries with their families, their children who now treated them like children, doubting their ability to stand on their own two feet; and to embrace the full range of emotions they felt, including anger, without judging themselves. I calmed them when they would feel anxious about what was next, about the holiday gatherings they did not want to attend, or the pressure they felt to tend to others' needs before their own. I gave them the permission they needed to prioritize their own lives outside of what the world taught them was expected of women and widows.

"This is your time now," I told them.

"You don't owe explanations or time to anyone," I said.

"Do what you need for your soul. Do what makes you feel good and nothing else."

Many of them had never known that any of this was an option to them and felt liberated by the idea that they could put themselves first in their healing journey, and in their lives moving forward.

This was one of my most unexpected accomplishments from my Thirty in Thirty list. I had expected my volunteer time to come in the form of finding another search and rescue team to be a member of. Axel and I had done this in Cheyenne and I found it to be rewarding and so healthy for both of us since it required miles of hiking to train and work together in the quiet wilderness, sometimes for hours. But my bag of supplies and gear had been destroyed by the tear gas and my fear of ever seeing Axel indicate a cadaver find again, after seeing him do it on

Clay's own blood, caused my stomach to turn.

I couldn't move from the place I was in, avoiding it despite missing that part of our lives. But here, in the grief support group, I could encourage and inspire these women to find themselves after loss. I could take what I was learning and the resources I was so fortunate to have and strengthen others who had not been so prepared to suffer their losses. I brought in art supplies and encouraged them to make their own comfort kits, sat with them through guided meditations, and taught them to remain in the moment and grieve, all things I was learning to do for myself at the same time. Since this year of firsts, I have found other rewarding ways to give my time as well, but none as rewarding as this.

* * *

One of the less constructive items on my list was to get a tattoo. I wouldn't recommend such a permanent decision for anyone who is suffering a major loss, although I don't regret it.

After losing Clay and Hunter, one of the earliest warnings I received from a good friend was, "Don't make any major purchases and don't get a tattoo." Maybe that was two early warnings. Either way, I disregarded both right away.

I had to replace my furniture, and insurance wasn't going to cover any of it. "Was it damaged in the scuffle?" they would ask. If it wasn't something specifically damaged "in the scuffle," per their policy, they weren't paying for it.

Bed destroyed by hours of soaking in blood from someone dying on it? Nope, since it wasn't my blood, from a "scuffle", they weren't paying for it.

All my makeup, toiletries, towels, hair tools destroyed by pepper spray from law enforcement's efforts to apprehend a criminal and save lives? Nope, it was a scuffle, but not *my* scuffle, so no dice. So, furniture soaked in tear gas didn't mean a thing to them either, per their policy.

In the end, they took responsibility for very little since nowhere in their policy did they cover the suicide of someone not living in the apartment, or domestic violence, or damage caused by a criminal coming into the home, or really anything at all besides scuffles and explosions. "Well, there was an explosion when the gun went off, causing my whole bedroom to be destroyed in the biohazard caused by the explosion." They laughed at me when I said this. Like a real, laugh out loud, hearty chuckle at my predicament while they refused to cover a thing.

I hadn't meant for this to be funny, my room was truly covered in the biohazard of someone I loved dearly and I was desperately trying to get coverage on my belongings so that I could begin my recovery. I threw the phone across the room, screaming in frustration and anguish. How anybody, least of all a nameless insurance agent, could imagine laughing at someone living through the nightmare that I was experiencing was so far beyond me, I didn't know what to do besides fall apart all over again.

I had owned one lone couch when all of this went down, but it was my couch. I had picked it without anyone else's opinion and paid for it with cash that I had worked hard for. I was proud of that couch. It was a small sectional so Clay and I could both fit long-ways on it and Hunter could lie across. We all fit, curled up together, without it taking too much space in my tiny apartment; it was perfect. That couch is where I was lying, doing my homework, when Clay came to kill me. We had our fight over the gun on that couch. I had almost been murdered on that couch. It was in those cushions that law enforcement found a magazine full of .9mm ammo and an extra round from me unloading a gun while getting my ass kicked. I didn't want that couch back even if it hadn't been completely saturated from the tear gas bombs.

When I went shopping to replace it, what I bought felt like a justified large purchase. I went with another gray couch in a darker shade and opted away from a sectional style. I didn't want anything that would look too similar and bring back memories, either good or bad. The expensive albeit stylish, yellow accent chair, on the other hand? Completely unnecessary trauma purchase.

I spent more on this one silly chair than I did on my whole couch, and at the time, I didn't even like the color. I didn't own anything else yellow, and it didn't go with any of the decor I already had in my home, especially not the accents of blues and reds I had started decorating with. But, you guys, it rocked back and forth and spun in a full circle, and it was wide enough that I could sit cross legged in it *while* rocking and spinning, which sounded very soothing. Something inside me told me I needed to spend all that money and I had to have that yellow chair. Looking back now, that something was probably the desire for a little retail therapy and an attempt at masking the trauma of needing to replace everything in my home.

Even at the time, it felt frivolous; but for the next whole year, it became my go-to place for every single meditation. I sat in that chair when I needed somewhere to fold over crying when I found jewelry, covered in flakes of dried blood, that Clay and Hunter had given me as gifts. I zoned out for hours rocking in that chair and read my Bible in that chair. I would sit on the gray couch to do homework, watch TV, or even, many times, to eat dinner. But when I really needed to rock myself into some emotional regulation, I would curl up in the comfort of that chair.

I had my tattoo planned out pretty much immediately. Even before I was warned against it, I had decided I would be getting one. Ever since that moment in the church when I felt so much peace and calm wash over me, I had been grasping to that feeling and seeking every opportunity to refill myself with it. I knew that maintaining peace with my situation was the only way I was going to survive it.

Philippians 4:7 became my go-to Bible verse. It was my mantra. One version of the verse goes like this: "And the peace of God, which surpasses all understanding, will guard your hearts and your minds in Christ Jesus" (ESV). I didn't know how I could possibly have felt so calm during that fight for my life with Clay or in the fight for my life in the days, weeks, and months after. There were many times when I didn't think I could endure the pain for even one more second and may never live to see the other side. In those moments, I would seek out that peace and reassurance so that I could know again the day was coming when all of this would make sense. I would understand why I had to be the one living through this; why I had to keep going.

Clay had several tattoos, but the tattoo on his right arm was his most prized. It was a long eagle feather that stretched from his shoulder down his bicep, and along each side of it he had "strength" and "integrity" written in the Seneca language. Later, he would get the word "Seneca" tattooed above the feather. He was so proud of his Native American heritage and was forever reading books about the Iroquois and Seneca people, watching movies, and researching his ancestry. One of my bigger regrets is that I did not pay more attention to those conversations or ask more questions. It is a part of him I wish I had known more about. From the little bit I do remember, I could probably identify a painting of Red Jacket and give a brief synopsis of his story, but very little else. I hope desperately that his family kept his books and his research for Hunter.

For my tattoo, I chose a replica of Clay's eagle feather. Almost every photo I had of him, he was in a cut-off T-shirt and gym shorts, so it was easy to find a good image of his tattoo. I brought it to the artist so the feather's curvature would fall exactly the same and the fonts would match. Only, instead of "strength" and "integrity," I chose "peace" on one side and on the other, "perseverance," translated in Seneca, mirroring his tattoo almost exactly from his arm onto my rib cage.

That night, I had a terrifying nightmare. Clay had barged into my home, violently throwing open the door and storming into my bedroom, coming close to scream in my face about a man I supposedly had in my home. When he reached out angrily to grab me by the shoulders, I sat straight up in bed, waking abruptly with a scream and covered in a cold sweat.

Afraid to close my eyes and fall back asleep, I got out of bed for the day and tried to make myself the breakfast that he would have made—a large pancake with a perfectly fried egg sitting on top. Except I couldn't flip the pancake in the air like he did, and so it came out shaped funny and folded up, only partially cooked through and raw in the thicker sections. My egg ended up undercooked but I didn't notice until it had made it to the top of my pancake. Frustrated, I zapped the entire thing in the microwave, which only made it worse and upset me even more. Clay had always made the best breakfasts.

10

For the Love of Travel

My final straw, my must-have-divorce moment, came while I was traveling. It had been a year and a half since the secret DUI, and while the anxiety had never subsided, I was learning to live with it as my normal; I had to since my work still required short trips throughout the state every few months. This time was different though, it was a personal trip, optional. I had been promising my niece from early in their high school career that I would take them on their junior year trip when the time came. That spring, I took them to New York City and Washington DC on what would be my first time out of state without Clay and Hunter since the trip to Maryland.

I missed my own junior trip in high school because I had been bullied so consistently that the idea of traveling across the country with students bent on making my life miserable for their own enjoyment sounded like a nightmare. Faye was facing the same dilemma and I didn't want them to make the same sacrifice, especially knowing by now how important travel is. So, I saved all my per diem from my work trips and the "fun money" I was allocated each month so I could pay for my half of the trip without taking a dime from our family budget. I sold some gift cards, scraped by without my normal coffee shop stops, and raised enough money so I could go comfortably and enjoy two cities that neither Faye nor I had ever explored. Just the two of us, we adapted the school's itinerary to only visit the sights we wanted to see and eat at significantly better restaurants. Then we took off for eight days of East Coast adventures.

We pulled off the trip amazingly, navigating the subway systems and walking through the city streets with the locals and other tourists. The whole trip was a dream until our last two days in DC. Faye was not in the kind of physical shape it takes to walk 20,000 steps a day, and the weather had been way colder than what we had packed for. Not having been raised with the resilience or the social capacity to handle these challenges, they had a meltdown. After six days of discovering what the world had to offer them and starting to hear their own heart tug at them to follow their dreams past the county lines, they fell apart. They called their mom, cried, yelled at me that they'd never be anything worthwhile in life, and the whole thing imploded.

When I reached out to their mother and mine for support, both women gave their boilerplate, peace-keeping response of, "It's Faye; they're just not equipped for this. You can't expect anything more from them." There was zero encouragement provided to either of us and every bit of the enablement that had led to Faye having these challenges in the first place. In fact, this attitude had set their mother up for the same low expectations. The same standard, the very low bar that had been set for me when I was Faye's age, was being set for Faye. In education, in social awareness, and now with travel, they were getting the same discouragement from doing anything outside of the very small box they had been raised in. The similarities to my own life left me exasperated and frustrated. Hadn't anybody learned from my accomplishments that we can grow? That we can do better? I was out in the world fighting so hard to be more than what I had been raised to be and nobody considered that maybe Faye could too. Nobody wanted to hear how this limited mindset had been poisoning the women in our family for generations.

This was not the first time I looked at my family and wondered whether they had learned anything from watching me leave. Clay had always been there to calm me when I felt wildly disappointed with their seemingly unreasonable grasp to a life with invisible limitations. Sometimes he was a peacekeeper and would talk me down from my determined attempts at making them see the world around them. Bottling it up never helped and only resulted in more conflict as I fumed my frustration.

I felt nobody would ever appreciate what I knew about life even after everything I had overcome. I desperately wanted them to see me and to acknowledge the lessons I had already learned the hard way, so that they could also break the cycles of fear and ignorance, poverty even, and make better decisions for themselves. Instead, they gaslighted my experiences and minimized my emotions. Clay always empathetically agreed with me that yes, they were being unreasonable, and no, there was likely nothing I could do to change their minds so there was no point in engaging in conflict with them.

Originally when I called him from the hotel lobby in DC, he told me what I needed to hear, that yes, everyone was acting unreasonably.

"Abby, you can't act like you didn't know this was going to happen. They have never understood you and it was only a matter of time."

"But they're treating me like this is all my fault! Like I've done something wrong, and all I wanted was for Faye to get to see the country. All they have to do is encourage them, and instead they're supporting them in quitting! Like they've always done for them, for me!" I was shaking with emotion but trying to keep my voice under control.

"Why would you have thought this would be different? They have always let you take the blame for what goes wrong; you have always been the one to take responsibility for their actions. I never thought this trip was going to be any different."

Overwhelmed, I didn't know what to do. I felt like the right answer was to keep fighting this, to beg my mother and sister to encourage Faye, to calm them down and convince them that they did not want to miss the final days of the trip.

"It isn't going to do any good, Abby. You can't change them and you can't let them ruin your last days in the city. Go get on the metro and do what you planned. Faye knows how to reach you if they change their mind."

So, I did just that. With a heavy heart and layers of emotion bringing up all the hurt I had piled up from my upbringing, I found my way onto the metro and rode into the center of DC. I texted Clay throughout the morning, and he continued to reassure me that I was doing the right thing, but I could tell he was still very upset with my family for having always treated me this way. As the day went on, his tone gradually changed, reflecting more of his own hurt and frustration with them. Even while he talked me out of those same feelings, his were still bubbling to the top.

Sometime that mid-afternoon, something snapped. I have no idea at what point he began drinking, but it was a classic crutch moment and I might have seen it coming; I knew that feeling out of control was a trigger for him. Ironically, he always started drinking when he knew I was hurting and he couldn't do anything to make it better. He knew what he was saying was true, that no matter how hard I had worked to give Faye this opportunity, my family was never going to thank or appreciate me for it. And there was nothing either of us could do to change that. He wanted to be mad at my family, and at the same time, he recognized them as his own family, since they had often been there for him when his hadn't been. So, at a loss and out of options, and hurting from decades of family trauma, he started drinking.

The worst part about all of it was that he had been sober. We had just celebrated his six months of sobriety, the longest he had ever gone without drinking his entire adult life. But I was gone, traveling, and he was triggered. The fight with my family sent him over the edge, if he wasn't already there.

He called me to tell me he'd just gotten off the phone with his mom. Reluctantly, having recognized the gradual shift in the conversation throughout the day, I asked what he had talked to her about. He said he told her that I didn't have a good mom to turn to when I needed someone. He asked her if she would be there for me, if she would be a mom figure to me so I would have one to reach out to when I needed someone.

I cringed at the idea of his mom being pulled into this, and more so at the idea of him thinking she would be there for me. Our whole relationship, I had wanted his family to love me, yearning for a family to belong to and be close with. But they had always been cold toward me.

"Clay, that was very sweet of you to reach out to her for me," I said cautiously. "But for years, I have been calling your mom every time I'm in Riverton, and I get her voicemail every time." He already knew that not even one of those calls had ever been returned.

"So really, thank you but no thank you. I am sure your mom would say anything right now to make you feel better, but I'll be fine without either toxic mom relationship."

Maybe I was taking out years of hurt from having never felt like I belonged in either family. Perhaps I was just embarrassed that Melinda might believe I was somehow in a position to need her sympathy, whether genuine or not. But Clay hated this response and began raging back at me with years of his own painful memories fueling his anger.

I do not remember everything he said to me after that, just that his phone calls would not stop. He called and screamed at me about how unreasonable I was being, calling me names and demanding I call his mother. This went on for the next hour. Eventually, I put my phone away and stopped answering it at all, his calls and those from my family who were still upset with me for having pushed Faye "beyond her limits."

As I sat on one of the cement benches at the edge of the National Mall, across the street from the White House, looking up at the Washington Monument, echoes of him screaming "psychotic bitch" into the phone over and over again ringing in my ears, it occurred to me that this was finally it. I suddenly felt my moment of absolute clarity, an understanding that if I was ever going to provide nice trips for myself, travel, and grow my mind, and if I was ever going to be able to follow my dreams in peace, then I could not allow this to happen every time I left the house for more than a night. I was going to need to get a divorce if I was ever going to be able to find my own happiness.

The next afternoon, I received a call from Hunter's school. Nobody was there to pick him up, and the staff were all going home for the day. I called Clay, but he was passed out, drunk. I called Kim, and she was unavailable, working. I had to call a coworker to pick him up and take him back to my office with her, where he sat until Kim came to get him almost two hours later. She called me, apologizing profusely that she had missed her day to pick him up. I didn't tell her it was actually Clay's day to get Hunter, but that he had been drinking continuously for two days.

Clay called an hour after this, again furious with me, crying and screaming at me for having interfered with the way he was raising his son. He was so upset with himself for having let his drinking inhibit his parenting and he blamed me for it. He drove to Kim's house, wasted, and picked up Hunter. But he was so incapable of calming down after his blunder that she soon needed to pick him up again and keep him until the next morning.

* * *

When I got home from DC two days later, my mother and sister were already in Cheyenne to take my niece back home. When they asked if I was okay after everyone's blowups and breakdowns, I was able to answer calmly, yes, I was fine. Because I was. I had absolute peace with my decision that I should no longer be married, that I could no longer allow the toxicity of either my family's lifestyle choices or Clay's drinking to hold me back from my dreams of travel and work, or any other dreams that might come up along the way. The way I had been treated for the past few days was my breaking point and I knew if I didn't set the boundary now, then I might never have the life that I deserved. I would no longer allow the drama and dysfunction to depress me and cause anxiety. I could not control it and I would stop trying. From now on, I was going to only live my life for me.

I wish I could say this peace made that conversation easier. It didn't. My family gave the same response they always had, only I was more prepared to respond to it. Something had clicked to give me uncanny clarity. When I told my sister my plans for divorce, she said desperately to me, "Can't you just give him another chance?" My mother responded with judgment: "I thought you would understand after hearing how much pressure he was under while you were gone."

After almost ten years of being verbally abused every time I traveled, and even when I hadn't been away, when I'd been home doing everything I was "supposed" to be doing; after fighting for years to continue loving myself while the man who should have been my best friend tore me down every time he struggled with his own life, here they both stood. They wanted me to be more understanding. They wanted me to believe it was appropriate to offer him some forgiveness and pretend like it had never happened. As if I could just "understand" why anyone could ever be justified to talk to me the way he did.

I kept my composure even as my heart sank with the disappointment of their responses. The two women in my life who should have protectively had my back more so than anyone else in this world were asking me to continue to put up with it. Why?

"Because what is going to happen to Hunter if you leave?" "You're not thinking of him."

And, said with so much disappointment and guilt-laying from my mother, "I just never know when I'm going to leave here and never see Hunter again because of your choices."

Crushed, I explained to them both, with as much residual calm as I could muster, that after ten years of "chances," no, I didn't have to try to understand why someone should get to talk to me that way ever again. It was never again going to be okay for someone to treat me this way.

I filed for divorce the following Monday, two days after returning home. My hand didn't shake when I signed my name; I didn't cry. Clay signed the papers with the statement, "There's nothing I can do to stop you anyway. You've already made the decision for us." I was at absolute peace with the entire process. In the end, I knew I could never be the person God had set out for me to be, I could never be fulfilled in myself or have a global impact helping people, had I not left. I never could have reached my fullest potential while being surrounded by so much negativity and suffering from so much fear and anxiety, constantly living in survival mode. I wouldn't find my personal legend with all the negativity drowning out the sound of my heart speaking to me.

The day after I filed the initial paperwork for my divorce, I received a call from an agency I had been trying to get hired with for years. I had submitted dozens of resumes and applications and had even interviewed with them a year prior, around the same time I had been told to look at the example of holiday romance movies as a better standard for my life. But the timing of getting the job had never been quite right, and had I been offered the position at the time, I don't know that I would have left Clay yet. I hadn't reached my breaking point, and I had already given up several other opportunities to try to prevent the drinking and fighting that came with the idea of us moving for my career.

"We have an opening on our team and think you would be perfect for it." The timing was finally right, literally to the moment. Prior to the divorce, Clay would have been so far outside of his comfort zone and he would have drunk himself stupid in anticipation of our life changing, even if it would have ultimately benefited us. He would have raged for days, calling on my family to interfere, placing blame on me for my selfishness and threatening me with Hunter until I gave in to find peace and relief from it all. Then he would have sobered up and I would have thanked him for keeping me "grounded" and "rational." "You're welcome," he would have said. "Thank god you have me."

Finally, the timing was right. Not only because I was soon to be single and wouldn't be held back from my dreams anymore but because the universe had made it so. In acknowledgment of the grit and strength it took to say, "Damn them all and their opinions of me," and to take that step out into my own life, the universe awarded me with everything that had been waiting just beyond the shadows.

Clay and I sold the house only weeks after listing it, for cash and with enough equity that we could split the difference and I still had plenty to quit my current job at just the right moment, when the toxicity had reached its highest point. I dropped my two weeks' notice and walked out. The cash allowed me to transition comfortably to life in Denver doing exactly what it was I had always dreamed of doing—travel and emergency management.

11

Letter to Kim

"Kim, Hunter has been trying to contact me. He wants me in his life. Please allow him to contact me."

"Don't call or text this number again Abby, ever."

"I am responding to him contacting me first, he needs me right now. I will respect your wishes, but you have to know that you're hurting him with this decision. And I know I can't protect him anymore. But you have to know what it is that you're doing to him."

"You have tried to reach him through friends before."

"Only in response to him trying to reach me first, you blocked my number."

"I'm not about to get into a pissing match with you. Hunter's dad is dead and it's not because of me. He will not see you or talk to you again, you are not good for him. You will not take him away from his family like you tried to do in the beginning. It's not going to happen. He's where he belongs. Goodbye."

"You know none of that is true. You've been in law enforcement long enough to know that none of this is my fault. And I have all the documentation I need showing he is trying to reach me. You think he won't know what you've done. He'll learn."

"Well thanks to you he knows everything now. And he knows he is not to talk to you or anybody in your family. And if I ever find out that he is, I will get law enforcement involved. So I suggest you tell everybody in your family not to text him or call him. You're not getting your grubby hands on my son Abby ever again."

* * *

April 26, 2019

Dear Kim,

You may think I am the one who is not sleeping at night. You may think you got me good this time and that you are living out some sort of vindication awarded to you despite having fallen short in your own role as a mother. Your jealousy was always so evident, yet it was never enough motivation for you to show up for Hunter and be a part of his life. You left that role to me but at the same time despised me for it.

All you had to do was step in, on a single sick day, for a parent-teacher conference, you could have come to one birthday party. We could have been partners in this. Instead, you now live in fear. Because you know that in the end, you're the one who will be exposed. You made your choice for how your son's life would be after his dad died, flexed your "rights" to him as his biological mother and kept him from me even while he reached for me, cried for me, and you did so out of pride and anger. You alone threw away the remainder of his childhood, knowing full well he would not be afforded the same opportunities for sports, the same attention to his education, the love and comfort of a mother he had been given for almost ten years prior to this. Have you ever once thought about what was best for him?

Deep down in your heart, you know you can't hide forever from what you've done. You know that one day he will be brave enough to start asking questions, he'll start to search for information on his father, and then he'll look for me on social media, wanting answers that were never afforded to him in your cold silence. He'll learn the truth, and you will have to answer to him for why you behaved the way that you did. You couldn't have stopped him from losing his father, but you chose to take away his mother just because you could and for no other reason. Do you appreciate that you have a respectful, polite, and hardworking young man in your home? You're welcome.

On the other hand, I sleep just fine at night while you stay up and count your days until he's old enough to know better. Do you stare up at the ceiling while you wait for him to find out what a fraud you are, that you kept him from the family who raised him; for him to realize you never wanted the responsibility of a child in the first place?

When that day comes, and he's finished grieving over his lost childhood, when I can finally be there for him and he doesn't want you anywhere near, I will hold him close and hug him like you never could, and I will encourage him to forgive you when he is ready. Not because you deserve it or because it will ever come easy to him but because I don't want him to live with the resentment that sits in your heart, eating away at you every day. I don't want him to live in the cycle of bitterness that has surrounded him during this nightmare of his. I don't want it to tear up his life and haunt him like it has yours, leading him to betray family and ruin friendships.

As for me and my forgiveness for you? No, I think I'll just sit here behind my hypocrisy and tell you to go fuck yourself.

From Karma and I both,
Abby

* * *

Hunter finally called me. It was in the afternoon on July 30.

"It's been a while since I've heard from you. I thought I should probably call," he said, sounding so grown up.

"Hi, buddy! I've been trying to see you. I want to hug you so tightly right now. As soon as I heard about your daddy, I drove straight to Cheyenne to be with you, but I couldn't get to you." I choked back tears, trying to sound as brave as he did. "Have you been getting any of my texts?"

"No, I haven't gotten any texts." I knew then that my number had been blocked.

"I'm visiting my cousin, Dalton, and my elders now." His mom must have sent him to Riverton to stay with his grandparents, Clay's mom and dad. "Mom is working night shift so she can't keep me right now. But she's paying a person for me to talk to about things. I've gone twice."

I hesitated, not wanting my frustration with his mom to come out in my voice. That couldn't be his burden. "I'm glad you have someone to talk to right now, sweetie. But be honest with me, please tell me how you're really feeling."

There was a long pause after this, but before he could answer, he told me there was someone there who wanted to talk to me.

"Abby, I don't think his mom wants you to contact Hunter at all," I heard Clay's sister, Blanche, say.

"Blanche, Hunter called me. He needs me right now."

"No! He doesn't need you, and you're forcing yourself on him. He doesn't want to hear from you!" At this point, she was yelling into the phone and repeating over and over again that I was not allowed to call Hunter. Then she started threatening me with a stalking order.

Large, silent tears rolled down my face, but I kept my voice steady. "He contacted me; that isn't how stalking orders work."

"Don't you threaten me with what I can and can't do!" she yelled, seething into the phone.

"Blanche, he's my son."

"No, he's not! You did this to him!" she screamed back hysterically. A long pause followed, and I heard a voice in the background; Hunter had followed her into the other room. With a false, cheerful voice, she said into the phone, "Mhmm, okay, great! I'll talk to you later!" masking the blame and hate she had been raging on me only just a moment ago, and then she hung up, hiding from Hunter that she was the one keeping me from him.

Later that day, Hunter sent me a text with just six emojis in it. There were two crying emojis, one kissing emoji, a father and son standing together, prayer hands, and a heart. I tried to text him back, but the text went undelivered. Still blocked.

A couple of days later, on the morning of August 2, he texted me again and said, "You're coming to the funeral, right?"

I texted him back and said, "Are you getting my texts?"

I never got a response. I tried to reach him on my work phone, but it had also been blocked. I found out later that day that Kim was still in Cheyenne; she hadn't bothered to take the day off to attend the funeral with her son.

In the days immediately after Clay's death when I had tried reaching out to Clay's mother, she had made it very, very clear to me that I was not invited to the funeral and that it would be in my best interest not to show up. Hunter stood there at his daddy's funeral without the person he needed the most, surrounded by this family's bitterness and without me or his biological mother to hold him. At twelve years old, he faced this day alone so his mother, grandmother, and aunt could stand in their pride and vindication, all the while betraying what had always been most important to Clay—his son.

12

Letter to Colonel Pritt

August 3, 2018

Dear Colonel Pritt,

    I would like to bring to your attention the poor personal conduct of one of your troopers, Kimberly Johnson. Kim is the biological mother of Hunter Caldwell, a twelve-year-old boy whom I have raised since he was three years old, since the time Kim left him and his father Clay. You may recall that Kim divorced then Wilson County Sheriff's Deputy, Clay Caldwell, after she began an affair with Trooper Tom Johnson, who has since passed.

....

    For the past nine years, I have been co-parenting Hunter as a girlfriend, wife, and then even as an ex-wife to Clay as we both recognized the importance of my role in Hunter's life as a mother even after our marriage ended. For nine years, I have participated in every aspect of his life, including clothing him for school, missing work on his sick days, teaching him to read and write and everything in between. In fact, many people who knew our family and even the relationship that we have had since the divorce would say that Hunter reflects far more of my personality and characteristics than either of his biological parents'. While Kim has always taken the majority of her visitation rights seriously, she has had very little interaction and involvement with Hunter outside of that time, including any interest in his health or education. This past summer, she gave up a lot of her visitation due to a new relationship and the inconvenience it would have caused to take Hunter to and from summer school.

Now, however, after a series of the most unfortunate events imaginable, Clay has passed away. He died by suicide on July 15, 2018.

...

Unfortunately, Kim explained to the troopers assisting her with the news that she did not think I should come around Hunter that day, and she immediately blocked my phone number so I could not contact him. It has now been almost three weeks, and she has continued to block me from contacting him, despite his continuous outreach to me for comfort.

...

On August 2, Clay's family held a funeral for him, which I was asked not to attend due to their assumptions that I was to blame for the suicide. When Hunter texted to ask me if I would be there with him, I was unable to respond since I was still blocked. When I asked friends to reach out to him to make sure he had the comfort and the support he needed, we were again told that Hunter's mom did not want me speaking to him, leaving him to believe I was not responding and not coming to the funeral by choice. Not only was I asked not to attend or to offer any sort of comfort to Hunter, or to let him know the reason I could not be there for him, Kim chose not to attend as well, leaving Hunter on his own to grieve his father during this difficult time.

I understand none of these things constitute Kim being an unfit mother. However, as she has never shown any interest in being Hunter's mother full-time, I do have to wonder why she is putting her son through such a difficult situation with nothing short of negligence to his emotional and psychological state of being. As Kim does not know Hunter as well as I do, she may not understand that he is already being treated for depression as he suffers from her abandoning him as a child and her inconsistency in his life since then. She may also not understand that he holds his fears and sadness very close to his chest so as not to hurt others and that he is less willing to share them with adults whom he does not know well, including Kim. She may not have any idea the abuse that is taking place by her selfish actions and that they may very well cause long-term side effects to her child's well-being. However, she will need to become aware soon as her child is hurting and clearly not getting the care and love he needs during this difficult time. As a result of what I would consider jealousy of my relationship with her son, she is neglecting him to hurt me and to prove a point.

....

I am asking for your assistance to help bring to an end the neglect of this young man's emotions by correcting Kim's personal conduct. .... I am sure Kim Johnson is a wonderful officer, as that has always been her first passion, but she may need assistance in seeing that she is only hurting her child with her pride, especially when more than anything right now, he needs to be surrounded by love.

Thank you, sir, for your assistance in addressing this trooper and bringing Hunter home so he can enjoy the same quality of life and love that he had prior to his father's death.

Counting on your help with everything I have left,
Abby

* * *

Colonel Pritt's Letter to Me

August 27, 2018

Dear Ms. Eichorn,

I am in receipt of your August 3, 2018, letter regarding concern for your previous stepson, Hunter. I am happy to respond to your letter, though I will be brief.

As you mentioned in your letter, Kimberly Johnson is a trooper with the Wyoming Highway Patrol. You are correct in assuming that Trooper Kimberly Johnson conducts her duties in a professional manner. What you may not know is that Trooper Johnson is a veteran Trooper with almost twenty years of service and is considered not only one of the highest performing troopers in the state but a "go to" and esteemed trooper for the Wyoming Highway Patrol. As a result, I hold Trooper Johnson in high regard.

Your concerns surrounding your former stepson, Hunter, appear to be more personal regarding Trooper Johnson. As such, I believe your concerns regarding Hunter's welfare are civil in nature. Should you decide to pursue your concerns, you would need to proceed civilly through the legal process in Laramie County, Wyoming, since Trooper Johnson is the biological mother of Hunter.

This has truly been an overwhelming and taxing situation regarding the tragic death of Clay Caldwell. I am sincerely sorry for everyone's loss, particularly for Hunter.

Sincerely,
Colonel Pritt, Administrator

* * *

After I received this letter from Colonel Pritt, along with a returned photo of Hunter and me that I had included in my original letter, I cried harder than I had since Clay died. I couldn't stop crying. It felt like my last opportunity to get anyone to understand what was happening to Hunter, my last chance to get to him and hold him and make this better; his last chance of having the resources he needed to survive this. I cried for the entire hour drive to my therapist, found that she had double booked our appointment, and cried all the way home before collapsing into tears and crying myself asleep on the couch.

LETTER TO COLONEL PRITT

* * *

After Clay lost his job and his brothers in blue, he sat on the couch, drunk for four years, gradually dying from a broken heart and loss of self. He wasted away, feeding the same bad habits that had once been an acceptable trade-off in exchange for the loyalty he gave to his department. None of them ever reached out to him. Nobody worries about what happens to Hunter, to the families, and to society, when the officers give up the badge but can't give up all the trauma they are left with in return.

I think back to that SWAT officer in the breakroom of the police station. "Just some fucking drunk," he had said. How many officers did he know and work with who went home and washed away their days with too many drinks? Were they different because they came to work every day and covered down on him when he was having a "long night"? He couldn't have been over thirty years old and was already so cold and indifferent to this man who could have once taught him so much. Apathetic to the loss of life he had just witnessed and the families that would be so deeply impacted. Who would he be in another twenty years after many more of these "drunks" had finally pushed him into leaving the force? How much soul would he even have left at that point?

Of course, all agencies say they provide "support" to their officers while they are in the department. Some truly do, offering debriefings and counseling services, insisting that officers participate without judgment or retaliation. But there is a very long way to go before the culture has shifted into a truly safe space, and many agencies have not even started that conversation with their officers. Especially not the ones sweeping something like child negligence under the rug in the name of good performance. This was Kim's reward for having never complained, never needing resources for her own mental health, coming right back to work after Tom died, never throwing another officer under the bus for their actions. You keep your mouth shut and you get protected. What do you think happens when that circle of protection goes away, paired with the physiological response from the post-traumatic stress of serving?

I can tell you what happens from experience. They die. Maybe not right away, and some will transition better than others. Some may live very long lives after their service, but they have lost such a huge part of who they were that they struggle the entire time to establish a new identity, becoming a stranger to themselves and their families. But even after a very natural, "agency supported" retirement, most officers will have died within five years of leaving.[12] Having lost the very definition of who they are, many dive into a deep depression, isolation, and grief for having lost the camaraderie and belonging they had with their agency.[13]

For those four years after Clay left law enforcement, he struggled with the heaviest alcoholism of his life, but he kept the framed artwork on his bedroom wall of the sniper, covered in camouflage and hiding in the grass on a hill above the scene, looking out over his brothers. He felt as if they were all so ashamed of him, and maybe some of them were, having forgotten how they themselves had spent many nights drinking far too many beers and driving home afterward. They had forgotten about the Christmas parties and the barhopping through their small town and the fist fights, DUIs, and domestic abuse calls they had been called to on one another that had gone unreported. But at least they hadn't been exposed, and there lay Clay's mistake. Being pushed out of law enforcement and abandoned by these men haunted Clay for years as he wondered how he had gone from golden boy to being a stranger to all of them.

Like Kim, like all the other officers who one day find themselves in court, in divorces, or sitting on the couch surrounded by darkness, they wonder what it is that they've done wrong when all along their behavior was normalized for them. They weren't convicted or investigated; in many situations, they were not even questioned. Instead, they were given a smirk, and at the worst, a scolding, and then tossed back out onto the street with their weapons, never a thought to how their actions could have been hurting anybody else.

Clay sat there on the couch, his brothers having washed their hands of him when they were exposed by his actions. He sat there for years watching his life pass him by; he never went hunting again after that, never took another big fishing trip. He stopped enjoying all the things that had once defined him, and he sat there addicted to the alcohol and the movie streaming and the sadness until he couldn't take it any longer. He sat there while his son grew up and his wife walked away, too lost in the haze to do anything to stop any of it, until finally, he had lost so much that he felt he had nothing else to live for. He had given the best years of his life to his department and his community, and in turn, they protected him from the real world for years. When they turned him out into the unknown of civilian life, he realized it wasn't a place he could adapt and live in. Like so many officers, he was abandoned to himself, and he didn't have the tools to survive it.

Maybe Kim knows about this common fate and so she will never leave law enforcement. She will continue to shut up and put her head down and take the trauma out on her relationships and those around her. If she doesn't, who knows what will become of her without that protection and identity? Will anyone notice what happens to her son during this time? Or are they just going to wait until she's not wearing the badge anymore to finally admit what she did to him?

You're not protecting them, Colonel. You're hurting them. And you're hurting their families and their communities while you're at it.

13

The First Time

I stayed consistently busy with work travel prior to Clay's death. Any chance I got, I wanted to be on a plane headed to any state that would have me, for disaster response, training, and exercises. I could travel freely now and had a supportive agency that would take me anywhere I needed to go. Clay was gracious enough to still keep Axel for me while I was gone, making some extra cash from the dog-sitting and the added-on surcharge for lint rollers. On the weekends I was home, I saw Hunter.

I wanted to believe that being away was forcing Clay to get better. He finally had to be there for Hunter because I was on the road or in Denver, and Kim hadn't stepped up to help at all during the transition. He had tried depending on her, taking Hunter over to her house on the days he needed to work. But she still demanded he be the one to come in the mornings and take him to school, no matter what time Clay had gotten off work.

This would typically consist of bringing Hunter a healthy breakfast and a change of clothes because neither would be made available at her house. All of this required him to stop drinking significantly more than he had. He was noticeably healthier and so much more enjoyable to be around when he was sober; he had more light in his eyes and joined in on the fun experiences with his son, something that had been sporadic for years prior.

Since our time together was so limited, and often centered around me getting time with Hunter, he would stay sober for the weekend, and the three of us could build memories instead of spending the time as we had been before. He was convinced this new harmony meant we were going to be able to make things right, and permanent, between us again. He would talk about the possibilities of moving to Denver; he could transfer to the railyard there, and he would tell me about all the help he would need with Hunter in these quickly approaching teenage years.

But I was nowhere near ready to give up this newfound independence yet. I had finally learned I could provide myself with the safety and security, financially and otherwise, that I had been searching for in relationships my entire life. I no longer felt I needed a man to provide these things. Clay was not healthy enough yet to be able to join me, and I was not about to take the risk and give up this feeling now that I had it.

Besides this, my travel would still trigger him at times. In October of 2017, I was on the East Coast. Even though he and Hunter would be visiting me soon, he was altering his anti-depressant dosages and hadn't stopped combining them with the occasional drink, leaving him in a heap of emotions, crying heavily about even the smallest things, and I couldn't calm him. When he confessed that he had asked his doctor to increase his dosage, without happening to mention to him that he was also struggling with alcoholism, I convinced him to go back to his original dosage, the one that had been prescribed at rehab by doctors who knew about his addiction. I encouraged him to talk to his doctor about some of what was really bothering him so they could make more informed decisions together about his medication. He went back to his original dose but never told his doctor that he was struggling with alcoholism.

In April of 2018, Clay made his first attempt on my life. Our team was assigned to Puerto Rico on a special project after Hurricane Maria had wreaked havoc across the island; we would be leaving for a month to the island. I had been dabbling in the dating scene and had been honest with Clay about it, explaining exhaustively about my hesitations with his unstable sobriety and my unwillingness to put myself back in a dangerous situation while he continued to struggle with it. He was in complete denial that I had ever been in danger or that his actions had ever led to abuse. I still don't know if he really didn't understand the harm of his actions or if he saw them and refused to acknowledge it. His whole life he had been enabled by loved ones, with family making and accepting excuses for his actions, so maybe he genuinely thought this was normal. Either way, he couldn't understand why I wouldn't come back to him.

The night before I left for Puerto Rico, I packed my bags and went to bed early for my morning flight. Arrangements had been made for Axel; in fact, he was at Clay's house. I slept easy, even with the excitement of yet another fascinating trip on the horizon. Then I received the call.

"Abby, is Clay with you?" I shot up from the bed; Clay's roommate Phil was on the other end of the line. My heart pounded from the abrupt awakening and the odd question.

"No, Phil. Clay isn't with me. What's wrong?" I could hear the concern in his voice, and I leapt off the bed, my anxiety increasing.

"He left a couple of hours ago. He wasn't in a good way, Abby. He wasn't good." He didn't want to say it, but I knew what he was implying.

I snapped into action, the same way I had every time Clay had sat blacked out on the couch or had taken off on his motorcycle after way too many drinks, staying calm and remaining in control. The same action I was so familiar with now in my own career: What needs to be done first? What next? Methodical in the chaos.

I managed to keep my voice calm as I looked through my bedroom's blinds to my front porch; I saw nobody. "Phil. I need you to go into Clay's bedroom. Is his Kimber laying on his nightstand? To the left of his bed, is his gun there?"

A very long moment of silence followed while Phil ran down the stairs to the primary bedroom. "No. I don't see a gun there."

I had only just been there a few days prior to drop off Axel. I had noticed the gun lying there on the nightstand. There was no other reason for it to have moved.

"I have to go." I hung up the phone and picked up my shotgun, checking to be sure a round was in the chamber. Then I checked the locks on the front door and positioned myself away from the windows and called 911. I explained my fear to them, that my ex-husband may be on his way to my apartment and could be arriving any minute, that he had been drinking. I told them what Phil had said. I asked for officers to come watch for his truck, describing everything about it, including his license plate number so they knew what to look for.

Sitting with my heart beating out of my chest, pounding so hard it reverberated in my throat and made me want to throw up, I struggled to stay calm and made some more phone calls. Once I reached the Colorado Highway Patrol, I knew for sure what I had feared was true. Clay had just been pulled over an hour prior on a side road off the main highway, headed south toward Denver. He had been arrested and was being charged not only for drinking and driving but for drinking while in possession of a firearm.

When I explained to the arresting officer that I had feared he was on his way to cause me harm, she said, "Well what he was saying makes more sense then." I never learned what he had said to her. I called the local police department and let them know they could stand down.

I called Phil, and in true dependent, enabling fashion, asked him to contact a trusted manager at Clay's work, someone who could work with him through this and excuse his absence for the next couple of days and I made arrangements to get Hunter to and from school the next day. I went back to bed and barely slept the rest of the night. The next morning, I boarded a plane for Puerto Rico with great relief that I would be outside of his reach for the next thirty days.

I knew then that if Clay had reached me, he would have tried to kill me.

I would have been sound asleep. I wouldn't have heard or seen the very quiet turning of the lock on the door. I didn't have my dog there to growl or to let me know that things were not right. I would have slept right through everything and would have never known what had happened to me; would have never had a chance to defend myself.

Later, my therapist would ask, "But why was your immediate thought that he might be on his way to kill you?" I realized I didn't have an answer to that. Instead of the assumption that he had taken off on one of his irresponsible, night drunk drives like he had so many times, instead of the immediate fear that he was going to hurt himself, I knew. I knew it was me this time, and I have no idea how I knew this, only that I did. And still, when he told me that he had only been out letting off steam, shooting at road signs for sport, I wanted so badly to believe him.

14

Letter to Passersby

July 5, 2019

Dear Passersby,

What a journey it has been. So many of you had no idea what I was going through when you met me, walked by me and noticed my red, swollen face, yelled at me from your cars and your bikes, held me and wondered what the hell was wrong with me. From each of you, I have learned that no matter what I may be experiencing in my own life, I can never know what someone else is facing in theirs. I have gained so much more empathy and compassion from those of you who gave it so freely and from those of you who judged me so harshly.

If I pulled out in front of you, drove too slowly, didn't hear you yell "on the left!" from behind, I was drowning in, or drowning out, my many sorrows, fighting my demons, and just trying to get home and out of your way so I could grieve. You probably couldn't see the large tears blurring my vision while you were honking, yelling and flipping me off for taking a yellow light a little too late. I was desperately looking for somewhere safe to pull over until I could get myself back together to finish my drive. I was just trying to survive, and your lack of patience with me, your cruel words and nasty hand gestures that before would have never even fazed me, blinded me with more grief. Try acting on the understanding that you don't know what that other person is going through, ever, and maybe don't be such an asshole.

For those of you who I simply ignored or couldn't engage with, I'm sorry. To the nice man at the breakfast bar in Rapid City, I know you were trying, but I couldn't give you the time of day. I was already far too gone in my own thoughts and just couldn't find the energy to pull myself back to the moment. To my coworkers and friends who had their own struggles, breakups, miscarriages, family deaths, I couldn't be there for you; I wanted to be so badly and didn't have the emotional capacity for it. I feel awful for that, but at the time, I couldn't find even the smallest reserves inside of me to give. Believe me, I was trying. I have been a lackluster acquaintance and friend, and not an easy person to get to know or to spend time with; it was never you. Well, it was mostly never you; it was more likely me, and I promise to do better.

For those of you who had an endless amount of patience and love for me, whether you even knew me or not, I am eternally grateful. So many of you crossed my path exactly when I needed you. To save me from being alone on Christmas day in a strange city or to pace around the parking lot with me when I didn't know how to stop crying. For those of you who weren't that close to me prior to this and still stuck with me to become my friend, best friends even, in the face of all my grief, I will never forget you.

Finally, to Angela in North Carolina, for holding me so closely to your chest, tightly clasping my shaking head to your bosom, brushing the hair off my wet face and singing "It Is Well" to me while I cried, bawled, and convulsed into your loving arms when I heard the song for the first time since Clay's memorial, sung by the church worship team. You couldn't have known it at the time, but that young woman, that stranger who you held so dearly, needed you more than anything in that moment, and God sent you to sit right next to me that Sunday morning.

With gratitude,
Abby

***

I guess if I were to admit to either being an optimist or a pessimist when it comes to my view on humanity, I would confess without shame that I am a realist. Some of the most important people in my life growing up have turned out to have terrible morals; I can't follow them on social media during trialing times of politics, racial tension or, really, any other time because I have become so disappointed in their hatefulness for those who are different from them.

Ironically, without them having ever been in my life during the time they were, I also wouldn't be the healthy, well-rounded human I am today. Many of them were the most influential people in my life growing up. My mentors, my parents, best friends over the years, basically the entire Christian church, have all at one point or another fallen far from the pedestals I once placed them on during my time of limited world views and life experiences. But I wouldn't want to know who I would be today if I hadn't known them and had their influence in my life.

Throughout my year of firsts, I came to realize that the groups of people my small-town, Christian upbringing would have taught me to judge, and even hate, would come into my life for beautiful purposes and that they were profoundly good humans, loving on me and holding me up in unexpected ways. Though I had been away from that small setting for some time, people who I was raised to believe were different, quirky, or extreme became unexpected blessings during times when I needed them most. I stood in amazement as I came to terms with the idea that there is a whole population of people who hate those who are different than them based on appearance, religion, and political beliefs, when humanity can be so good and full of so much love.

People who I thought would always be there for me, those who I would have expected to do what is good and holy, if not for the world, at least for me, a friend, instead chose selfishness and jealousy. Family deserted me. Friends appeared to forget about me. But strangers stepped in and held me, brought me along, and blessed me in ways they may never know the full impact of.

I've come to learn through my trauma journey that the majority of humanity is not inherently bad, but nor is it inherently good. Since I was not allowed to attend Clay's funeral, I held a memorial for him myself. The morning of the memorial, my former workplace, the toxic one I had left so suddenly before, sent a large bouquet of flowers, and my former boss came to show his support. It had been over a year since I had left, and I had still been so hurt by the torment and toxicity that they had shown me, the times they knew I was struggling at home and used that opportunity to capitalize on my weaknesses, yet in this time of need, they stood there by me.

In that same moment, my own mother turned against me at the memorial. After two weeks of holding me, driving all over Denver and Cheyenne and everywhere in between, helping me get my life back together and comforting me through all my fear, anxiety, and pain, she did the one thing I had asked her not to do—she talked about Clay's attack at his memorial. I had very specifically asked my family to not make the day about me, to let Clay have his time and be remembered for who he had been before those last twelve hours.

When I overheard her loudly recounting my horror to another guest, I snapped at her, "This is not the time or place for that." She walked out, and took my whole family with her, abandoning me to continue welcoming guests alone and almost refusing to sit in the front of the church with me once they finally returned.

"You need to consider all that she has been through these past weeks, Abby," my sister scolded me.

Clay had been a devoted father and community police officer. He mentored students, school administrators befriended and trusted him, and his community knew he could be depended on to keep them safe.

Yet he was struggling, fighting to have a life free of addiction, and after years of teaching me to manage my finances, work hard, and navigate adulthood's challenges, he tried to kill me. Who are we to judge and say whether a person is good or bad without knowing their life story?

Expecting a person to be polarized, either all good or all bad, is not only unfair to them, but it sets everyone up for inevitable disappointment and heartache when unrealistic expectations are not met. When faced with survival, people will make selfish decisions. And since everyone's risk level is a little different, and not everyone has the same resources to manage life's challenges, it might not take much before they are in a dark place, pushing others away but then wondering where their support group went.

Others who have lived a whole life of selfishness and greed may unexpectedly find themselves in a position to bless another person. Did this person now earn unconditional forgiveness and respect from their judges? Is it really up to any of us to place that standard of behavior on anyone for what "good" and "bad" even means?

I say all of this to actually say that my Random Acts of Kindness goal in my Thirty for Thirty list turned out to be one of the most challenging tasks I had set for myself. While I should have been surprised by this, I wasn't. When I first set this goal, I had taken for granted how easy it would be to find ways to be extra kind in the world while also maintaining the motivation to feel generous to others. Throughout the month I chose to focus on this goal, I learned so much about humanity and came to understand how it can be so difficult to be a light in a world that sometimes seems so dark.

This had been one of my social media goals, meaning someone else from my network had given it to me and I originally took it on as a great idea. I had planned to complete all thirty acts continuously for the month of October, my favorite month of the year. I looked forward to it, planned for it, and attempted to set up a list of things I could do daily that could offer some kindness to someone else's life. From past experiences, I knew that nothing could cheer up a bad day more than turning someone else's day into a good one. But for reasons I would never have expected, it turned out to be a lot more difficult than I thought it would be. Not to mention, I was deployed to a hurricane response as well, meaning long days and being far from home.

I didn't walk into the month nearly as prepared with ideas as I thought I would be and trying to "make" kindness happen every day turned out to feel unnatural, fake, and awkward. Struggling to build my list of ways to offer unexpected kindness to others, I reached out again on social media and searched for ideas on the internet. My research left me so disappointed in humanity. "Hold the door for someone." "Smile at a stranger." "Say please and thank you."

Wait. These aren't random acts of kindness! These are things you do to just be a decent human! The internet thinks it's random kindness to not let the door close on the person behind you? Is this the standard we have set for spreading kindness? That not being a jerk means you are being randomly nice? Is somebody passing out gold stars for using our manners?

I'll be honest here—I'm not your most thoughtful friend. I'm not very good at remembering birthdays, and I never pay attention to someone's favorite...anything, really. It takes me a lot of *very* deliberate attention to know how to pick out a great gift for someone else, and I always forget to buy a card. But basic humanity is something I do believe I am pretty good at; I'm in public service, for crying out loud. Saying please and thank you just seems like a given to me. I wasn't about to start taking credit for things I already considered a normal part of my day.

Just like requesting good karma from the universe but never really deserving it, forcing out kindness just to check it off a list is never going to go well. On the first day of my random acts of kindness month, using a trick I had found from my online searches, I attempted to leave $1.50

in the vending machine at the office. Not much, but it was enough to have surprised the next person to come along with whichever snack they desired. That would have made me happy. I stood there for a stupid amount of time while the machine cycled my last two quarters endlessly. I'd place them into the slot just to have them dropped right back in the change receptacle again. I ended up walking away annoyed, having left only 75 cents sitting in the machine. "Whatever, I tried at least." Kindness achieved.

Day two was an oldie but a goodie. I bought a gift card at Starbucks when I was buying my own coffee and left it for the next person who came through the door. This is one of my favorites, and if you've never tried it, please do. It's a great feeling. When I started doing this years ago, I noticed an increase in the number of times I'm in line in the drive through and someone else has paid for my drink. It's fun and it feels good, especially to drive away and know that the only way the person can thank you is by paying it forward.

By day three, though, I blew it. A coworker had left to get coffee and came back with about fifteen of them for the whole group on assignment. Looking for a way to be thoughtful, I paid close attention to one drink in particular, the one ordered by my very least favorite person on the team. When the order came back, I grabbed the grande peppermint mocha, no-whip and walked it across the room to him with a smile on my face.

He was having a casual conversation with one of our partners. When I reached out to pass him his coffee, he put his finger up in my face, and in his most demeaning voice, told me to wait because he was in the middle of a conversation. Forgetting kindness month, I called him a dick under my breath and walked his coffee back across the room and left it with the others. Good riddance.

After that, I tried to keep up with doling out kindness as often as I could, offering extra appreciation for someone's hard work when

I could tell it was going underappreciated by others, setting up an Amazon Smile account so the ridiculous amount of shopping I did online could help fund a favorite nonprofit. I bought several more coffees for strangers and coworkers, though this was quickly becoming my go-to and was starting to feel disingenuous. I went back to scrolling my phone for ideas on how to be extra kind to others.

About a week into this awkward struggle to force both "kind" and "random" to happen, I met Carly. Carly and her family were staying in the hotel after a tree had fallen on their home during the recent hurricane. I had seen Carly several times in the elevator with her family, and while I had made small talk with her parents, I had not talked directly with her yet. To be honest, I was nervous about saying the wrong thing to her. You see, Carly had Down syndrome.

In college, I had nannied a young girl with Down syndrome, and her impact on my life had been so profound that when I saw Carly standing there, smiling sweetly, I just wanted to hug her and tell her that everything was going to be okay and that they would be home soon. But I knew that wouldn't be appropriate. At all. And so I would just stand there awkwardly, and when they left the elevator, I'd kick myself for not including her in the conversation.

When I saw her that Sunday again, I wasn't sure if she recognized me. She had come downstairs to buy herself a soda, and with that same sweet smile, she said hello as we got onto the elevator together. I was desperate to somehow brighten her day, knowing she must be stressed from all the uncertainty that comes with moving into a hotel after losing your home in a disaster; who wouldn't be? So, I complimented her pretty sandals. Almost before I had finished my statement, she had brightened up so completely with a huge smile, thanked me, and dove into an animated conversation with me about her grandmother buying them for her.

We had a lively conversation after that, riding up to our top floors together, talking about shoes, birthdays, family, somehow managing to cover a variety of topics with excitement over the short elevator ride. My heart was full, and I hoped the glow on her face meant hers was too; I don't know who received more joy from that conversation, her or me. But I knew this was the type of innocent kindness I wanted to be able to show to the world, the natural, loving kindness that Carly had just shown to me on the elevator.

After this, I tried to pay special attention to going above and beyond while I continued showing kindness, but I did so when it came naturally and stopped trying to force it. I stopped checking the box every day and quit tracking my actions. I left a few encouraging notes for people around me, bought and sent a couple of postcards, including one to Hunter, although I found out later that it was never given to him. I went out of my way to pick up a Pepsi for a coworker when the café we ordered from only had Coke available. I even paid for a women's conference scholarship when I realized I wouldn't be able to go myself.

I had fun shopping for Toys for Tots with some ladies after work one evening and sent a nice Christmas meat and cheese tray to the police department that had run lead on my encounter with Clay. I made homemade bagels for my office and bought a glass cello from an island outside of Italy for a young girl when I realized she wouldn't make it out to the glass factories herself. I donated Girl Scout cookies to a nearby fire department and gave up my spot in a self-defense class to a young woman so she and her mother could attend together after I found out there were no more openings left.

But I was no longer trying to do all these things only in the month of October. In fact, I dragged this out through the rest of the year, looking for opportunities that came up naturally but no longer doing them for the sole purpose of writing a book or bragging on social media about it. I'm not sure if I ever even made it to thirty, though by now the habit of going out of my way for others when I can has made up for it, even if I stopped counting a long time ago.

In the end, keeping score had been taking the joy out of it. Not to mention, there were still so many days when I barely functioned. Not as consistent now but scattered throughout those months were days when surviving was all I had the emotional capacity to do. Being kind was not something I could muster from the floor of my bedroom, and so I would just lie there and try again the next day.

On the days when I did have the energy to go out into the world, complimenting the time and energy someone took in putting together their outfit, or for maintaining their hair in a bold color, or, like me, simply managing to get themselves out of bed that day, lifted my spirits and gave me purpose. When I knew I was making the world a better place, even for one person for that one moment, I knew there was still a reason for me to be alive; that the world still needed me in it for those moments.

I also came to understand how impactful somebody's rudeness can be. I learned through my worst days that sometimes an act of kindness is really just giving somebody grace whether you think they deserve it or not. There were times when I'd leave work and hurriedly rush to my car in the middle of the day to keep anyone from seeing the ugly sobbing that was about to occur. I'd pull myself together enough to see straight so I could get home, wanting to fall to pieces some more in bed once I got there. And in my flustered state, maybe I'd cut someone off by accident or take a light a little too into the yellow stage, keeping someone a split second from their green light.

I've had people run me down, flip me off, and honk incessantly at what was a small blunder. Only a moment of their day had been inconvenienced, and I would be left questioning my place in this world. I would wonder why I even wanted to be a part of humanity with all its darkness. Dramatic, I know. But these were dramatic times, and I was in a bad place more often than I was in a good place, especially in the beginning.

My runs felt long, and my body heavy, and it would take everything I had to drag myself out the door, often after falling into fits of tears while pulling on my shoes, crippled at the front door. On a particularly dark day, I had literally forced myself off the floor, knowing I might not live through the coming hours if I stayed in my pool of tears much longer. In an attempt to drown out all the demons screaming blame and guilt into my soul, I had turned up my headphones louder than normal.

I was barely putting one foot in front of the other, praying my endorphins would kick in and fuel me in my efforts to mask the pain loudly reverberating in my mind. I had also apparently covered up a call from an approaching biker behind me. As she finally passed me, she screamed insults and obscenities at my lack of consideration for not moving right on the trail. I stopped in my tracks and broke into tears all over again. It took everything I had to find the energy to drag myself back home and back into bed.

On another occasion, I sat at an airport waiting for my flight while I tried my best to ignore a woman sitting nearby raging loudly into her phone about the fight she had just had with her partner, describing in detail how he had broken into her apartment. It wasn't a big airport, so I tried to find a different seat near the gate where I couldn't hear her, but the entire waiting crowd was unwillingly getting every violent detail rehashed to them. I sat there and tried to keep myself from reliving the flashbacks of my own traumatizing situation as she debriefed her whole experience to the person on the other end of the phone.

Kindness doesn't mean enabling, letting others take advantage of you, or allowing yourself to stay in an unsafe or uncomfortable position to not come across as "mean." It is still appropriate to set boundaries, stand up for yourself, and walk away if the situation is unhealthy for you, and often these things can be done while showing respect and consideration in how you communicate these things. Just because you've told a person something they didn't want to hear doesn't mean you weren't kind about it. And sometimes, being kind to yourself is the most important kindness you can offer to the world.

But let me assure you, your own happiness is not at risk by smiling at the mother of a screaming child on an airplane or walking your grocery cart back to the return bin. Let pedestrians have the right of way, especially on rainy days while you sit in your warm car. And for the love, remember the privilege you have when you're sitting at a restaurant, the nail salon, or having your coffee delivered to your home by a delivery service, and tip well. Keep in mind that the small things you consider "random" may be the only things that keep someone together on a bad day. It doesn't have to cost you anything, it doesn't have to be planned.

* * *

The Random Acts of Kindness goal was suggested to me by my community, and my community—including the strangers who crossed my path—were a huge part of my healing process. I'm grateful for this addition to my list and the experiences it brought me especially because my goals were, like me, a little more practical.

Paying off my 4Runner was a big one. I put this goal at the top of my Thirty in Thirty list because if I was going to do it, it would require me to buckle down in all areas of my finances to pull it off. The last thing I wanted was to fall back into my old spending habits in the name of retail therapy and grief. Paying off the car, on top of everything else I wanted to do, would be my ultimate opportunity to show myself that I had learned money management and self-control when it came to spending. It would also show me that I had the financial discipline to achieve the other goals on my list, like traveling.

When I started responding to federal-level disasters after the divorce, I was making so much overtime, and the only thing I wanted to do was to pay off that 4Runner, more to prove that I could than anything else. I wrote large checks, covering months of payments at a time, so I could chunk it down faster.

The winter before Clay's death, I received what I considered a decently large income tax return, which would have taken down the balance to almost nothing, putting me only a couple short months away from paying it off. Clay and I were still seeing each other on the weekends, coparenting Hunter, and I confided in him when I had something exciting to share. When I told him my plan for the money, he asked me to take a pause on it, to consider putting that money aside to grow my emergency fund. Sober again and in a moment of his old financial wisdom, he said, "If anything unexpected happens, you're really going to wish you had that money on hand. Save it for a rainy day and keep making payments on the car instead."

I listened to him. And that following July, when I found myself without an apartment, my brand-new mattress and bed frame destroyed, my entire bathroom in the garbage, paying for a memorial and replacing all the things that insurance did not want to cover, I had that emergency fund to take care of my needs. I was able to recover almost immediately, at least tangibly, because I had the money set aside to cover all my needs and even several creature comforts for my emotional recovery while I battled with the insurance company, applied for victims' compensation, and eventually recovered some of those funds. The paperwork and reimbursements took months, months I wouldn't have survived waiting for the stability of my home and getting my belongings back. The emergency fund enabled me to focus on recovering my brain and heart.

Now that I was deeper into my recovery process, paying off the 4Runner had climbed back up my priority list. It meant a few things. First, I had finally learned some self-control around my shopping habits, where I used to be so incredibly out of control. And I did it without punishing or shorting myself on my needs. I don't remember a single time in the three years it took me to pay off the car, and especially not during the year of my Thirty in Thirty, that I ever paid full price for an item of clothing. I didn't punish myself with so much self-control that I could never have nice things, but I certainly got really good at bargain hunting, and I only shopped for items I genuinely needed.

I proved to myself that I could stay disciplined in other areas of my life as well. I cut out my gym membership, which was about 180 dollars a month. But instead of expecting that I would go from one of the most motivating atmospheres known to the women's gym scene to suddenly working out alone cold turkey at 5 a.m., I cut the 180 dollars to only 100 dollars and earmarked it for the month as a "fitness reward" line item. If I hit my fitness goal for the entire month, I could spend that money on whatever I wanted to, no judgment. I set goals like working out for a certain amount of minutes weekly, drinking my gallon of water a day, logging my meals every day for the month (with cheat days, of course), and then I built onto those goals every month until they became as second nature as waking up to go to a gym that I was paying almost twice as much for.

A lot of times throughout this journey, I did tell myself no. Self-control is like a muscle, and it needs to be exercised to get stronger, and this takes time.[14] But like anything hard, it will never get easy until you start practicing it. To show self-control in my shopping, I did all the standards like making a list before I went to the store, setting aside the more expensive grocery stores for only scheduled special occasions, and budgeting my splurging. Stores I knew were triggers for excessive shopping, I just didn't enter. The things I needed from those stores, I purchased online and picked up curbside or shopped at a different store where I could get what I needed without all the other distractions.

Sometimes, if I really wanted to get the urge to shop out of my system, I would get online and do a ton of shopping for all the things I wanted to buy. I would put all the items in the cart, gape at the total, and decide against it—not in the budget. I would think about the things on my Thirty in Thirty list I still needed to pay for and could put that money toward instead. Typically, just putting it in the cart was enough for me to decide I didn't really need it. If several days later I caught myself still thinking about an item I found in my faux-shopping spree, I would add it to my list for judgment-free shopping with my earned fitness money and I would prioritize this wish list at the end of the month.

If I found something that really called to me while I was in the store, I would carry it around for a while, finish the rest of my shopping, then take a picture of it and put it back on the rack. After a few days, I could decide whether it was something I could justify actually needing. If a week or two went by and I found myself reaching for that item and felt significantly inconvenienced without its purchase, I would go back and get it. Normally, I owned something already that made a very reasonable substitute or I could find it for a significantly better price elsewhere. And more often than not, I forgot about the item altogether after a couple of days.

For large purchases, trips, or items that were purely a splurge, I started a list titled "Things you can buy after you pay off the 4Runner" and I would write them there. Once the vehicle was paid off, I could go back and see what was on the list that I had once wanted so badly and decide if it was still a priority. Many of these things didn't even rise to that level of importance by then, and I was so grateful I had not spent the money when I had originally thought I wanted to.

There was a time in my life when I had to dig change out of my car seats to pay for enough gas to get to my next stop. I would get upset if someone came over and rinsed their dishes using hot water instead of cold because every dollar of my gas bill meant something to me, and I knew I would be stretched to pay it. Financial stability is freedom. Paying off my 4Runner and having my control of my financial life was an important step in my healing process. It meant that I could always rely on one person in my life to keep me safe and protected: me.

15

Sitting in the Muck

When I first added the yoga and meditation goal to the Thirty in Thirty list, I vaguely understood why it would be important in my recovery journey. I had attended enough yoga classes to know it was a form of mindfulness practice and was supposed to be a great way to relieve stress, not just physically but mentally. Up until this point, I had used it only to increase flexibility and cross train for other sports, like Spartans and running, or for stretching and recovery after races. I knew there was a deeper value if I wanted it for that purpose, but it wasn't what I had been looking for at the time.

I had the same experience with meditation. I had toyed with it, at best. Hunter and I often used it as a tool when, after Kim's partner Tom died, Kim moved to Cheyenne, disrupting Hunter's routine and confusing him again with her gaslighting. His emotions were so dysregulated from the abrupt changes in his life that he began getting into fights at school and acting out by throwing fits of rage when he wouldn't get what he wanted at home. He would burst into tears at the smallest of conflicts and was confused about why he was even sad or angry in the first place.

We started a meditation practice together using a mindfulness app that was made for children. He could select his feelings from the day, and then we would sit in quiet meditation together. He even found a small LED candle that he would turn on and place in between us to set the scene. The meditation seemed to help calm and regulate his emotions, yet so did Kim's distraction with a new boyfriend, which meant Hunter's time with her ceased and his life became more consistent again.

From all this, I had a baseline knowledge that mindfulness, journaling, and yoga for more than just stretching would likely prepare me for what was coming in the months and years to come. I didn't understand the science at the time, but I do now, and I can't say enough about how beneficial these practices are.

For my year of firsts, I needed to force myself into that space. To "sit in the muck," as many others who had lived their own trauma advised. I would like to pretend like my Thirty in Thirty list was some sort of mindfulness practice in itself, the opportunity to live life to the fullest and sit in the moments that had almost been stolen from me. And that was partly the case. But truthfully, I know my tendency to force myself through life, jumping from milestone to milestone without embracing a single second in between.

A part of me at my core believed that if I could only keep busy, meeting goals and achieving great things, then I wouldn't have to live through what it was I was going through. If I could look back on my social media sites a year later, scroll through my photos and my journaling, and see all the exciting and super cool things I'd experienced, then I could ignore all the rest and pretend like the trauma and depression weren't settling into my brain, where I desperately didn't want them to be.

On the other hand, I am also an athlete at my core. I know if you get an injury and you refuse to rest it, it won't heal. Or it "heals" back, but it is weaker than it should be. A reinjury is almost inevitable. Rest, as frustrating as it can be for those who lack a little, or a lot, in patience, is 100 percent necessary for long-term, healthy healing.

The brain is no different than any other muscle, bone, or tendon I might have injured. My brain had taken more than just the physical impact from when I was knocked on the side of the head during our fight; it had also undergone some pretty severe trauma. Being attacked like that by somebody I loved so much, losing my home, things I held dear no matter how materialistic they might have been, the ongoing, long-term trauma of having lost my son to a bitter and angry family. Yeah, I could pretty much count on some brain damage from the unseen, non-physical impact of what I had just gone through.

I knew I had to rest it or it wouldn't heal back the way I needed it to so that I could live a healthy life after this. If I fought the healing, I would be suffering from the trauma my entire life. So, I set a goal—to not achieve anything at all, even if just for five or ten minutes a week.

My assumptions about mindfulness turned out to be right. For weeks after losing Hunter and Clay, I cried my eyes out every single day, unapologetic and ugly, often face down on my bedroom floor, sitting against my bathroom door, at my desk at work. As life kept moving forward—and I muscled through my Spartan races, forced myself back into the office for a few days a week, and eventually, not too long after the whole incident occurred, was deployed to respond to Hurricane Florence in North Carolina—I let myself get taken with the current of my life and tried to subsequently block out as much emotion as possible. I needed to focus on getting my life back. How was I going to learn a new language, plan a trip abroad, focus on all A's and maintain my work if I was breaking down all the time?

My yoga and meditation practice gave me the time to fall apart that I so desperately needed and had been avoiding; to sit in the trauma and just be with my emotions. And cry. There were times when I knew I had too much emotion held back in my body, I couldn't calm my mind and couldn't figure out what was wrong with me in the light of day, holding myself to the unreasonable expectation that I should have been able to control it. So, I would sit with myself, turn on a guided app or soft music and check in, and I would begin crying within seconds. It was just a matter of sitting still long enough and giving myself permission to feel what I needed to feel. Sometimes, all I needed was to cry for the five or ten minutes of meditation, then when the bell would ring, indicating the end of the guidance, my tears would stop, I would wipe them away, wash my face, and continue with my day.

After about six months, meditation had become a true practice. It became a tool I could use when I wasn't sure how else to accept all the emotions in my body. It became a way for me to schedule time to grieve instead of allowing the emotions to control my life. Without meditation, I'm not sure I would have ever made it back into the office or brought myself to achieve a single thing on my Thirty in Thirty list.

The sadness was a constant in my life for that whole first year, and the grief from all the loss I had suffered sat in the back of my throat like phlegm, threatening to trigger a gag reflex that cascaded into uncontrollable sobbing, often at the most inconvenient times. I learned that when I felt this oncoming explosion of emotions, I could take a deep breath, acknowledge what I was feeling, and then schedule some time for meditation the second I got home, left a meeting, finished a call, or completed a run. I just needed to get through the day and I could close my eyes and sit in my grief again.

If it hadn't been for meditation, I may not have found the feelings inside of me to process what had actually happened to me. For months, I had been processing the loss of Clay and the hurt of knowing Hunter couldn't reach out, that he couldn't know how much I missed him and wanted to be there for him. I broke down and cried for what had happened to them. Over three months later, I finally realized what had happened to me in all of this.

SITTING IN THE MUCK

* * *

It was October 30, 2018. And it was the first time I cried about almost dying.

Up until then, my body's response to almost dying was just a sickening fear, a little PTSD and adrenaline spike when someone walked up behind me in the dark, or walked up behind me at all. An original mantra of mine, from almost day one, was, "Nobody is actively trying to kill you." Despite this, I often found myself barricaded in my kitchen, gun in hand, waiting for someone to come flying through my front door, triggered by the sound of the neighbors fighting. Hearing fireworks in the month after Clay's death had me hiding in my bedroom closet.

Not too many weeks after he died, I heard the very reasonable sound of wind blowing through the crack in my non-squared front door, shuffling it back and forth ever so slightly in a storm. Very unreasonably, I thought it might be someone trying to get into the apartment. When I finally gathered enough courage to peak out my bedroom window and saw nobody there, my very next assumption was that it might be Clay's spirit trying to come in and finish what he had started. It took several more minutes for me to realize it was the wind and by that point, the adrenaline in my body was enough to keep me up the rest of the night.

But I had never cried about it. About almost losing me. I hadn't really, truly begun to process that I had almost lost my life that night. I had just returned to North Carolina to continue hurricane recovery after a brief break at home. It had been about four or five days and I was reflecting on how peaceful I once again felt.

I had an underlying recognition that Clay wasn't around anymore. I had wanted to call him the previous weekend when the Browns played the Steelers at their home stadium, the game that he and I had planned on attending together. The day of the game, a shooter entered a

Pittsburgh synagogue and shot and killed eleven people, wounding six more, the largest attack on the Jewish community in our nation's history. I wanted to call him and ask if he could believe it. We had almost been there and this horrific thing happened in that very city!

I knew I couldn't; he wouldn't know what had happened in his beloved city, and he would never get to visit Pittsburgh and see his favorite team play. But I acknowledged the feeling and moved on in a peaceful way that I might not have a couple weeks prior. There was none of the gut-wrenching sadness I had been feeling, and I didn't break down and sob about it like I would have expected.

October 30 was a good day. Productive in the recovery efforts but fun and light; I helped our interns decorate our desk spaces for the Halloween contest at the field office. Holidays on deployments have always been some of my favorite memories. That night when I went back to my hotel I still had a lot of energy and felt good about the light I was able to bring to our workplace that day.

But something must have triggered the sadness again—maybe fatigue as the dopamine from the day faded. I suddenly felt that overwhelming grief I had become so accustomed to and became so incredibly tired. I had a few school assignments to finish before I could give in to my night and I needed to be able to focus. I fell back to my meditation goal. Maybe I could dab on some essential oils, meditate, and rest my brain for a few minutes and be done with this feeling so I could get back to work.

I journaled first. The prompt in my meditation journal was to write out my three biggest fears, and then color over them until I couldn't see them anymore. I wrote that I was afraid of being sad forever, and that I was afraid Hunter would not be okay after all this. I couldn't think of a third fear. These were it. I never colored over them. Instead, I put the journal away.

I was still using a guided meditation app and an algorithm of suggestions to figure out how I should be meditating. Let's be real, even today I still use an app to guide me through the many long minutes of forced stillness. My app suggested a body scan, a practice I have learned is incredibly beneficial for those days when I can't pinpoint the negativity but know it's in there somewhere. It promotes awareness to those feelings, allows a person to find where in their body they are holding on to tension.

Something I am still learning is the "notice it without judging it" part. The point of a body scan is to just know, to recognize without judgment that there is stress and acknowledge it but then refocus your attention on your body and breathing. I still judge, but I am working on being more compassionate with myself, and I have a more peaceful meditation when I get that part right.

As I sat there that night and the peaceful voice in the app reminded me to focus on the weight of my seat in the chair and my breath coming in through my nose and out through my mouth, my focus automatically went back to the fun I had watching those girls decorate earlier in the day and how much youthful joy they had in what is normally such a tough environment.

Focus, Abby.

"Seat touching the chair, breathe in through the nose..." the voice brought me back in.

Then me: *Feel the cold air brush your nose hairs and expand your tummy to look like you've got the worst food baby...Focus, Abby.*

".... And then let it out through your mouth."

The soft voice told me to start the body scan: "Bring your attention to the top of your head."

Okay, done. Top of my head noted.

"Now bring your attention to the back and sides of your head and down to your ears..."

Something in this triggered me. From out of nowhere, I suddenly thought, *okay, head noted, but it was almost blown all over the back of my couch,* and then an even more panicked and abrupt thought, *I almost lost my head all over my living room, and I wouldn't have had a head on my body anymore!*

Soft meditation voice: "Bring your attention to your face."

Even more distracted from my seat in the chair and the breath in my body now, *why do I even complain about my oily skin and lines around my eyes?! My mother wouldn't have even gotten an open-casket funeral for her daughter! My parents would have had to cremate me because my beautiful face would have been completely gone with that bullet!*

But then the voice got more detailed: "Your forehead and eyebrows... your eyes, cheeks, mouth and jaw." As I moved my focus across my face, my mind's eye narrowed in on something else.

My eyes were closed, but I could see it clear as day. The gun in my face and the man standing in front of me, not there just to hurt me, not wanting to talk to me, yell at me, or even make me suffer for the way he was feeling, but there to kill me. That one shot from the gun, the millisecond it would have taken to pull that trigger, was meant to kill me. His plan was to not leave any chance of my survival or to let me say goodbye to anyone. The back and sides of my head would have been all over that couch and splattered against the wall. My eyebrows, eyes, and cheeks would have been unrecognizable, gone. Nobody would have ever seen my face again.

All these thoughts happened before the voice could continue and say, "Whatever is experienced, just allow it and let it be."

My heart had already sunk to my stomach in the unmistakable fear for my life I had been feeling so often, and my eyes shot open. Panicked, I looked around for the gun I had seen in my mind, and realized I was still alone in my hotel room, staring across the room at the blank television, sitting on my bed. I gasped frantically for air and felt like I might not ever catch my breath. I hit pause on the now incredibly irritating mediation voice and, knowing it was coming anyway, gave in to the tears. And I bawled. For the first time since almost dying, I cried hard, solely for myself and the life I almost never had. Not so much that the man I loved almost killed me. And not because I lost him while I lived. But because I came so close to a bullet in my face that would have ended everything without a second chance. Before I turned thirty. Before I got to experience another hurricane season.

Life would have gone on without me. I wouldn't have been here three weeks ago to encourage my coworker when she was worried about her career and to congratulate her when she got promoted on the deployment. I wouldn't have been here to show those girls how to enjoy themselves a little at work while brightening up everyone's day and bringing our team together. Hurricane Florence would have happened, and nobody at the North Carolina field office would have noticed I was missing, but I would have been. Everything I'd been able to bring to this mission and these communities would have been missing.

I would have missed out on my life. All the goals I had listed on my Thirty in Thirty list, leaving the country, motivating others like me; learning to snowboard or sitting in another coffee shop writing out my untold story, they wouldn't have happened. I wouldn't have practiced yoga in the famous Red Rocks Amphitheater at sunrise watching the purple, pink, and blue sky light up the mountains and the red rocks around me that following summer. I pulled my knees in close to me and sat on the bed crying my eyes out for hours before finally collapsing to sleep in exhaustion.

16

Letters to Clay

February 14, 2018

Abby,

You are the love of my life. I find myself missing you more and more each day, and I anticipate the next time I get to see you or even talk to you. Like I've said before....I'm very, very sorry I'm late to the party. I've found within myself that the last thing I wanted was to get a divorce, but I think that's what it took for me. Still, it's very, very hard if not impossible to feel thankful. Someday I pray that you can forgive some of my behavior and find your way back to me. Nothing in the world would make me happier.

I love you so very, very much, my valentine.

Clay

July 22, 2018: Clay, I wonder how many times I am going to reach out to you and realize you're not here anymore. I'm about to successfully pull off a great memorial service for you. You would be very proud of me. And I think it's exactly the way you would have wanted it.

July 24, 2018: I love you, Clay. Today, I sent you away. I held a beautiful memorial for you so you can be laid to peace having been celebrated and *knowing you were loved and forgiven. Everyone loved it. You would have loved it so much. I wore my Steelers jersey, and we had Steelers and Harley Davidson colors. The flowers were lovely, and we played some great songs. We celebrated you as a great daddy. It was exactly the way you would have wanted it to be. I just wish your family could have been there. And Hunter. I love you and forgive you.*

July 24, 2018: *I know you've always loved the way I write. So, I wrote you a beautiful eulogy, and then I gave it for you.*

July 26, 2018: *Clay. You tried to kill me. Are you fucking kidding me?!*

July 27, 2018: *I'm so incredibly sad all the time because I don't have you in my life anymore. Because I lost Hunter. Because you loved me so much, and I don't have that anymore. But then I realize that you tried to kill me. And I don't know how to be sad about both. You should be here today, though. We should be running this Spartan together. I love you.*

July 27, 2018: *Your son loved you so much. How could you hurt him like this? How could you take away his daddy? He loved you so much. You were his best friend!*

July 30, 2018: *I hope you didn't cry. I hope you didn't have enough thought left in your head for fear and sadness, and I hope you were just that fucking drunk that you didn't even think about it. I hope you didn't do it because you thought I hated you. I could never hate you, even after this. I just pray that you didn't cry, that you didn't have a fucking clue. I love you, and I wish you were here. I'm going to get our son back, and I'll be sure he remembers his daddy.*

July 31, 2018: *I still can't accept that you're gone. Every once in a while, it hits me. That I don't have you anymore. That you're dead. But then it's like I have to turn it back off again because I still need to fight. I still have trauma to survive, and I need to get Hunter back to safety. But in brief moments, I miss you and love you so much. I'm sorry you spent your life surrounded by such awful and unloving people. I know now that I could never have loved you enough to undo the damage they caused you. I'm sorry for your childhood. They couldn't love you. But you were loved by so many others so much more than you will ever know.*

August 6, 2018: *I'm trusting that you and God are working out the game plan to get Hunter back to me.*

August 7, 2018: *Clay, I wish you were here to tell me that this isn't my fault. I wish you could remind me of your terrible years as a little boy, never earning your father's love and approval. About being so poor in college that you were practically begging for food. To remind me of all your hard years in law enforcement where I know you sacrificed all that was left of your soul to people who ultimately betrayed you, people who expected you to do and handle the unthinkable and then shamed you for hurting, ignoring your illness.*

I know deep down I was the only one to ever show you real, unconditional love, and even I screwed that up more than once. I hurt every time I think of any of the roles I played in hurting you. I loved you so much that I put up with the pain and hurt that you had for the rest of the world. I let you take that out on me because I wanted to absorb the hurt and pain for you, and when I ultimately gave up on being that for you.

Then the hurt was too strong and the pain was too much, and you didn't have anywhere else to put it. I wish I had been stronger. I knew the happiness I gave you was only temporary. If I had just stuck it out with you, if I had chosen you and we went back to being us, would you still be here? Could we have maintained your happiness? I know it isn't my fault. But it sure feels like it is. I'm so sorry for hurting you. I miss you so much.

August 8, 2018: I miss spreading my things all over your house on the weekends, curling up on your couch and falling asleep watching movies. I miss the comfort of the love that we had together. I hope you are so happy in heaven, getting all the love you never received on earth.

August 27, 2018: Clay, I miss you so much. And I wish you could have known how they were all going to treat Hunter and me. You would have done something. You would have put it on paper if you would have known how they were going to brainwash him. I wish you would have chosen rehab instead of death. I would take on all the fear in the world to know you were still alive and that Hunter was safe.

    I wish I would have stayed with you the night of the Fourth instead of driving home, so that we could have had just one more of those nights where you laid your head on my chest and fell asleep there. I'm sorry for the nights I fell asleep on the couch instead of coming to bed with you. I wish I would have never wasted a single second of our time. You could have gotten help. You could have asked for it at any point over those last few days. Anyone would have helped you. You should have told someone—anyone—what you planned on doing that night in April. You could have gone to rehab and gotten better; you would still be alive. Hunter would be safe and would still have a daddy.

    How could you choose your sickness and pride over him? You thought that by not going away for rehab that you would be there for him instead? Why wouldn't you just let me move on? You knew you weren't better. Why couldn't you have just let me go and let me be happy? What right did you have to steal that from me? And as a result of you trying to control my life, you've now ruined Hunter's. How could you do that to both of us? We were your FAMILY. WE were the people who loved you unconditionally!!! I am *sorry that nobody else could. I'm sorry that your father beat you and your mother let him and Kim left you and your brothers abandoned you, but WE loved you. It was Hunter and I who fought those demons with you and suffered with you and loved you through it. WE loved you. WE were your family! And it was OUR lives you ruined!!! And WHAT THE FUCK is wrong with your fucked up family? Seriously, what the fuck, man?!*

17

Italy

After giving so much of myself to others, in both my life and in my healing process, it was time for me to do something scary.

Put my own dreams first.

Next on my Thirty in Thirty list was a big one: Travel alone abroad.

Everyone around me seemed to have an opinion on my international travel experience—or lack thereof. "Oh, you've never been outside of the country? How interesting..."

It seemed as if everyone I knew had been to Italy. Friends younger than me had traveled there alone as graduation gifts or internships, like it was completely normal. When I started to truly explore the idea of visiting other countries, everyone had advice from places they had been to, what they did there, and how many more trips they were planning. I realized only then how much I had limited myself with my own mindset, focused on work, family, and college without any thought of how much discovery and education I could be getting from international travel. I knew I loved to travel domestically, but like Clay, it had never occurred to me that there was anything to be missed by never going to another country.

Now, I asked myself, how much *had* I been missing out on by doing everything I thought I should be doing and none of what I was meant to be doing? Had I died that night, I wouldn't have been that much more traveled than Clay was and wouldn't have known any different.

So I planned my own trip to Italy.

The days leading up to the trip, I was filled with nervous excitement. At the same time, I was filled with fear. If Clay were alive, there would be no way he would let me leave to travel abroad. On his best days, he was discouraging, scoffing at the "unrealistic" idea of taking off to another country by myself. "Is this where you got this bright idea?" he had asked when I told him about a coworker who had just returned from her own empowering solo trip to Italy and Greece. He reminded me how frivolous it was to think about doing such a thing, and it filled me with doubt about whether I could even afford it or whether I would make my way around safely. On his worst days, he might have shown up in the middle of the night like he had tried to that April and stopped me from going anywhere ever again. My PTSD had me unreasonably fearful that his family might show up instead of him. That somehow they might know I was leaving and, wanting to keep me from ever finding happiness again, would interfere and finish what Clay had started.

Even more unreasonably, I feared that Clay's ghost might show up in the middle of the night and finish his work. I don't even know if I believe in spirits, but this wouldn't be the first or last time that I wondered very seriously if I was experiencing some presence of him, left angry on earth, not sure what had happened that night and wandering around looking for answers or justice for his death. I slept uneasily and wouldn't let myself get too excited about the trip, staying on guard in case there really was somebody who would try to stop me, from this world or from another.

* * *

Once I was safely in Italy, many of those fears passed. Entire days would go by, and I would be missing Clay again, longing to talk to him. I wanted to be sharing this experience with him, and I was heartbroken that he never took his own trips or followed his own dreams. I wanted to tell him how much I loved him and to apologize for every petty fight we had ever had. Every moment of missing him, though, was mixed with overwhelming gratitude that I had broken free from our relationship and from the grasp of death to experience something so magnificent as Italy.

From the first moments of walking into the Sistine Chapel, I knew this was what I had been fighting for this entire time. This was why I fought so hard to stay alive that night. Standing underneath the brilliant work of ancient artists, surrounded by walls that had been so intricately and painfully painted over the course of so many years, I stood and admired them in awe, and I realized just how small I was. I wondered whether Michelangelo knew that his paintings would survive for hundreds of years and that millions of people would travel across the world to admire them.

Comprehending this made me feel like a single unit in the entire workings of the universe, and I realized that the moments when my pain felt like the only pain in the entire world, I was actually surrounded by thousands of people who had stories of their own. Human suffering has been ongoing throughout history since the beginning of time and these ancient walls around me whispered that history to me. I took in every detail, knowing I had lived so I could experience every part of the world just like this, safe, in the moment, without rush or fear.

My second night in Rome I had a nightmare, a scene that would become common in my sleep for years to come. Clay was being released from prison and coming home, to our home. My fear of what this might mean for me had me tossing in my sleep. In this particular dream, as in some others, Clay willingly unloaded and handed over all the guns so I would feel safe. I cried and cried, begging him to let me see Hunter again, explaining to him what had happened since he had gone away. In some dreams, he would be furious at how his family and ex-wife had treated his son. In other dreams, the nightmares, I wouldn't be so lucky.

In the dreams when I would see Hunter at last, I'd hold him tight in a hug and tell him how hard I had tried to reach him; that I wanted everything for him but that his mother wouldn't let me be there for him. Every time, he would reassure me, "I know." In every dream, for years, he understood the truth and he told me he knew all along.

I woke up crying from my dream and looked over at the postcard I had bought for him from the Vatican. It would be one of dozens of postcards that I would come to buy over the years, knowing I could never send them but collecting them so that one day, one day soon, he would receive them and know I was thinking of him every single day. Then I looked around my room and reminded myself I was in Rome, I was safe, and I forced myself to go back to sleep.

* * *

I am a master of checklists and am always looking for ways to strike things off my lists. So when planning my trip to Italy, I took a good look at my Thirty in Thirty goals to find what else I might achieve while I was abroad. In preparation, I had studied Italian on my months-long disaster deployment. With hours spent driving alone on the dark North Carolina roads, my language books on tape kept me company as I repeated phrases and statements to myself to stay awake. Once in Italy, I nervously practiced my Italian as I navigated my way through the country. But I knew I could officially check the goal off the list when in Bologna I successfully conversed with a shop owner over the price of a beautifully made piece of pottery shaped like Mother Mary and her nativity scene. I chatted with her about the prices of other nativity scenes available and she showed me a magnet, also made of pottery, depicting the local towers.

Apparently, I sounded like I knew well enough what I was doing. As I stood at the counter waiting to finish my purchase, a small elderly man with a flat hat on his head, a curly gray mustache, and grandfatherly smile bantered with another man in line, as well as the lady I had just been talking to. I stood there next to them waiting for my turn to purchase my new treasures, enjoying his cheerful demeanor. As he told his story in Italian, he paused throughout it as everyone listening laughed heartily at the details, tossing their heads back, the old man slapping his knee as his face brightened and he entertained everyone. I laughed along, unsure of what was going on but enjoying the overall atmosphere and not wanting to look like a blank-faced American.

Then, unexpectedly, he turned to me and asked me a question. I was caught. I looked sheepishly at him, embarrassed that he would now know the truth—that I did not have a single clue what his story had just been about, and I said in my best practiced Italian, in a slow, American accent, "I am sorry, I do not understand much Italian."

At this, he looked surprised, tilting his head at the realization of what I had just said. And then he tipped his head so far back that he was looking straight up at the ceiling as he let out his loudest, merriest laugh. "Where are you from?" he asked in clear, fluent English.

"Denver, United States," I said, still feeling a little sheepish but relieved that he had found my ignorance amusing rather than offensive. "Oh yes!" He knew of Denver and had been to the United States several times. He spoke in more quick Italian to the others and wished me "Prego" as he headed out the door and I finished my purchase.

* * *

Since this was my first trip abroad and I wanted to do it right, I spent months researching what cities I would visit, what sights I would see, and most importantly, what food I would eat while I was there. I had my trip so well pinned down with a plan by the time I got on the plane that my only concern was whether I would be hungry enough to eat all the gelato, pastries, cannoli, and pasta I planned on consuming while I was there. One of the main reasons for choosing Italy, besides all the glorious history, art and architecture, was for the food.

As I toured the cafes and restaurants of Italy, downing entire pizzas with large glasses of wine and slipping into corner stores on a whim for their window pastries, I posted my food journey on social media, and to my surprise, received an overwhelming number of comments from other women along the lines of "Oh my goodness, I could never!" They fretted about how if they were to do that, they may gain weight, and they commented on how hard they would need to work out to make up for all those sweets, how they envied me for getting to enjoy those things without the guilt.

I was dumbfounded. I mean, yes, I've struggled with my own body shame and society's standards of beauty just like anybody else. Women are constantly stressing about everything we consume, worrying about how we look, what others think of us, the size of our clothes, and the numbers on the scale. I get it, I'm not immune. But seriously? ITALY.

I was saddened to think there could never be an acceptable time for women to not be worried about their body image so they could just enjoy their lives. I couldn't get over how so many women in this same position would let that shame rob them of the experience of exploring a foreign country and the food culture it has to offer. It's a travesty to think that society and beauty standards have had such an influence on any person that they might visit a country like Italy for the first time and not eat gelato every time they walked by a shop or skip the cannoli in the window because of the calories it will add to the day's total.

There was no way in the world I was going to let shame keep me from enjoying myself 110 percent on this trip. I didn't spend all this money and wait so long to get there so I could waste the opportunity worrying about what others might think of me if I gained a couple of pounds.

Part of my food journey, I had decided, would be to get the full Italian Christmas Eve dinner experience: a traditional, six-course seafood banquet at a Venetian restaurant on the canal. I had done my research and booked my reservation months in advance. When I walked in, they must have been waiting for me—I had the only table for one for the entire night—because I was greeted with a glass of champagne. They took my coat to check, already making this the fanciest restaurant I had ever been to.

I wanted the meal to be authentic, the full traditional experience, so I declined the menu and requested the chef's recommendation for the evening. The staff was attentive, bringing each course out and waiting by for my first bite to be sure I was satisfied. Offering salt and pepper because I'm an American but smiling approvingly when I turned it down. The plates were all so fancy with colorful drizzles and beautifully laid fish of all sorts, every detail perfectly designed for the dish. My wine glass was kept full and switched out by the glass as the courses transitioned and called for a different pairing until finally, a palate cleanser and then dessert was presented.

It was everything I could have ever wanted to top off my trip and to get through my first Christmas Eve, knowing I would not be seeing Clay or Hunter the next morning.

As I ate, I began to contemplate the champagne, the multiple glasses of wine getting switched out, the courses, and I started to add it up in my head, translating the total with the exchange rate. "Holy shit!" I almost choked. I was about to spend more on this meal than what I had ever spent on dinner for even the three of us. Never had I spent this amount of money on myself for something as frivolous as a meal, or honestly, for anything. But the thought fleeted just as quickly as it had come, and I quickly pulled out my phone to make a note to myself.

"This. This is my reward for staying alive. This whole trip really, but I get to have this night because this is my treat for living. I could have let him kill me very easily, but I didn't. I fought, and I stayed alive. I could have failed that night, but instead, I chose to fight, and I continue to choose to fight. Yes, this night is for me now." I put my phone away, feeling empowered to treat myself for all the work I was doing in my recovery, and then I just didn't look at the bill when it came.

* * *

Many times throughout my recovery, my judgment became irrationally skewed, and my need to achieve everything on my Thirty in Thirty list was sometimes neurotic and even a little dangerous. Determined to "Learn a New Skill," I signed up for a pasta-making lesson with a local Italian chef. I was so focused on the idea of learning to make homemade pasta and tiramisu while drinking Italian wine that it never occurred to me to think through the logistics. It was two days before Christmas, and apparently, pasta classes weren't on anyone else's mind.

As I sat in the café waiting for the chef to meet me so we could walk to his apartment's kitchen, I looked around for the other tourists who would be joining us for the evening. Only then did it dawn on me that this event may not have sold out so close to a big holiday. I started debating whether I should back out. If I walked out now, nobody would know. I could just pick a different skill to learn another time. But often, I get far too focused on the achievement and am not always reasonable with myself, especially with the waves of overconfidence that would hit me every once in a while since, you know, I had saved my own life and all.

I decided to stay. It was a terrible decision.

The chef walked in, far taller and in way better shape than Clay. I realized immediately I wouldn't be able to take this guy if I needed to. *Yes, but pasta! And cheeses*...and he had already recognized me as the only American in the room and was walking up to introduce himself and begin the evening. I followed him to his apartment after a quick espresso, a snack, and a little small talk at the café.

Seriously, I'm not proud of it. I immediately made a pact with myself that if I survived the night, I would never tell my girlfriends or my mother that I followed a strange, large man to his apartment at the promise of wine and pasta, but I did. I followed him right into the building, up the narrow staircase, and into his small Bologna apartment. I tried to send my location to a girlfriend and realized I didn't have a single bar of cell service on my phone. *Well*, I thought, *it's been real, but this one might actually be lights out this time.*

The poor guy was incredibly kind, patiently showing me how to mix the eggs, flour, and water, testing it for the right consistency, how to lay out the dough and pull it to make it the right size for the pasta attachment clamped to his kitchen counter. He talked to me about the process of making tiramisu just right and which wines should be paired with which sauces. He took photos of me with my carefully folded Cappelletti as I smiled the best I could in my chef's hat and apron.

And the entire time I stood, tense, my hands at the ready, taking a step back every time he picked up a knife, ready for a fight, watching my exit. He had to have thought I was the most awkward person he had ever met with the way I cautiously made small talk and refused to relax the entire time, not drinking the wine or ever turning my back to him. By the time I left, I practically ran across the city back to my Airbnb, sprinting up every flight of stairs, and bolting the door behind me.

He later sent me an email with the recipes and directions for the food we made, but I was too embarrassed and ashamed of myself to open the email. It was a reminder of how irresponsible I had been and how uncomfortable I must have made him in return. I'm not sure it is considered a "new skill" officially, I haven't tried to repeat it since. It is on my future list of recovery goals to one day make homemade pasta again but in the safety of my own home this time.

18

A Mother's Plea

When my attempts to contact Hunter failed, my mother reached out to Clay's mom, pleading with her to intervene. She never received a response to this letter.

September 23, 2018

Dear Melinda,

I have tried and tried and tried some more to process this loss and I am struggling. It's been over two months now and I cannot seem to get back to being myself emotionally. I'm frustrated, angry, distracted, and sad and trying to obtain joy while in the midst of overwhelming turmoil and sadness.

I find myself thinking about Clay every single day. I wake up during the night and think about Clay and worry about Hunter and struggle to go back to sleep. Sometimes I manage to relax and go back to sleep and sometimes, like this morning at 4 a.m., I get up because sadness overpowers me, and I become restless and cannot sleep.

I find myself searching for the right words to say in reaching out to you even as I know you do not want to hear from me. And why should you? We don't know each other even though I always wanted to meet you as Clay spoke very lovingly and highly of you as his mom. I always imagined *sitting down with a cup of coffee and visiting and getting to know each other someday. I think we would have found we had things in common and actually enjoyed visiting. I talk myself out of writing to you but then continue to think about everything I would like to say and realize that until I do reach out, I will not find any sort of peace. I won't say I'm sorry for your loss anymore because I know you don't want to hear that from me, even though it will never cease to be true.*

I miss Clay. We all miss Clay. Clay was a part of our family well before he and Abby married, as well as while they were married and he continued to be a part of our family even after they divorced. He was always welcomed with open arms, and I looked forward to his hugs when we got together and before we parted.

He was part of a weight loss challenge with various members of my family, which lasts a year and ends on January 1 of each year with an announcement of the winner and a prize. He won't be here this year to participate in that on January 1, and I'm going to know it, and it's going to hurt that he is not present. That's my family's Christmas, and last year we had such a great time, but it won't be the same this year without Clay, and I know the memories will come flooding back.

I have memories of talks with Clay on the phone and spending time together, memories of traveling around Wyoming with him and Abby and Hunter, and laughter when we all competed in board games. He was competitive, and I loved that about him. I remember meals spent together and how he loved to cook and made the best breakfasts and how he hated it if he spent time cooking and everyone did not immediately show up to eat. I remember a weekend that he and I spent off and on for an entire weekend putting together a puzzle as we could neither one accept not having it finished and visiting while we looked for all the pieces and then throwing up our hands when there was a duplicate piece and the last piece was missing.

I remember visiting when I was in Clinton for a few days. Clay still worked for the Sheriff's Department and worked evenings. I had fallen asleep on the couch, and he came home late at night. I woke just enough to know he had arrived home and to watch as he quietly went down the hall without a word and returned with a throw and put it across me so I would stay warm. Clay was such a good guy, and I remember feeling very cared for and loving him for caring for my comfort.

I remember a trip we all took to Branson, Missouri, to Silver Dollar City. It was cold and miserable, and Clay didn't feel well. One of the rides was a roller coaster that went through a dark cave-like room and was terrifying to watch as it looped and rolled. At first, Clay didn't want to participate since he was sick, but with Hunter's encouragement, he decided to ride it once. He had such a great time on a ride that absolutely terrifies me that he kept going back over and over again despite not feeling well and each time got off with such a big grin on his face.

I watched Clay grow as a Christian and grow in his desire to become a better Christian. It was heartwarming to have him lead prayer before we ate, especially since that ability and desire to do so had developed during the time we got to know Clay, or to have him ask Hunter to do so and watch Hunter lead the prayer. He was a great dad and was teaching Hunter that praying out loud was not something to be afraid to do.

He once asked me about the book of Esther as the pastor at his church had made reference to that book of the Bible, so I was able to visit with him about her and her incredible bravery at such a young age. Her willingness to protect those she loved and her family above her desire to protect herself or give in to her fears and emotions.

I gave him a new personalized Bible and Bible cover and some Christian CDs for Christmas one year. Something happened and he lost the CDs, and so the next Christmas, he asked me if I could replace them for him as a gift. His favorite song on those CDs was "Not My Home" by Building 129. Abby said he and Hunter danced around the kitchen to that song. We used it as one of the songs at his celebration of life service.

Clay actively spent time on the phone every Saturday night with his friend

Rich in Bible study. They were last studying Ephesians. Rich said Clay had a real desire to know the Lord better and to become closer in his walk with the Lord. Rich told me Clay said that "he found the best time for him to pray was driving to and from work. He would pray out loud in the car and have a conversation with the Lord as if He were sitting right next to him." He said, "I know that Clay desired a closer walk with the Lord."

A day did not go by that I didn't include Clay in my prayers with the rest of my family because he was and still is family. I lost a family member—someone I cared very deeply for. I remember receiving a call from Clay a few years ago. He was distressed and anxious as he wasn't sure whether law enforcement wouldn't show up on his doorstep to arrest him. I believe I wrote to you then, with his permission, as I was very concerned about him and what might happen to him.

When he called, I was working at my store, and after visiting for a few minutes and realizing how upset he was and finding myself equally upset with the situation, I went to the door and locked it. I put up my closed sign and went to a back room where customers would not see that I was in the store, and we prayed together on the phone. Praying with others out loud is not something I do very often as it is a little out of my comfort zone, but this was important to me and to Clay, and it helped us both. Once Clay knew how much I cared, he always called me to let me know whenever he would be in the mountains for a few days and have no cell service so I would not panic if I could not reach him. He knew I cared, and I always worked at showing him unconditional love no matter what happened.

We have all lost so much. You have lost your youngest son and a piece of your heart with that loss. The loss of a child for a mother is heart wrenching. You have those memories of Clay growing up and what his childhood was like and watching the man he became and all his accomplishments. That is something that no one else has.

I have lost a friend and a member of my family who was no less important to me than the rest of my family. I have lost my son-in-law. I still considered him my son-in-law and never would have stopped doing so. Once my family, always my family. I miss him so much. And I have lost touch with my precious grandson, which is devastating and heartbreaking. And yes, again, always my grandson. He called me Grandma Donna before I actually became so during the marriage, and he continued to do so after Clay and Abby divorced. He will always be my grandson. During one of the times Clay and Abby split up, Clay asked Hunter about his Grandma Donna, and Hunter told him, "I will never forget my Grandma Donna." My heart is breaking from worrying about Hunter, and I find myself in tears so much of the time over this entire situation.

Abby has lost someone whom she considered her best friend as there was not a day that went by that they did not talk on the phone and not a weekend or holiday that went by that they did not spend time as a family, even once they divorced. They still very much loved each other. They just could not be married. Clay called her every day just to let her know how his day had gone. You briefly hit on it when you said, "Well, maybe it was mutual" in their not leaving each other alone.

Clay very much wanted Abby to remain a part of his life, and she never wanted them to stop being friends. Abby has also lost contact with someone whom she loves and adores in losing contact with Hunter. Hunter has reached out to her twice now, and there is no way for her to let him know she has not willingly left him or to offer him any kind of comfort. She cannot assure him she has not abandoned him when he has needed to hear from her.

But in everyone's loss, Hunter has lost the most and at such a young age, and I am overwhelmed worrying about him and thinking about his sadness and what he is going through. He has lost the person who was the closest and most important to him—his dad. The person he adored and looked up to and counted on to always be there for him. His heart has to be hurting every day over that loss. He is such a sweet little boy, and I'm hopeful he is sharing his sadness with someone so he is not trying to cope and process his loss on his own. I know he never wants anyone to feel sad, so he might not share his own sadness easily with others.

Then he has lost the next person closest to him, the person who has had the role of mom to him for the last nine years—from the beginning of his memory. He knew that even if Dad was not available that Abby was there for him and he could count on her. Abby has had that role of mom for Hunter before Clay and she married, during the years of being married, and even after they divorced.

That relationship was always important to Hunter and has always remained intact. She took care of him when he was sick, helped him learn to read when he struggled, went to parent-teacher conferences, did homework with him, read to him, and taught him to read recipes and cook. He loves to cook. She made sure his birthdays were always celebrated with special events. She took him camping, fishing, and participated in his sports and in Scouts with him. She took him on 5Ks and runs and offered him encouragement when he struggled. She loved on him when he hurt and let him know how proud she was of him in his accomplishments. They shared adventures together. She took him to church on Sundays and encouraged him in his love for Jesus.

The weekend before Clay passed away, we had all spent the weekend together up until Saturday afternoon. Clay had to leave early as Phil had called to let him know there was a water leak at the house, so Clay had to return to Cheyenne. On Saturday night, we were planning a trip to the Denver Zoo the next day. We figured we would get up early and go to the zoo before it got too hot.

Hunter came into the room and asked Abby to help him pick out his clothes for church the next morning. She explained to Hunter that we had thought about skipping church so we could get to the zoo early, but if he wanted to go to church first, then that was what we would do. Always eager to please everyone, he looked around the room at everyone, trying to determine what we wanted to do. Abby told him whatever he chose to do would be what *everyone would love to do and it was totally up to him.*

His decision was to go to church first and then go to the zoo. Twelve years old and his choice was church first over the zoo. I am so proud of him and for the young man he is becoming. I hope someone is still nurturing his desire to go to church and learn more about how good God is, especially now. It terrifies me that he might be struggling and losing faith in God right now.

Hunter has lost contact with his Grandma Donna and Grandpa Steve and cousins Faye and Alec as well as aunts and uncles that love and miss him. He struggled to make friends in school, but through contact with Abby's friends, he made friends with their children. Children who shared in fun with him. He is missing out on that part of his life and those vital relationships. He needs friends his own age as well as family right now.

As adults, we can all work at processing our loss. In my case, I study my Bible and pray and listen to Christian music and am currently reading a book entitled Hope in the Dark: Believing God Is Good When Life Is Not. *Even though I continue to struggle, and nothing helps completely, it seems to be offering me hope and encouragement. I sent a copy to Abby as she continues to struggle and mourn the loss of Clay and needs some sort of measure of peace, hope, and comfort.*

Hunter has lost so much in such a short amount of time and at such a young age. This was an absolute major tragedy for this little boy. A devastating loss. He has to be filled with sadness and confusion and a total sense of loss. How does a twelve-year-old boy cope with such loss? Is he talking to someone or keeping it all bottled up inside? Is he wondering where all those people who he considered friends and family are at and why they are not reaching out to him? Is anyone able to fill those roles that he has now lost? Is anyone encouraging and nurturing his love for God during a time when he is hurting and wondering about God's goodness?

There is nothing anyone could have done to prevent Clay from making the decision that he did. There is nothing that could have stopped my brother. There is nothing that could have stopped the young lady that was a classmate to my son or the young teenager—the daughter of one of my customers who always seemed so happy on the outside or the teacher that everyone really loved that started a community garden and taught Sunday school to college age students. No one could have stopped their decisions. They could have reached out, but they didn't. Clay saw a counselor on a weekly basis and had just done so days before—he could have told her how sad he was, but he didn't. He had a friend he did a weekly Bible study with and could have reached out but didn't. He could have let you know, and he could have reached out to me or let Abby or Phil know. But he didn't.

Rarely does anyone who takes their own life tell anyone they are actually going to do it. The ones who generally threaten it are the ones seeking attention and who may or may not succeed in doing so by accidentally succeeding in their cry for help. But the ones who actually do plan to do it seldom ever tell anyone their plans. Seldom is there any real warning of what is about to happen. There is nothing anyone could have done to prevent this tremendous and horrible loss for Hunter.

But the rest of the loss he is experiencing is preventable. The adults in Hunter's life determine how much loss he has to continue to experience. He doesn't have to experience the loss of Abby from his life. Simple phone calls would keep him from feeling abandoned and from having that sense of having lost everyone in his life. There would be comfort in hearing from Abby and knowing she still loves him.

He doesn't have to experience the loss of this entire side of his family from his grandma and grandpa and his cousins and his friends that he developed with Abby's friends and their children. The loss doesn't have to be this great for him. His family, the adults in his life, determine how much loss they want him to cope with and to endure. His family determines the amount of pain he must feel and go through. As a mother and a grandmother, I would never want my children or grandchildren to go through any more pain than they had to and would do whatever possible to prevent unnecessary pain and grief and loss. If you and I share nothing else in common, hopefully the love for our family far exceeds any personal emotions for ourselves, whether it be sadness, bitterness or anger.

I'm not discounting the family that he has—the family that he has always had. Grandpa and Grandma Caldwell, Aunt Blanche, Uncle Ivan and their families. His mom, Kim, and Phil, who can fill some of the void. That part of his life remains intact. But an entire part of his life was wiped away suddenly and is missing and doesn't have to be. Because of Clay and Abby's relationship, Hunter has an entire other family who loves and cares for him. Everyone has a role in Hunter's life, and no one can replace the role that each person had. To first lose his dad and then to have an entire part of his family wiped away has to be more than he can handle emotionally. It would be difficult for an adult—but for a young child?

One final thought before I end here—hopefully you know and are assured that Clay is in heaven right now worshiping and loving God. I plan to see him again someday, and even though I don't know completely what happens when we get to heaven, if I'm allowed, I plan to hug his neck and tell him how much I love him.

There is a misconception out there, and hopefully this is not your belief, that if someone dies by suicide, they do not go to heaven. This is so untrue. When I lost my brother, I struggled with this question. I had heard it preached and I had seen it in movies. Would I ever see my brother again or was he lost to me forever? So many people believe this, I want to make sure that you are not one of them. I have read the Bible through, and I have searched and I have talked to other Christians. It is not in the Bible that is what happens. Clay's heart was right with God when he left this earth. He is loved, forgiven, and cherished by the Father and is currently walking with Jesus and worshiping the Lord. And I can hardly wait to see him again.

I lost my mother in August of 2016 right before Clay lost his grandpa. It was a hard loss and still is. Viola was deeply loved by everyone. She was little but tough and honest to a fault, and it is one of the traits she passed on to me. My mother was the matriarch of our family and others looked up to her for guidance and wisdom. She fought for the "principle of the thing" when things mattered the most. When she passed, even though I did not seek the role and did not expect it, as the oldest daughter, I became the next matriarch. Everyone looks to me for guidance in family matters. I am logical and honest to a fault and believe in the "principle of the thing" and my family means the world to me. I would sacrifice myself and give up my rights if it would protect my family and prevent them from unnecessary pain.

Unlike my mother, you are still here. You are the matriarch of your family—looked up to and respected and looked to for guidance. And again, like me, I know you would protect your family and not allow them to go through something you could prevent like the extreme amount of loss that Hunter is going through. I am asking you to help Hunter by not allowing him to deal with any further loss than is necessary and any more than what he has experienced with the loss of his precious dad. He has family and friends and a support system outside of what he is currently experiencing. And while I know he is loved and cared for by your family, I also know he has lost a huge part of the family and friends who have come to love him and been a big part of his life. There are some people that filled roles in his life that cannot be filled by anyone else.

My intentions in writing were never to upset you. There needs to be healing all around, but especially for Hunter. I am tired of loss of sleep. I'm tired of acting like everything is fine on the outside only to be hit by waves of sadness and grief when I least expect it. I am exhausted from worrying about this little boy. I wish you and I could have gotten to know each other under different circumstances. Communication would have been so much easier, and we might have had a better understanding of each other. We may have actually liked each other rather than assuming the worst about the other based on this whole awful situation.

I have found myself praying many times over the past years for Clay, for Clay and Abby, for Hunter, for Blanche when she found out she had breast *cancer and when Clay shared other concerns for his family. I prayed for him during the loss of his grandfather even as I mourned the loss of my mother. I have prayed for your husband as Clay shared health concerns for him as of late. The things that Clay was concerned about concerned me. I thanked God when Clay gave me good news concerning his family.*

I recently saw something that said it is not a sin to be down and out, but it is a sin to not get back up. I'm going to get back up even though I'm struggling with it now. I'm going to continue to have faith in the goodness, kindness, and mercy of people. I'm going to continue to hope, and I'm going to continue to pray for everyone concerned including myself as I try to cope and heal.

May God bless your family each and every day.

Donna

19

Learning to Snowboard and Other Life Lessons

Next up on my Thirty in Thirty: Go snowboarding.

I had just arrived in Vail, Colorado safely, despite a gorgeous snowstorm through the canyon and stop and go weekend traffic. For the first time, I had the opportunity to throw my 4Runner in gears I had only ever wondered about but hadn't had the chance to utilize. It felt good to use the SUV for what I bought it for—having safe outdoor fun and getting to places that not everybody gets to go to.

When I was hesitant to drive in this type of weather in the past, on these slushy, wet, sometimes icy road conditions, Clay would tell me, "Abby, you own the best snow vehicle money can buy." Whether that was actually true or not, it felt good to have provided something so capable for myself; I just didn't know how to drive it. Looking back, I wonder if he was just saying that to boost my winter driving confidence. Growing up in Kansas on flat, long, straight highways and country roads, I hadn't learned how to drive through mountains, on snow, how to back a trailer or shift down on my...gear shifter?...when heading down steep grades.

For some reason, my asking always frustrated Clay to no end. He would get visibly angry with me, probably because I needed to ask him more than once and usually waited until I was mid-steep grade before bringing it up. Also, because he was terribly impatient with me to begin with. For some reason, he felt like many of these skills should have been inherent—driving through the mountains, backing a trailer—and I was secretly looking forward to when the time came that he would be teaching Hunter to drive and would realize people aren't just born with these skills.

When he lost patience with me, I typically got mad back at him, it felt he was talking down to me like I was an idiot for not understanding. We would end up in an argument and whatever he said about when and how to downshift would have been lost on me once again. This was the case with so many of his lessons and after I lost him, I had many more moments of wishing he was here just one more time to teach me again, feeling unsure of myself. When I finally came into the canyon on I-70 and saw all the semi-trucks pulling off to put chains on, I knew I only had one choice: to figure it out.

As it turns out, I really had picked up on what Clay was talking about when he showed me how to use the gears to keep myself safe on the slick roads. That whole time we had been arguing when it was my turn to drive at elevation, it turns out I was learning it all along. Was it because I was too stubborn or stressed out to want to listen to him? Lacking in my own confidence despite the tough-girl persona? Did teaching me bring up his own frustrations from having not had father teach him these things? Or did he really think I lacked the common sense it takes to know the skills that came so easily to him? It didn't matter anymore. What mattered was that the whole time, despite the hurt and anger and frustration with one another, he had been the one to teach me so much about how to do life, and this was just one more stupid topic I wished we would have never wasted time fighting about.

Here I was, though, rolling down a slushy hill with weekend ski traffic all around me, and I could hear him reassuring me, "Ab, you can do this. I taught you how to do this." So I did it. I flicked the gear shifter into fourth gear and immediately felt the transmission hold itself back. I could cruise down this hill without riding my brakes and feel more in control on the wet, snowy roads. After I figured out how it was supposed to feel for my massive SUV to hold itself back from just rolling right through a sea of Subarus, it felt great. I turned on some music and cruised along in confidence, shifting up and down depending on traffic, road conditions, and the feel of my vehicle.

Maybe a small feat for some—many, even—but it felt empowering to bring some of that hard-earned, tough-love knowledge and use it to take myself into the mountains alone. It was one of those moments where I thought, *Clay might have been proud of me for this*! Realistically, he would never have said it or shown it. I like to think, though, that he would have thought it.

* * *

Sitting in the warm coffee shop, still missing Hunter, I reflected again on how grateful I was to have my life.

I am in Vail, Colorado. I drove here in a super badass vehicle that is now covered in mud and beautiful in all its beastliness, and I got here safely.

That night, I planned to attend a parade of skiers in the Tenth Mountain Legacy Parade, an event I hadn't planned on but after seeing posters all over town, realized I should really check out. The next day, I would be taking snowboarding lessons in one of the most sought-after ski resorts in the world!

I can sit here in this cozy cafe and can provide for myself this overpriced latte, I thought. *I am grateful to be alive.*

I sat there for a couple of hours, watching the ice skaters spin around in the rink outside the shop, making notes for this chapter in the book.

LEARNING TO SNOWBOARD AND OTHER LIFE LESSONS

* * *

When I first moved to Wyoming over ten years ago, I told myself I would learn to snowboard and go to a cattle branding because both of those things sounded very "Wyoming" to me. Well, my first branding was actually in Montana, and it turned out the only ski resort near me had been closed down for sanitation reasons. I still don't think you can ski or snowboard in most of Wyoming, besides Jackson and Laramie, and at the time, I lived near neither of those locations.

For years, I let this goal fade away. Once Clay and I were in full swing, and then married, I was busy trying to prove myself as a mother and a wife and gradually I lost myself, no longer having my own hobbies. I did try to go snowboarding with Hunter one time when we had lived in Cheyenne. We had some friends who lived on the local Air Force base, and they were taking a discounted trip to the local resort, about an hour and a half away. Awesome. Bucket list item: *check*!

Unfortunately, this was about a year into our marriage, and I had already put my health at the bottom of my priority list to focus on being a mother, and it would be another four months before I would break down and get a HIIT gym membership that would change my life. So the first time I tried snowboarding, I probably couldn't have squatted more than once if I wanted to, and I certainly wasn't going to go from sitting on my butt to standing on a snowboard in any sort of graceful motion.

As children do, Hunter caught on quickly and fearlessly and even went on some of the more challenging slopes with our friends. Meanwhile, I spent the entire time on my butt in the snow. I was trying, very hard, to get to a standing position and make it down the hill. But every time I fell, it was another long, hard struggle to get back on my feet. It turned out to be miserable.

I did not have the leg, core, or glute strength to stand from sitting while attached to my board. As an alternative, I would chaotically fish-flop onto my belly, and then try to plank walk up to standing, inch-worming my way up, backward to the slope. If I did make it up, I would have to get turned back around to face the right direction which would promptly land me flat on my tail again, resulting in zero progress down the hill. If I tried to take my board off to stand, I ended up chasing it as it slid smoothly down the mountain without me. When I got home, I felt like I had been hit by a truck, and I never went again.

* * *

Until now. This trip—let me tell you, you could have bounced a quarter off my ass. I mean that in the humblest of ways, but since first joining the gym, finding my group of girlfriends with similar goals and consequently, all our Spartan obstacle course races, I had been working hard for this booty, and I was proud of it. This strong body had saved my life when I had to wrestle a gun from a large, grown man.

Was I also in leggings because it was too hard to get this ass into the same size snowboard pants I had worn four years ago? Absolutely. Muscle takes up a little more space in those things and I filled them out more than I once did. And let's just say I may secretly have had to go with only one snap on my pants instead of two the next day when I finally did squeeze into them.

In exchange, though, thank the Lord, my body was now built to stand up on a snowboard. My legs were stronger, my core was solid, and I knew how to move and use my body like I never had before I started prioritizing my health along with being a mother and a wife. As I looked proudly at myself, at my ass, in the mirror while getting dressed the next morning, taking in all my healthy glory, I realized what an incredible blast I was going to have. I was going to take back my dream of learning to snowboard that weekend.

***

The evening before, when I first arrived in town, I wandered up to the base of the mountain to attend the Tenth Mountain Division Legacy Parade. I thought the event might have been in recognition of the history of skiing as a sport. I had only briefly glanced at the signs and the Vail tourism website before deciding I would walk over that night, and I quickly learned it was about so much more than "just skiing."

It turned out the Tenth Mountain Division was, and still is today, an elite light infantry division of the United States Army. They could likely be considered some of the original survivalists, as a group of men trained to fight specifically in mountains and arctic conditions. I was blown away when I learned this. They originally fought in the wintry mountains of Italy during World War II, playing a huge role during the final months and the German surrender.[15] They then went home, mostly to Colorado, to open ski resorts and popularize the sport. I had no idea the sport of skiing had such a fierce history!

To honor these brave men and athletes, skiers dressed in glowing orange, bright enough to light up the dark night sky, descended down the ski slope in a beautiful serpentine while fireworks lit behind them. All the while, speakers, music, and videos played in the background, emphasizing the amazing story behind this legacy. You can hear me laugh a little in the video I took, but there was nothing funny about the situation. That was, without a doubt, my avoidance laugh; my "I'm not crying, you're crying" nervous laugh as I got caught up in the beauty of the moment.

When the production was complete, the announcer told everyone he had a surprise for them and he introduced an elderly gentleman sitting in the passenger seat of a topless old Jeep nearby, he was one of the division's original infantry men. The man sat humbly but with a proud smile on his face as he waved at the clapping spectators. To top it off, his son was standing in front of the Jeep as a veteran of the same division, presenting the Tenth Mountain Division flag. It was a beautiful sight and brought even more tears to my eyes as I took in the beauty of the lives of the people around me. These hard-earned, resilient lives of people who had also been through so much and could now stand at the base of this mountain, proud of what they had survived and accomplished.

If walking into the Sistine Chapel was one of the moments that I lived for when I was fighting for my life initially, this was one of the moments I was fighting for in my day-to-day recovery from all the secondary impacts of the fight, the depression, anxiety, and trauma brain that haunted me daily. My Thirty in Thirty list was made for these moments, these moments when I push myself outside of my comfort zone into worlds completely unfamiliar to me and experience a universe so much larger and more important than I could ever be.

The role I play in my life is large. I am the main character, as I should be. But the role I play in the world is small and can only get bigger as I recognize the sufferings and experiences of those around me, and from throughout our vast history as humans. My impact here on this earth can only get broader if I continue putting myself in these positions where I am learning and growing my empathy and understanding for humanity outside of myself. I needed those moments.

Hell, I still need them as I battle the depression, all the hurt, trauma, and questions about *what if?* and *should I have?* I need to have these moments where I can see all the good and happiness in the world and experience love, hope and joy all around me. This is why I needed a list to pull myself back up and push myself forward. For moments like these that would save my heart.

* * *

Snowboarding turned out to be so rewarding and enjoyable that I extended my trip a second day and went back two weekends later to do it again. To have the financial freedom to throw down for a day-two lesson and then the hotel points to stay another night was a true blessing. These were the times when I stepped back, looked at my life, and was overwhelmed with gratitude for the way the universe was conspiring to help me achieve my goals.

Over the course of those three lessons, here's what went incredibly well with snowboarding, and everything else I learned that had nothing at all to do with the snow: when I allowed myself to let go of my previously set expectations, and face something head-on without fear, I grew. When I doubted myself, I missed important opportunities; and sometimes missing out on those opportunities was the lesson all along and I actually hadn't missed a thing.

Since this was one of my pricier bucket list items, I really wanted to get my full money's worth so I decided to go all out on the slope. When my instructor told me to dig my toes, I dug them hard. When he said to dig my heels, I did that too. Sometimes I dug too hard and threw myself face down, or landed hard, flat on my back. I would go rolling and tumbling down the hill, board flying over my head, jerking my legs abruptly in weird directions. And I just let it happen. If I was falling, I didn't try to catch myself; I just let the hill have me and tucked and held on until my body stopped throwing itself down the slope.

Then I stood up, took some coaching, focused on my skills, and went at it again. I was fearless. And you know what, I learned. By the end of day one, my instructor was so impressed with how much I had improved, especially considering just that morning I hadn't known how to tighten my boots or which direction the snowboard should face when I was putting my boots in it. By the afternoon, I was turning and coming down the hill backward, standing upright.

That night, I could hardly sleep. I was excited to hit the slopes again the next morning and didn't want to sleep in. To be real—I was kind of excited to spend another day with my instructor too.

As impressed as he had been with how quickly I picked up my snowboarding skills, I was impressed with his smooth movements down the hill, the way he patiently held the more apprehensive students' hands, and I really, really liked his mountain-man style. I had imagined us chatting it up on the lift and spending some one-on-one time developing my skills. The rest of the class would have to go with another instructor who could continue nudging them down the bunny slope. I was so sure of myself, in snowboarding and flirting apparently, that I looked forward to the next day with great apprehension and significant confidence that it was going to be life changing.

The next day didn't go nearly as planned. I got to the mountain early, but I was still nervous about going up on my own, so instead of taking the initiative to get up the hill and start warming up, I waited for our class to gather. I could tell the instructor was trying to get the two of us to break off from the group because I had been so far ahead of the rest of the class the day before. Unfortunately, I heard another instructor, the one who I had imagined taking the other beginners, saying it wasn't that she "didn't want to work" but she would rather not be working with the Level 1 snowboarders. She'd rather be riding on her own that day. He talked her into letting us all do a first run and if "any one" of us stood out, she would stick around with the beginners and he could take the more advanced students with him.

I rode up with the rest of the group, nervous about my newly gained skills but knowing that my time alone with the handsome instructor depended on me remembering my turns and my balance. When it was my turn, I self-assuredly performed my fish-flop and planked up to standing on my board (I still couldn't stand up facing forward for whatever reason; coordination, likely). I spun around confidently, started down the bunny slope, and immediately face-planted into the snow, my legs unceremoniously flying into the air, board-over-head, cold snow covering my face. I flipped again, planked back up, and started down again, and toppled over, again.

My skills from the day before had come late in the day, after hours of practice. Because I had been suddenly so unsure of myself, I hadn't gone out to practice at all before class. I didn't have it down yet, at least not well enough to do it without a warmup. The other instructor, the one who didn't want to work with us "Level One" students, bailed. I was stuck watching my crush holding the others' hands as they scooted nervously down the hill and I spent the day alone off to the side, working on my turns and spinning backward, hoping to catch his distracted eye, having now warmed up and regained some confidence.

After a couple of hours, he was able to advance us to a steeper hill and let the others board a little more independently, which gave him some time to focus on my progress. By the end of the day, I had my chance to ride up in the lift with him, taking it to the top of a blue, but still beginner, slope. When we got off the lift, one of the other students inconveniently panicked, and he had to ride along with her while I came down behind.

As we advanced down the hill and mounted the top of the next section, the one with the blue circle on the sign, we all stopped to reassemble as a group and check in. When we were ready to continue, I was the first back on my feet, still hoping to get some more one-on-one time with him. When none of the others followed us down, he paused to turn back and I took off slowly down the mountain alone, expecting they would eventually fall in behind us.

What I didn't realize when I took off, apparently not paying attention to anything other than my instructor's backside, is that we were meant to route ourselves to the left, and finish on a less aggressive slope. Instead, I continued down the much steeper section, tumbling harder than I had been the whole day before as I struggled to keep my speed under control on the grade. After falling board-over-head several more times, I finally came to a clumsy stop at the bottom of the hill, wet and out of breath. And I waited. And waited.

After what felt like twenty minutes, I saw them coming down the beginner slope, several yards away from me, so I wandered over, slowly dragging my board and scooting my loose foot clunkily along behind it. It wasn't until I arrived that I learned I had boarded down a significantly more advanced slope than the instructor had intended for me. He was impressed, and I shrugged it off coolly. He talked me into going back up the lift alone to do it again while he continued working with the rest of the group. He said he'd watch me, and I flirtatiously told him not to because it made me nervous, completely expecting that he would, of course. I was determined to look significantly more graceful the second time down.

When I made it back to the bottom once again, shaking off a few more violent falls, I looked around proudly, expecting to see him waiting. He was nowhere to be found. It was the end of the day on the second day of class. Sunday afternoon was quickly turning into Sunday evening. He had already dismissed everyone else and took off to get in a few real rides of his own before the lifts stopped running. It wasn't like I was expecting a high five; a flirtatious "good job" would have sufficed. If nothing else, I thought he would at least need to know as an instructor that I had reached the bottom safely. Either way, I had read the signs wrong for two days and all my flirting hadn't paid off in the way I hoped it might.

Thinking back on my two successful days of snowboarding, and my lack of success in wooing my instructor, on my drive home the next morning, I asked myself, *what was it about that man that I was so attracted to?* What was it about this Midwest kid from Iowa who came to Vail every winter to teach snowboarding that seemed so appealing? Then it occurred to me, he reminded me so much of Brad, the guy I had been seeing when Clay passed, that it made my heart hurt.

My relationship with Brad hadn't worked out—not only because of the traumatic experience I'd gone through, but because he'd turned out to be a married man with a family, cheating. I didn't know anything about this instructor as a person, as I obviously didn't know Brad either. But what I did know, from our two days together and a little bit of social research, is that, like Brad, he also had kind eyes that stood out behind a shaggy, mountain man beard and nicely gelled, styled hair, parted on the side. He loved adventure and camping and photography and seemed like someone to go on road trips with and explore the world fearlessly. And he was so amazingly graceful when he glided down the mountain on his snowboard, like a dancer, swerving back and forth with perfect posture.

All these were things I thought I had also known to be true about Brad, even though I know now that the man I thought he was had never existed. And I also know now, post-trauma, that these things are not holistic of a person anyway, and I was really just searching for someone safe, and so opposite of Clay. I was also in no position to be trying to form a new connection with anyone in a romantic way anyway.

Meeting this snowboard instructor taught me there were going to be many men who came along to meet those qualities. I live in Colorado, for goodness' sake. Adventure, hiking, and photography are probably going come with the standard package. I would say most of the men I meet travel, especially those I meet while I'm on the road. And in Colorado, you really can't throw a rock without hitting a man with a great mountain man beard and wearing a little bit of flannel.

More seriously though, meeting this man put into perspective that the things I liked about Brad, the "Brad" I was still missing, could be found in hundreds of men, more even, because there had not been any depth in what I knew about him, only surface level, first impressions that were filled with my own assumptions about who he was as a person.

The Brad I thought I had lost didn't really exist. I had made him up from a few brief encounters and then clung to him in my trauma. These features were not independent to him, or even to cute snowboard instructors.

What I've learned to look for is someone who is kind to everyone, and while probably not perfect, will have way more good days than bad. Whether he has a beard or not will never matter, because what I'm looking for goes so far beyond shallow physical traits. Knowing this, I can be far more intentional, and picky, the next time around.

There was one more revelation that I came to when I imagined myself winning over the heart of this snowboard instructor. From my "social research" in the evenings, I knew he would be somebody who ski-bummed in the winter, worked in landscaping during the summer, and then traveled, doing photography in his free time. This wasn't the money-making breadwinner I had been raised to expect in a husband. As it turned out, I was okay with this. Thinking about whether I could make something like this work, I realized, if *only* I could find a man to love who truly loved his own life and followed his own passions intently, how much more rewarding the relationship could be.

I looked at this potential situation I was dreaming up for myself and came to the conclusion, if I was the only person who ever made a single dime between the two of us, but for the love of God, he enjoyed his life and felt fulfilled, that was all I could ask for in a healthy relationship. Ambition does not have to be connected to income. It can easily relate to simply having a passion for life and following one's dreams even if they never make a paycheck worth writing home about. The love for life is all you need, and after a decade of trying to talk Clay into loving himself and his life, it is all I would ever hope for.

* * *

The morning I was set to leave Vail and head back to Denver, I felt good. Well, my body didn't. I finally felt all the violent falls down the side of the mountain and my tailbone, particularly the left side, felt so bruised it was difficult to sit for the long drive home. But I was feeling pretty confident in myself. Not only had I learned how to snowboard, relatively speaking, given only two days of instruction, but I had checked another great accomplishment off my Thirty in Thirty list. I accomplished it alone, when I wanted to, where I wanted to, and I had crushed it. I felt strong and independent and very capable, both from the act of snowboarding but also from the whole empowerment of the trip.

 I hadn't washed my hair in days and by now was smelling a little funny, given I had stayed an extra day and hadn't brought a blow dryer or an extra set of clothes. But I looked in the mirror that morning, after forcing my tangled, windblown hair into a side bun and pulling my stocking cap on to cover the matted down roots, and thought, "Dude, you're a beautiful badass. Why are you worried about meeting somebody? You're amazing as you are."

20

Letter to My Best Friends

May 21, 2019

To my best friends,
  You know who you are. My best friends, my circle, my people. I had lived in Wyoming for years before I found you, but once I did, it was like we had been sisters our entire lives. Every morning at 5 a.m., it was just us, getting our thirty-minute workouts in, taking just that short time for us so we could run off and be wives and mothers for the rest of the day. We ran 5k races every weekend it seemed, spent hundreds of dollars on coffee dates, and suffered through long, grueling, mountain obstacle course races for fun, carrying each other through while we talked about all the food we would eat when we crossed the finish line. I remember going to my first concert at Red Rocks together, after everything had happened, and we all pretended not to be crying, but we were. Because we were together that night, and less than a year prior, we had come only a split second from losing me from the group.
  And I know, without a shadow of a doubt, that I would never have survived those first weeks without you. I still feel the warmth of your tight, scared, strong hugs that lasted for whole minutes when I walked through Juni's door that first day. The relief that flooded over all of you confused me. I was

still lost in my grief and guilt about why I had survived when Clay had to go. I know you didn't understand; why would you have? Your best friend, your sister, was standing there alive after someone you barely knew had tried to steal her from you. How could she be lost and sad and how could you have felt anything other than anger and relief? Besides, it's not like you hadn't lived through your own atrocious grief.

You were no stranger to loss and you understood firsthand how much time it takes to see clearly, to piece together the truth. You knew what it was to clean up your loved ones and bury them, to face their abusers, and many of you had never had access to the resources or the support that I was about to receive to help me through. And still you were there for me, by my side, to love me through all my loss, to feed me and hold me, to pool together everyone's extra resources to pass my way.

I came to you, and you let me grieve and hurt and work through all my confusion, and you never once judged me or questioned my strength. You stood by me and supported Clay's memorial with all the grace in the world. All the while, I could see your concern on your faces, and I know you didn't understand my love for him. I love you for never once questioning it out loud and letting me sit in that love.

Then the communication stopped. Not suddenly, but over time, I stopped hearing from you, and I didn't reach out anymore. I have missed birthdays and weddings, retirements, big moves, and you have too. I've learned that this is one of the unfortunate side effects of grief. It drags on and on in some people's lives and fades in others. It rears its ugly head in the form of blame, depression, unfair expectations, and it confuses loved ones, overwhelms them. Grief makes once strong relationships awkward and uncomfortable.

At least it did for us. For months, years even, I grieved the loss of Clay without accepting the full blessing of my life or the acceptance of what I had been through that night. But why would you grieve my ex-husband? You knew I had left him because of the drinking and the abuse. On top of that, he tried to take me from you all and came so close to being successful. I tried *to understand why you wouldn't feel the same way for my almost-killer, but to me, he was so much more than that. The decade we spent together had been so dynamic, confusing, both the best and worst years of my life. So I couldn't make the grief stop and I couldn't make anyone understand, and so I felt alone, so alone in my grief, and stopped reaching out to you.*

Where I really got off track with our friendship was when I thought you would all have been there for me in my loss of Hunter. Because at the time, that felt so avoidable. I genuinely felt in my heart that we could have fought for him, as a team, with all our combined resources and influences, and we could have won. I guess that is what I expected to happen. I never wanted your husbands' loyalties to the blue line, to their own law enforcement brothers, to be questioned, their careers rocky for putting themselves in the middle of things. I know cops back up cops. I lived that life too, for many years. I suffered the consequences of thinking what is right and moral would ever overcome that loyalty.

But I know you still see her, run into her. That you say hello to her at work, knowing my son is home alone without the love of a mother to get him through this life. I know you still see him at school, that your children pass him in the hallways. Did I really think you would put yourself in that awkward position though, to get in the middle of a family feud, especially with a fellow law enforcement officer? That you could pass my messages of love and support of him through your kids? I guess I really did or at least hoped you would. In the light of day, I know that I have rarely ever set reasonable expectations for those around me. It's been a challenge my entire life, expecting others to be comfortable with risk like I am. My expectations that others will respond and act as I do and will reach to my irrational idea of perfection has always put a huge strain on my relationships.

So, it isn't fair that I blame you for not joining my crusade, to have expected that you would have risked so much for me, for Hunter. But I do; and it couples with my jealousy that you still have your families. That your children get to grow up baking together, playing sports, celebrating holidays with you, and getting your love and guidance every day; that they grow up healthy and loved. Knowing that your husbands see and work with Kim every day, write her schedule and performance evaluations, that you see her at events; Hunter is only just beyond your reach and still believes I have abandoned him and left him alone during the worst days of his life, I can't let the hurt go. I know it's not your fault. But I can't get it out of my mind. And for that, I am so sorry. I miss every one of you so much.

With so much love,
Abby

* * *

Journal Entry. September 4, 2018

   Prompt: List five things that always, and immediately, bring a smile to your face.
   Mountains, sunflowers, friends, softball and 5Ks.
   I can meditate any place at any time. It doesn't have to be scheduled.
   Week One: I'm going to try to meditate more than once a week. Today was tough, though. Maybe because my mind is racing after just finishing therapy. Maybe it's because I'm sick. Because it's evening and I have other things I want to do instead. But I still did it. And I forced myself to sit with myself for seven minutes! Today that felt like forever.

Journal Entry. September 15, 2018.

   Meditation is teaching me to sit still in the moment. It is teaching me to bring myself back to the present when I have flashbacks. Hopefully it can help me process so I can heal.

Journal Entry. September 19, 2018.

   Quote from Journal: "A wise man loses nothing, if he but save himself." – Michel De Montaigne

Prompt: Think of something you lost recently. What are two positive insights you gained from the experience?
I lost Clay and Hunter. I have learned that I'm a hell of a lot stronger than I thought I was. Even though I already knew I was a badass. I learned that for ten years, I gave up everything, maybe even God's plan for me, to take on someone else's responsibility. Trusting that God is holding Hunter in His arms, maybe I can learn this is my time now. To not give up my career anymore. To own the things I have earned. And reach my goals. Trusting that Hunter is going to be okay through all this; maybe it is Kim's turn to give it all up.

Journal Entry. September 26, 2018.
Prompt: Color in this world map with the ten places you plan to visit.
I almost died before getting to see any of these places. Would anyone have noticed? They would have found my empty passport in my mailbox, unused. Last night I had a dream that I was so angry with Clay for what he did to Hunter. I know he couldn't control his actions by the time he pulled that trigger. But he knew when he started drinking. And he had so many outs. He didn't take any of them. Praying helped; meditation only reminded me that I needed to be praying more.

Journal Entry. October 5, 2018.
Prompt: Think of something that is currently troubling you and write about it here. Don't try to solve it; just focus on getting your thoughts out of your head and onto paper.
Losing Clay and Hunter. I want to know that God has Hunter, but I'm still very worried about him. I don't know that he has anyone there to truly love him, and I don't know if he has anyone to truly talk to. I wish I could at least get him in to see Rebecca so I know he has someone with a brain to talk to. The only thing I can do is keep praying for him.

And I miss Clay still. So much.

Journal Entry. October 12, 2018.
Every day, I'm learning something new. I love to learn. Something I'm trying to focus on learning is how to sit in the moment, how to bring myself back to the moment, and how to grieve. I have never needed to know how to grieve. I don't know how I have always dissociated loss in the past, but I have. And now I need to learn to grieve and sometimes sit in the suck. It's okay that I miss Clay. I'm going to miss him for a very long time. I still wish I could tell him how much I love him even after what he did. I can be mad at him but still love and miss him. Shit, that has been our whole life together!

Journal Entry. October 23, 2018
Prompt: Write down your favorite, most daring dream.
My most daring dream may have been to backpack across Europe. Very recently, this would have seemed outside of my reach. If Clay were here right now, I probably wouldn't be going. He would be criticizing how irresponsible and crazy this is. That this is something for rich college kids to do, not me. He would be making me feel bad and telling me this is money that should be spent on a vacation for all three of us. When we were married, there was never anything extra to put into a vacation fund, and I still wonder where our money was actually going. But the idea of saving and going somewhere, anywhere, was always far out of the question. I definitely would never have been able to do something so frivolous as to travel abroad. Even taking Faye to New York and DC had to be done on 'my pocket money' without spending family funds.

Journal Entry. October 27, 2018.
Prompt: What gives you light?
I'm alive. That is plenty to have light about. Against every single odd possible, God kept me alive to fight another day, to do great things. I'm positive my mind can't wrap itself around all the greatness that I have in front of me. God has huge plans for me. I should hang on to that.

Journal Entry. November 7, 2018
Meditation will keep me grounded and focused on my present even though I am hopeful and anxious for the future. I am so relieved that Hunter is reaching out again. I am so relieved because I feel like he's going to be okay. But I need to be wise and patient about contacting him. I don't want to get into any legal trouble (I mean, whatever), but I definitely don't want to be cut off again, meaning that everyone else gets blocked too. I have to stay focused on my present so I can continue to succeed for Hunter and me. So I can let God do His work without my interference.

Journal Entry. November 29, 2018.
Prompt: List four times you continued to try even though the odds were against you.
Leading in my career. My education. Fighting for my life. Fighting for Hunter. When people tell me they admire my resilience, I am surprised. But I think I just don't know how to respond to them because I have never been able to understand it myself. From leaving my home, to fighting for an education, to constantly being told I'm too young to lead, to surviving a literal attack on my life, and now in my fight for Hunter. Somehow, I have always survived and then thrived. That's my advantage over everyone who would try to stop me. My will to live is stronger than their will to kill me. I just wish I had an idea of where this came from. I certainly wasn't raised with it.

Journal Entry. December 11, 2018.
The outdoors has always been a place of imagination, discovery, and success for me. Of growth and peace. From playing outside as a child to 'hiking' on Grandma's farm to AmeriCorps, always outdoors. Running my first Spartan race gave me so much peace when Grandma died, and again when I lost Clay. But lately, when I am in nature, I am filled with gratitude. I am constantly surrounded by such beauty and God's amazing glory, and I have yet to miss the fortune and blessing it is to be outdoors and to be alive. Nothing has made me more aware of being alive and the blessing of being alive than when I am out in nature. Every time, I look around at the beauty that God has made, and I am grateful that I am not missing those moments. I am grateful to be alive.

Journal Entry. December 16, 2018.
Prompt: Things I want to be
A mom. Loved. A good friend.
Prompt: Why I want to be them
Because I'm a kickass mom.
Because, for real, I don't know if that has ever happened to me before. The most valuable thing to be in the whole world.
It has been so hard for me to find joy this past week. Transitioning home has been really hard, and I'm lonely. I am trying to give it to God but it's hard.

Journal Entry. December 31, 2018.
Prompt: Think of three ideas that you fundamentally disagree with, ideas that hurt your spirit and are harmful to your well-being.
That I need someone in my life to complete me or make me happy.

That I'm not good enough.

That I am limited.

Sometimes people come into our lives exactly when we need them to be there. But when they do not stay, it is not a reflection on me. They are just no longer needed for that chapter, and it is time to keep moving. If they are still needed, or needed again, they will return. But only if they're treated with honor and respect the first time. Let them move in and out freely. It is not because you are not good enough. It is because you are.

Journal Entry. January 7, 2019.

I don't even know why I am so depressed tonight but I am. I came home from work at four, too tired to do much of anything else, so I skimmed Facebook for an hour. I forced myself to eat dinner and laid in bed with my homework, staring at my computer, unable to focus on anything. I gave in and just went to bed without washing my face, without brushing my teeth. I didn't even take Axel out. I have zero energy to complete anything. But when I tried to go to bed at seven, I closed my eyes and all I could see was Clay blowing his head off. And I wanted to scream at him to stop before it was too late. I wanted to scream at him to come back and fix everything that he left broken. And I wanted to scream at him not to do this to his son. To me. To our family, as dysfunctional as it was. I ran back through my what ifs again. What could I have done differently to save him? To convince him of how loved he was?

Journal Entry. January 11, 2019.

The sun didn't shine today. It snowed. I was excited to telework in the snow, but instead I laid around and slept and cried most of the day. I cried for all the things I had to lose in exchange for my blessings. While I am grateful for the life I have, I often wonder if I would go back to my old life. If I would give up all the good I have and the good I know God is going to do in my life so I can have Clay and Hunter back. Maybe that's why I'm so depressed. Because I feel like my success is linked to their fate. But I tried. I tried so hard to bring them along. Clay had every excuse in the book for why this life wouldn't be good enough for them. I tried so hard to give them a better life. But it wasn't until Clay saw that I was so successful that he was ready to trust me. Maybe that's why he would get wasted when he saw me succeeding. Because he knew he had thrown it away.

Journal Entry. March 7, 2019.
Prompt: List three traits you'd like others to see in you.
That I'm fun to hang around.
That I care.
That I'm only competing with myself.
Tonight, I meditated for ten minutes! I didn't think I could sit still with myself for that long, but I did. It was a really good one too. I sat and breathed compassion into others who are suffering.
This came at a good time because I'm really struggling with how to process that others can't process their own grief. Why aren't they doing anything to fix how they feel? I'm confused, and at the same time, it leaves me feeling like maybe I'm the one who is wrong. I don't know how to respond, but I guess I can send compassion.

Journal Entry. March 14, 2019.
Prompt: What are your three most frequent thoughts?
I'm losing weight and I look good.
Why am I single?
I miss Clay.
Prompt: What do you wish they would be?
My body is beautiful every day because it is strong and capable.

Being single is a privilege and an adventure.
Clay was the only person in control of his choices. He is also not hurting anymore.

Journal Entry. March 22, 2019.
Prompt: List the resources (people, tools and ideas) that can help you on your journey.
My friends. And their resources. My sharp mind. My financial stability. My past trauma and experiences. My strong survival skills. My voice. My health. My sense of humor. My balls. Meditation. Yoga. Bath bombs. Face masks. Pedicures. Chocolate. Axel. Outdoors. Everything Clay taught me about life. My faith in God. My candid relationship with Him. My independence. My feminism. My grit. Running. Swimming. Travel. Lifting. Support groups.. Therapy. Journaling. My awesome job. Deployments.

Journal Entry. March 24, 2019.
Prompt: Desire.
Recover from grief.
Provide a good life for Hunter.
Share my story with others.
Fulfill the universal plan for my life.
Prompt: Action toward that desire.
Sit in grief without abandon or shame.
Keep myself mentally and physically healthy over the next five years. Write my book. Share my testimony. Network and build relationships. Wait patiently.

Journal Entry. April 5, 2019.
Prompt: What is your greatest motivation in life?
I lived when someone with the skills, resources, and intent tried to kill

me. I lived. That's my motivation. God let me live because He wasn't done with me yet. He has a magnificent life promised to me and needs me alive to live it.

Journal Entry. May 8, 2019.
Prompt: You've created so many things out of nothing. Write about one of them here.
I've created growth out of trauma. Yes, I might sleep more than I would like to. I impulse eat and shop. I occasionally lose sight of my healthy recovery. But I have developed awareness and focus, resources and strength. I have goals that are unwavering and a recovery that is progress and will come to fruition. I love who I used to be, and I am grateful for her and her experiences and strength. But now I choose a new identity of a different kind of strength and even more love and appreciation for my experience. I choose to grow and love me.

Journal Entry. May 9, 2019.
Tonight, I found the strength to do yoga and meditate instead of sleep. I found the strength to cry and process some of my hurt and to show compassion to Clay and Blanche for their upbringing and how it has impacted their lives. I am fortunate to know how to cry. To be able to cry without shame and retribution. I am blessed to cry and process so my trauma and the hurt from my life does not get to steal my joy. I haven't always had that. Clay didn't have that. I am strong because I cry.

Journal Entry. June 13, 2019.
Prompt: List three aspects of the human condition that you are grateful for.
The gift of a vast variety of complex emotions. I am grateful for the experience of feeling every single one of them, and I am blessed to not

be limited to any few. The ability and attraction to movement. I love that our bodies can move the way they do and even thrive from movement. Dancing, running, lifting, hiking. All of it. I love that we want health.

Love. Even when we 'shouldn't' and even when we hurt. It is still a natural tendency to love, and for that, we are fortunate.

Journal Entry. June 20, 2019.
Prompt: Make a wish and write it down here.
I wish I could have my son back.

Journal Entry. July 10, 2019.
Prompt: Remember yourself as a child; what piece of advice would you give your future self?
Love yourself. First. Endlessly. Without ever stopping. Unconditionally. No matter what.

Journal Entry. July 20, 2019.
Prompt: Writing in a stream-of-conscious style, describe the darkest pain that visits you from time to time.
The darkest pain is an easy one. But I have all the resources I need for managing that. What is really terrifying is when I can be living my absolute best life and still not bring to mind what I am grateful and happy for because I am afraid of not achieving one really terrifying goal on my list. So what if I'm not running thirty miles yet? One day. I have so much to be grateful and happy for that if I'm going to let one task keep me from feeling fulfilled, then I need to reevaluate why I am doing this in the first place. Seriously.

Journal Entry. July 25, 2019.
Quote: "There was another life that I might have had, but I'm

having this one." – Kazuo Ishiguro.

Prompt: Identify three parts of your life that you wish were different. Can you come up with a reason you are grateful for each?

I wish Clay were still alive.

I wish my parents would have had more ambition for me as a child.

I wish I could be in a loving, healthy relationship.

I could never be grateful for losing Clay, but I do recognize the freedom it has afforded me. As much as I miss him, I know he would have been discouraging me from almost every accomplishment this last year. If my parents would have expected more, I would have never developed my grit. And if I were in a relationship, it would probably distract me from all this great self-love I am giving myself.

* * *

After my year of firsts was over, I bought a second gratitude journal with the intention of continuing this practice, which I did, but much more infrequently than when I had first set it as a Thirty in Thirty goal. It should have been no surprise to me that I continued to struggle with sitting in my grief and healing from my trauma, and when these moments came, I did my best to practice yoga, meditation, and journaling.

It would be almost two years after completing this goal when I found myself back in my therapist's office asking, "Why?" Why am I still suffering from depression when I am trying so hard not to? Why are one or two jerks at work or small inconveniences ruining my week when I was once so resilient that I could fight to recover from such extreme adversity?

She explained to me that when a person suffers from extreme trauma, or multiple traumatic events over the course of their life, the effect on their brain begins to impact their hippocampus. The hippocampus is a small but super important part of the brain that is crucial for forming new memories and allowing those memories to dictate how we think of the future[16]. It also plays a big role in emotional regulation and stress response so, it is important that it remains healthy. She told me that from a trauma lens my hippocampus had likely been damaged over time, from the many experiences I had in my youth, living in an abusive relationship for a decade, and then, of course, the whole near death/suicide thing.

What I learned through therapy after three years of trying to muscle my way through this recovery was that I needed to step it up or find a different solution to healing my brain. I had been trying to force myself back to health with exercise, learning new languages, sitting in nature, and while every little bit was helping, I was still grasping at straws without really knowing what I was doing.

When Clay first died, I had poured myself into research about the brain but mostly about how his amygdala might have come "disconnected" (in layman's terms) from his frontal lobe, possibly causing a physiological snap that would have caused him to act as he did[17]. I needed a scientific, biological excuse, a logical explanation to try to understand why he may have made the decisions that he did that night.

Obviously, alcohol had something to do with this. When his blood had been tested, hours after his time of death, he was at a .315 percent blood alcohol content. At .4 percent the alcohol content in the blood becomes fatal and the chances are significant for comatose. So I'm sure that didn't help his brain function or decision-making skills.

Of course, I was not doing the same level of research about my own brain until after she had mentioned that mine was likely more damaged from the trauma than what I had originally expected. She got me started in this new journey for healing with a helpful tip: three things have been proven to rebuild the hippocampus over time—sixty minutes of meditation a day, sixty minutes or yoga a day, or psychotropic medications.

While relieved that rebuilding my hippocampus was an option, sixty minutes of meditation or yoga was so far beyond the initial effort I had been willing to give to this. For several reasons though, including the way I was raised to rely on prescriptions for almost every stuffy nose and sore throat, my terrible fear of losing my sharp cognitive function, and the idea of "increased suicidal tendencies" as a side effect, medications were a big, fat "no thanks" for me.

Let me quickly caveat: do not take my personal neurotic tendencies here as advice for how to manage your own trauma or therapeutic treatments. In fact, run very far away from it. Please talk with your therapist, a trained psychiatric doctor, and your personal physician before making the decision to either take or not take medication of any sort. It certainly has its place in the treatment of a series of brain chemistry functions. All I'm saying here is that I didn't want it to be my solution, against the advice of my therapist, because I have an irrational fear of the side effects. Instead, after a quick mental assessment of my schedule and a "Shit, are you sure it is sixty minutes a day?!" I decided to throw myself into taking meditation and yoga significantly more seriously.

New habits are not easy to build. I have a lot of work to do before I would consider myself an actual "yogi" and long before I can sit for sixty minutes, focusing only on my breath. But I am working on it and I am already seeing great improvements. The drama from coworkers and the thoughts of my dysfunctional family do not weigh on me and hijack my entire day anymore. When my brain takes off with anxiety about the things I cannot control, I am more aware of it and can (usually) bring myself back to the moment.

I want to remember my past. It is endearing and important to who I am. I want to look forward to my future instead of being anxious about it. I want to hold onto my memory well into my old age and not be struggling to maintain my brain health from this terrible thing that happened to me back when I was twenty-nine years old. And I want to maintain that resiliency, the strength in my mind that I had when I originally said, "No. Fuck you, trauma. I'm not giving in."

21

Clay's Eulogy

Every time I am asked what my book is about, I struggle to define it. I still don't like going into the details with strangers, but it is difficult to avoid at least a quick briefing when I tell them I am writing about trauma. Then I call it resilience; I am writing about resilience and recovery from trauma. Sometimes I say I am writing about the complexity of being a domestic abuse victim, the stereotypes behind those labels, and how even strong and very self-assured women can fall into these situations. It's about how society (and the Christian church) often pressure us into these situations and marriages that were never the right fit or even the safe choice for our lives.

Or I am writing about the toxic masculinity that forces our law enforcement officers into a state of anger and depression, ignoring their trauma and experiences, and then abandons them when the emotions finally surface as violence or addiction. I'm writing about the cycle of trauma that we all experience when our families, our friends, and even strangers we meet on the streets project their own unresolved suffering onto our lives. Then I realize that I probably can't have this many major themes but since I have never actually written an entire book before, maybe that isn't true either.

What it all really comes down to is that it is complex. In every one of these themes, the cycle of trauma is the foundation. It is why Clay and I, Clay's parents, their parents before them, my parents, our friends and coworkers, all responded the way they did to all of this, leading to the letters and stories in this book. Trauma, abuse, relationships, religion, resilience—it all means something different for everyone, and all those answers can be right or wrong based on the resources and life experiences that each person has had.

I once thought alcoholics were only men who sat shirtless with "beer bellies", lazy on the couch, screaming and yelling abusive things, drinking their cheap beer all day and not working to support their families. I couldn't identify it otherwise; this was what it looked like. And because Clay, or any former boyfriend for that matter, didn't look the part, I didn't know they were struggling to control their addictions. I couldn't understand that I was walking into a relationship driven by alcoholism because I didn't know how to identify it for what it was—an addiction and illness that can impact even the best people.

While recovering from my grief, I came to know others who were unable to survive on their own after trauma, could not pull themselves off the couch for years because of the pain of losing a loved one even decades prior. I met people who were falling to pieces over divorces or the impending loss of a sick spouse, and I quickly learned that just because I had gone through the traumatic and complex loss that I had, I could not underplay anybody else's grief. People are resourced so differently, with different emotional styles, financial understanding, life skills, and education, and what I might have considered to be an acute loss for others may be equally as traumatic and life-altering as my worst experiences. There is no way to measure grief and trauma; no comparison from one person's experiences to another's, and it all sucks for the person going through it.

Yes, Clay was abusive. He was also my guiding light for the years when I really needed to figure things out. I hadn't been raised to know how to manage money, how to work hard for what I have. I didn't know how to take care of myself and keep my car maintained, stand up for myself when working with realtors and insurance companies. I didn't know how to be an adult. I learned those things with Clay.

Clay didn't know how to love me. His father had chosen him out of the three siblings to beat endlessly, and his mother allowed it so she could keep the income and stability for herself and the other two children. He was never given an example of what healthy love looks like. I don't believe for a second that he didn't love me with all his heart. I also know that his inability to show love was not a reason for me to take his fear and insecurities onto my shoulders and live with abuse.

He pushed me around, poked me hard in the chest, and threw things at me. He also yelled at me, discouraged me from my dreams, and shamed me when I cried. None of this looked like what I thought an abuser would look like. He didn't punch me or kick me; there were never any bruises. I never had to lie about falling down the stairs or walking into something. And because I had relied on him to know how to be a grown-up, I believed him when he told me I was lucky to have him to keep me grounded. I didn't know that he was holding me back.

There is way too much complexity for any one person to define it all and get it right. But at least I can write my story and hope it reaches someone who has a parallel experience, or similar components, or knows someone who has been labeled as a victim, as an addict, as depressed, and they can understand there is so much more to it than what they see and understand. Maybe this book can allow others to stop being so critical of one another's demons.

I know one thing, though— Zora Neale Hurston was right; there really is no greater agony than an untold story inside of you, and even the idea of not finishing this book was the root of my anxiety many days. The thoughts and words that ran through my mind every minute of every day begged to be said out loud, to get out of my crazed mind and onto paper so I could release them to the world. I needed to say all the things I had hidden away for so many years to protect Clay, the things I silenced with blame when he died; I needed Hunter to know them so he might understand.

I didn't even come close to completing my book's first draft in that year after losing Clay. I did, however, take pages and pages of notes and drafted many chapters, and I journaled so, so much. Those were good to reference each time I found myself back at my desk, crafting the pages as they came together to form this book.

It turns out, writing an entire book is hard. It is hard for those who get to hole up and focus solely on writing as a career. It is difficult to prioritize while also writing a dissertation and completing a doctorate. It is even more challenging when you pile on the trauma brain, grief, desperate recovery, and then add a few disaster deployments. After a year of striving to meet this goal, I realized it was not going to be fair to expect myself to accomplish it. I am astonished that I once really believed it could be done, but I sit here in my umpteenth coffee shop writing yet again, now over seven years since Clay's death.

Even now that I have completed my doctorate and have taken what I would consider an acceptable period of rest before diving back into this goal, it still takes a level of energy to dig back into these memories that I don't have or want to give most days. For every hour of work I do bringing this trauma back up in my mind to get it down on paper, I spend the equivalent amount of time in a heavy sleep, the weight of my memories holding me down until my brain feels rested. In my sleep, dreams and nightmares reappear in my mind, and I see Clay flipping eggs for breakfast calmly while I cry and beg for him to try harder to stop drinking, and I feel the warmth of Hunter wrapped around me in a full, monkey-like hug like he would give me when I came home from a long work trip.

This one-to-one ratio of writing to sleep doesn't leave much room for long, extensive writing sessions and this isn't exactly my day job. So each time, I come back to this goal with compassion for myself, knowing that this untold story desperately needs to get out.

* * *

Clay's Eulogy

July 23, 2018

The very first thing Clay Caldwell said to me on our first date was, "There are two things you should know about me: I have a three-year old son and I am a huge, huge fan of the Pittsburgh Steelers." I responded with, "Is that a baseball team?" This was in 2009, and the Steelers had just won the Super Bowl a couple months prior. Fortunately, he stuck with me after that, and after a few more dates, I learned that his son, Hunter, and the Pittsburgh Steelers really were the most important things in Clay's life. Hunter was always along and there was almost always a Steeler's logo to be found in every hunting trip, fishing trip, and Harley ride.

One particular situation involving these two favorites was when Clay found out Brett Keisel (a Steelers defensive end at the time) would be at the Clinton Golf Course one afternoon. He was so excited that he pulled up and jumped out to get an autograph, completely forgetting that Hunter and I were child-locked in the back seat of his truck and couldn't get out to join them!

As Hunter got older, it got a little easier for Clay to do all his favorite things with his son. They enjoyed taking afternoon Harley Davidson bike rides and going on poker runs, eating ballpark hot dogs while watching the Colorado Rockies play at home, and making Clay's famous elk tacos. He was a great hunter, fisherman, Little League coach, and had just started running obstacle course races with the goal of completing a three-race trifecta. And every activity involved Hunter first. Hopefully, Hunter will continue to enjoy these things in remembrance of his daddy.

Clay lived a full life of public service, serving fifteen years in law enforcement for Wilson County, Clinton Police Department and Uptown Police Department. He was a great law enforcement officer, wholeheartedly believing in community policing and service to the public. He served as a sniper instructor and sniper for the Black Sheep Tac Team and took so much pride in teaching his fellow officers the tactics of rifle shooting.

While working in law enforcement, Clay received several awards for his service, including one for the largest methamphetamine seizure in the history of the department as well as a stolen vehicle seizure, which included an ambush and led to a multi-state response. Above all else, though, Clay took pride and enjoyed most the time he spent in Wilson County schools as a school resource officer, working with youth and teaching DARE classes to the kids.

More recently, Clay worked as a switchman for Union Pacific Railroad, where he enjoyed serving as the safety officer for his fellow yardmen. He was known as a dedicated employee and a good friend to those who knew and worked with him. Not surprising knowing Clay, but he was known as a quiet person who, when he did have something to say, spoke with purpose.

Clay came to know the Lord in 2011 and was always seeking to find a way to walk closer with God. Up until the time of his death, he studied the book of Ephesians with a close friend, learning that he is loved and blameless before the Lord because of what Jesus did for us on the cross. We know that he is now walking in the presence of the Lord.

Thank you for being here with us today to celebrate Clay.

* * *

Clay loved my writing, and so it only made sense that I would write and give his eulogy. Many of his closest friends did not show up to the memorial, nor did any of the members of Clay's home church. Word had gotten around about the circumstances of his death and Clay's family had already spoken with most of them, placing blame and making their accusations on me, disregarding Clay's lifetime of trauma and alcoholism as a potential factor. When I reached out to his friends, they wanted nothing to do with the memorial that *I* was giving him.

Hunter's mother wouldn't allow him to attend either, though so many showed up from his school to support him. For the past decade, Clay had complained about me to his coworkers and friends, seeking reassurance that he was in the right and I was wrong to control him and be angry with his drinking. So it comes as no surprise that I was the one they wanted to blame when in fact, I had been the one in the arena with him the entire time. It was he and I who fought through the battle of this addiction together. For a decade, I was the focus of his anger, his relief from the pain, his biggest supporter in his struggle to overcome the addiction. No matter what they wanted to say about me from the brief moments they had spent with him, I knew him best.

22

Letter to Clay's Friends

December 21, 2019

To Clay's Friends,
    I know you thought you were helping. He was the one who told you how controlling his wife was, how she didn't let him drink at home, wouldn't just let him relax. I can see how that can be frustrating for you boys; you don't let your wives tell you what to do, I'm sure. But you didn't live with him, and you weren't wise enough to know that there is always more than one side of the story.
    Here's mine: I was controlling. I was frantic and anxious and a screaming hot mess because I didn't know how else to keep him alive. I was sleep deprived and scared not just for my life but for our son and whether he would have a daddy until he was grown, whether we would keep the house with all that alcohol getting charged to our credit cards.
    When you thought you were being slick by slipping him a couple beers when he was at your house, you were actually kicking off a night of rage for him and fear for me. You see, he couldn't have just one or two once his demons surfaced. When you were talking him into getting blackout wasted with you, bringing over a handle of Wild Turkey and spending the whole weekend being too drunk to make it to the fishing trip that you had planned,

you didn't think twice about the wasteland you left there for me on Monday. You thought you were helping him, releasing him from his controlling wife, "She's the problem, man. Get rid of the problem and you'll stop drinking. But until then, fuck it." Nice advice, guys.

Here's the worst part. You all had the nerve to blame me for his death in the end. "The controlling bitch wife who didn't want him drinking." You idiots. He was blackout drunk when he pulled that trigger. You think I was trying to keep him sober just to keep him from enjoying his life?

He was miserable, but it wasn't because of me. He would stay up entire nights binge watching crap television with a bottle of vodka slid between the couch cushions. He would booty call old babysitters. He would get sloppy and he would cry and rage about his awful childhood, the senseless abuse he endured from his father, the dirty favors he did for his law enforcement brothers, covering up their mistakes and taking care of people the law wasn't going to, the memories he tried so desperately to erase with more drinking.

You know this. You got the 2 a.m. phone calls too. Who was always there, trying to stay calm and keep him stable, get him to bed? Not you. Many of you thought it was funny. Most of you thought it was situational, even after having grown up with Clay your entire life.

You all knew he was an alcoholic. "Must have been the controlling wife's fault." What was your excuse for him before I came along? He was surrounded by people telling him it was okay, so I had to stand alone to help him fight this addiction. I alone had to stand next to him all night, most nights, trying to hide keys and guns so I could keep him alive to finish raising his son. In my twenties. So yes, I'm sure I was a frantic, controlling wife. Sorry to ruin your fun, but I guess I lost and you won in the end anyway because he never did have to learn to control it and he never did have to take accountability for his drinking. Blame me for that too.

The part that really amazed me was when you sided with his family about Hunter. I heard you say, "His parents might be right; if he had wanted you to have Hunter, then why would he have been trying to kill you too? Maybe *he was trying to keep you from being around to get Hunter."*

I get it, everybody's looking for answers. But can we use a little common sense here, guys? His blood alcohol content was at .315 percent even hours after his death. Every ten seconds someone dies from alcohol-related causes. The way Clay was living his life, it was only a matter of time before he joined this statistic, and it was going to have nothing to do with his decisions about Hunter or me. He didn't think of anyone else besides himself when he drank; that's what it is to be an alcoholic.

By the time he got into his truck and drove to Denver, he was too blacked out to have some elaborate plan to save Hunter from having me as a mother for the rest of his life. If he had been thinking about his son at all, it's unlikely he would have gotten into that truck in the first place with his suspended license while on probation and after all that whiskey. That's not how being drunk works, boys.

No, he wasn't thinking of Hunter at all when he made those decisions. He wasn't thinking about me or himself or any plans for what life would look like for anybody after that night. He was too damn drunk to be planning any of this. You know who else wasn't thinking of Hunter? Clay's best friends and family when they chose not to see past their hurt and anger to observe any common sense.

And Ron, if you haven't sold it by now for your own drinking money, I'm sure Hunter would like to have his daddy's saddle back.

Fuck you very much,
Abby

* * *

There were many Thirty in Thirty goals that didn't happen that first year. The struggle to accept the lack of achievement taught me one of the biggest lessons of all: grace for myself.

When I first put "Run a Sprint Triathlon" on my Thirty in Thirty list, I didn't even own a road bike and I hadn't actually swum since I dropped out of swim lessons at seven years old. A reasonable person in my position would have chalked this one up as a "no thanks" and crossed it off the list. More than ever, though, I needed to get my mind off the pain and the grief, I needed wild goals to get me out of bed in the morning. There would be no slacking on my health if I were to teach myself to swim...and bike.

So, I bought a road bike, learned to clip in and out of my pedals in the grass at the park, and woke up early every morning for months to go swim back and forth dozens of times in my apartment complex pool. I picked a race that would be all women with a first-time competitors heat. I figured that as long as I could keep up, being surrounded by so many other strong women would be empowering. Plus, there were going to be shirtless firefighters along the route.

I was feeling pretty confident in my training when I suited up early that Saturday morning and headed to the lake. Unfortunately, before I got across town to where the race would take place, it started raining. A cold, heavy, constant rain poured onto my car, on the lake, on the bikes, and soaked the bags of clothes for changing in between each leg of the race. My body tensed. I knew not to tense, and I did anyway, my attitude about being cold and wet before even getting into the water impacting me more than I'd like to admit. Once there, many of us got into the lake before the start of the race to warm up, the rain coming down colder than the body of the water.

My heat was first, and I lined up, surrounded by probably twenty other women all excited to take off around the large square of buoys marking our course. The gun went off and we all started swimming. Before I even reached the first paddleboarder, serving as both a lifeguard and a guidepost, I panicked. I stopped swimming, realizing that I was terrified by all the flailing bodies around me and the fact that I had no wall to reach out to. It had dawned on me quite suddenly that if I couldn't do this, I would die. There was no quitting or resting here. I couldn't pull my mind from the anxiety that had unexpectedly capitalized on my mind; my nervous system raged, and I completely forgot all my training.

The paddleboarder came floating up to me so I could rest. "Is this your first triathlon?" she asked as I gasped for breath, clinging to the side of her board while trying not to bring her off balance. "The swim is always the hardest part. Just stay focused on the next paddleboard and take it one stop at a time. You'll get there!"

The next volunteer was more concerned. "Are you okay? Do you have any history of asthma or heart problems?"

"No," I attempted to reassure him, "I trained very hard for this. This isn't because I'm not in great physical shape," *this is a mental block*, I thought to myself.

One paddle board at a time, I continued in a sloppy doggy paddle, unable to put my face back in the water. As I struggled through the swim, I heard occasional gun shots signaling the start of the next heat and one by one, every other swimmer passed me until I became the 201st woman out of 201 women to leave the water.

Running to my bike, I found it to be the last one still parked, except for the bikes that had already returned from the ten-mile ride. Stripping out of my wet suit and throwing on my next outfit, soaked from the rain, I jumped onto my bike, clipped in my shoes, and took off on the course, catching up and passing biker after biker. When I returned to begin the run, I changed my shoes but kept all my layers since the cold rain and fatigue already had me shivering, and I began running as fast as my numb legs would take me. I ended up finishing, after coming in dead last out of the water, at about halfway through all the competitors, having passed about half of them on the bikes and 5k.

I was so proud of this accomplishment and maybe even more so because I had come so close to giving up and had fought through to the finish. On the other hand, it opened my eyes even more to the effects that depression, trauma and anxiety can have on the brain. Only a few weeks later I was scheduled to run the Spartan Ultra—a 31-mile mountain obstacle course race in Aspen, Colorado. At this point, I was still struggling to accomplish my goal to place in a 5k without the weight of the trauma holding me back and I now knew the fear of possibly being pulled from a race for not being able to finish.

I had already spent a couple hundred dollars signing up for this race and had purchased the additional gear for the longer distance. I put in for time off and was prepared to return to Colorado from the field to achieve this goal. Even more importantly, I had put it on my list and announced to the world that I would accomplish it that year. By this time, though, I questioned whether I might have learned my lesson. Was I really going to continue putting myself in a position where I was not at all mentally resourced to get through a self-imposed challenge?

I made one of the hardest decisions of the entire year—to quit something after I had committed to it—and I dropped out of the race. I knew by now that this was the smartest thing for me to do, a true demonstration of the compassion that I was, very slowly and painfully, learning to have for myself. Unfortunately, I hadn't quite gotten there with my mindset.

For days after skipping the race, I *wallowed* in self-pity. Grasping for understanding about why I was so upset, wanting to pull myself back out of the sadness, I reflected on why I could not accept this decision. It took me quite a bit of journaling, and therapy, before it came to me; it was never about whether I could complete the race, if I had trained or worked hard enough, or if I was ever going to overcome the trauma.

This overwhelming sense of inadequacy was literally all about failing to put a checkmark on a list. This race alone wasn't going to define whether or not I was going to be okay, and completing the entire, unrealistic list of goals was not going to determine who I would become after this first year. I was still in charge of all that without torturing myself, and no amount of checking-off was going to get me through this any better than a little self-love and compassion was going to. While I had understood the list was not fully realistic when I first developed it, for the first time in this whole year of recovery, I finally accepted that I didn't have to get everything accomplished.

I battled again with this concept when it came time to recognize that I had no business floating a kayak down a river and camping out overnight by myself. And again when I realized I wouldn't be going cattle branding. This had been a social media suggestion, and while it sounded like a lot of fun, I didn't even know anybody who branded cattle nor did I have the connections to find myself invited to a branding.

Thankfully I had come to the point of giving myself more grace by the time I realized I wouldn't be maintaining all A's in my doctorate program. My first hint should have been when, only days after losing Clay and prior to even regaining access to my computer, the school was already telling me, "I'm sorry to hear about what has happened to you but our late assignment policy does not have room for flexibility."

Even if that had not originally deterred me, I had been steadily failing to understand my quantitative research assignments despite having reached out for tutoring. I dropped the class that quarter to save myself from the F and the following term I let the B happen and forgave myself for it, knowing it wasn't worth the mental capacity that it would have taken just to check a box.

I used to get so angry with Clay for all the time he spent sitting on the couch binging television, not for hours but literally for days at a time, not sleeping for nights at a time with a bottle of vodka snuck in between the cushions. I would scream at him about not helping around the house or with Hunter's activities and homework. I couldn't understand why he could not overcome his depression by just going for a run, eating healthier, or taking a shower for God's sakes. I had completely underestimated the power that mental illness has on the brain and how exhausting the daily fight for survival can be. Finding this compassion for myself through my Thirty in Thirty list created an emotion that was a mix of guilt and shame for not having more understanding and grace for Clay in his struggle to overcome his illness.

23

Finding Humility in Costa Rica

Considering that public service is basically what I do for a living, my Thirty in Thirty goal to go on a mission trip was way outside of my comfort zone, for many reasons. The first one being I really wasn't sure whether I could hide my dark humor and foul mouth from the young, innocent souls I would be traveling to another country with for an entire week.

Walking into the church for my first trip meeting, I was totally intimidated by how young they were. Most of the women didn't look like they had started losing their teenage metabolism yet, and I quickly discovered that one of the guys didn't even know whether he hung the toilet paper over or under at his house because his mom did that for him. *Great, my old soul is going to fit in nicely*, I thought snidely.

My biggest fear going into this was that it was going to be just like all my bad memories from youth group. What if we broke out into a random Christian musical and prayed out loud at every possible occasion? Maybe there would be interpretive dance and constant laying of hands. Were they going to judge me critically for my past decisions or for my lack of bible verse memorization? This was going to be just like every Wednesday night in high school all over again. Which, by the way, hadn't been a stellar experience for me.

At this initial gathering, we went around the table to share our blessing from the week, and most of the responses were something really lovely and spiritual, like the impact the pastor had on their hearts during the young adult service they all attended together, a service I had aged out of long before I even knew it existed. Which was fine, because from the sound of it, they did end that week's service in a spontaneous Christian musical dance party. *No thanks.*

I shared about a highlight in my week from my job. And so here I was, back where I had always started in the church—not singing and smiling and baking, but focusing on my secular career, "sinner." I had learned a long time ago that being a woman with a career in church seemed to raise eyebrows. "What do you mean you're too busy to bake ten dozen cookies this week for the bake sale?" "Does anybody have any prayer requests? Oh, I mean for others or for your health...not the promotion you're hoping for." "Do you realize every time you have a prayer request it's work related?"

None of these comments happened in this group. This was all internal dialog I had with myself while I judged the young people around me based on my past experiences. Beyond already feeling uncomfortable about being one of the oldest in the group, a thirty-year old among twenty-year olds, a difference you only really understand once you're thirty, it had also occurred to me that I had never shared my testimony out loud before. Heck, I didn't even think I had a testimony until this past July. On top of this, I didn't pray out loud. At all, like ever.

I was raised Baptist, and we just didn't do that in our church. I don't know if that's all Baptists or if it was just where I grew up. But we didn't ever pray out loud—not at church, not at the dinner table, not even at bedtime. Oh, and one more thing—I didn't know any scripture to quote. I mean, I knew it, but I didn't have it memorized. Bible trivia was always another great source of shame for me in Sunday school, always too slow compared to the other children whose mothers seemed to have all the time in the world to practice with them at home. My mom was "the working kind" with three kids at home, so her "priorities" were different.

Basically, when I finally left home at eighteen, I thought I had left behind all those people who judged me, who judged my family, my mother working full time, my past decisions about life and marriage, our inability to fit the mold they were looking for. Sure, I continued attending church. I even struggled to fit into a few throughout Wyoming by baking some of the prettiest dishes, volunteering to help with the children, and even by getting married, hoping for some sort of acceptance, but everywhere I went, I still saw the same kind of judgment.

Older women in the church would tell me stories about crying themselves to sleep for weeks when their husbands moved them from their home community to middle-of-nowhere-Wyoming for work, when they decided they would sell their homes and rebuild outside of town, when they gave up their careers as doctors and teachers to stay home with their children so their husbands could follow their dreams. The stories always ended with, "But I'm so grateful I was an obedient wife because I can see now that it was God's will." Was it, though? Or was it the equilibrium that you finally came around to once you stopped listening to your heart speak to you? I never really felt like I could have all of it—a career, education, and family—without feeling like I was either not being true to the church or not being true to myself.

So really, what was I even doing there? I didn't fit in with these young adults. I was divorced and hardened in my soul against the church, against being indulgent, against having any fun because I had to stay grounded, competent. Partly from living with Clay for so long, I had picked up many of his bad habits, believing that people who were goofy, fun, too loving or open, were a threat of some sort; that acting silly or having too much of a good time was frivolous and even somewhat beneath us. I wasn't about to stick a dozen marshmallows in my mouth to giggle "chubby bunnies," and so help me, I was not about to get into an interpretive dance contest to the song "Awesome God." My life's goal was not to find a man, sold-out for God or otherwise, and I really didn't know that abstinence before marriage was still a topic of discussion in 2019. Are they really still teaching this stuff to kids? And how in the world was I going to get through an entire week without inadvertently dropping an F-bomb?

The truth is, going on a mission trip had come up as a social media suggestion when I put my Thirty in Thirty list out for votes. That was it. Since I wasn't about to shame the idea of a mission trip in a public forum, I felt obligated to put it on the list, and then figured I would make an effort to volunteer at a homeless shelter during a deployment sometime. That way, I would be traveling and serving, *check*! Sounds like a mission trip to me!

I wasn't planning on a real, legitimate mission trip at all. It didn't sound like something I could fund while paying off the 4Runner in addition to the trip abroad. Not to mention the twenty-eight other accomplishments that were yet to be determined. And more than anything, I was obviously still pretty cynical in the God department when it came to relating with other Christians. I felt closer to God than I had ever been after He saved my life that night and had given me the wake-up call I needed. But I still felt judged and hurt enough by legalism and religion to last me a lifetime; I didn't need to pay to spend a week immersed in it.

Then something happened. It was Christmas morning and I was lying in bed scrolling through social media because, even though I was in Venice, I was depressed at waking up alone that morning without Clay and Hunter. I lay there and tried to distract myself from facing my day. And then, there it was: a social media post advertising a mission trip to Costa Rica through the church I had been attending since moving to Denver.

"Huh. Okay, well that's interesting. I mean, it is Costa Rica...but I have no idea how I'm going to pay for all this. I guess I'll apply for it, and if they don't pick me, at least I can say I tried." I took my leap of faith, knowing that if I was going, I was going to have to fundraise for the entire trip, another idea that had me reeling with uncertainty. A few weeks later, I interviewed for a spot on the team, and they picked me. Reluctantly, I was going to have to face all my cynicism about the church body, meeting new people, and relaxing and enjoying myself, areas where I had been burned in every possible way for the past decade. I didn't know if I could do it, if I would get through it, except for checking it off that damn list.

Sure enough, there were cheesy icebreaker games and sharing circles and long, journaling sessions with worship music playing, and piece by piece, these activities began to melt away a little at my heart each meeting. I still sat there though and wondered what street cred these kids could bring to the table.

We sat around planning how we would organize our women's ministry, and when someone offered that we should bring nail polish and paint the ladies' nails, I was floored. How could this be empowering? Were they kidding me? We negotiated our ideas, and I finally settled for painting nails while writing words of affirmation on small hand mirrors for them to carry around.

As the months went by, I wrapped my mind around my testimony. I had never felt like I had one before, but I wanted this to be my motivational speech, again, checking something off the list because otherwise, there was no way I was going to open up with that kind of vulnerability. But as I wrote it out and began sharing small pieces of it bit by bit with the group, I started to realize my story was going to truly change lives.

As hard as it was to think about sharing my testimony with perfect strangers, in a culture so different than mine, in a language other than my own, I kept honing it and perfected what I would say and how much I could share. But as I started to open up gradually throughout the months leading up to the trip, I ran into the same problem I had whenever I was forced to talk about what had happened to me with others. How was I going to share my story and still protect Clay? What could I say to make them understand that he was sick? How could I share with the church that I was divorced and truly with all my heart felt that it was the *right* thing to do? This trip was pushing me outside of my comfort zone in every possible way; even *planning* for this trip was making me uncomfortable.

Finally, the day came to leave for Costa Rica. There were many things I would come to learn I was so, very wrong about when feeling apprehension for this trip but I was right about some things, including all the singing and dancing, praying out loud and laying of hands. Our first night in the country, we were immediately immersed. The church put on a special service for us with joyful and loud singing and dancing. It was hard not to get caught up in the excitement and since the tunes were familiar, we all sang and danced along with the rest of the congregation, even though we didn't know any of the words in Spanish.

All day every day we were interacting with the church and members of the community and every time we met someone new there was a prayer, which always involved laying hands no matter how sweaty and humid we all felt gathered closely together. On top of that, everything we said was being translated, so it took twice as long to get it all said, making the pain of vulnerability drag out that much longer. And the forty-five-minute bus rides to and from the community we were working in were basically loud karaoke sessions every day. One day, there was even a spontaneous interpretive dance contest between several of the members of our group, right in the middle of our work project, which I opted not to participate in but did watch with a smile on my face.

What I *was* wrong about was how pretentious I had felt about all of this. After almost ten years of being a full-time working mother, living with all those skeletons in my closet and the homelessness, abuse, and shame I had survived just trying to reach my dreams, I was so snobby when I thought about relating with this team of young adults. Getting to know each of them that week, I learned that they understood so much more about life than I had when I was in my twenties and I was the one who had been missing out on experiencing the world.

Many of them already had established careers, but even then, they weren't taking life too seriously. They played in the church's sports ministry and knew all the bars down Denver's 16th street; they loved without any hesitation and sang and danced and had way more energy than I had had in years. On top of that, many of them also had very hard life experiences that they were recovering from.

Despite their trauma, they were living their best lives by embracing their youth and enjoying every day of it, and I came to realize that there had been an entire decade of my life I had missed out on. Not only had I not experienced my coming-of-age decade with the freedom and support that every one of these beautiful souls apparently had, but I realized how much I had missed myself and who I could have been in my twenties had I not been trying to make everyone else around me feel happy and comfortable.

That Wednesday, I shared my testimony with the five local women who showed up to hear about how worthy they were despite their own daily struggles to survive. We painted their nails, and I realized again my ignorance. These weren't women who knew anything about being pampered, all of them having lived much harder lives than I had. They were supporting their children and, often, their mothers, many of them with absent or abusive husbands and fathers. Survival was an everyday part of their lives, and nail polish didn't even come close to making the list when they were trying to keep their kids in school and food on the table. I felt ashamed, and blessed, to know yet again that there was an entire world out there where families are resilient despite odds that I couldn't even imagine, yet they love with their whole hearts and are gracious and giving in ways that are inconceivable to many.

That night, I led the group's ladies in a dance party, singing "All the Single Ladies" while we danced around the tiny outdoor kitchen in the humid Costa Rican night. And later that week, at our going away sermon, I danced my heart out to the worship music, jumping up and down to every song while sweat plastered my hair to my face and shoulders and my dress stuck to me in the heat. We even danced a conga line around the church with the members of the community with completely unabashed love and enjoyment for life, something I never thought I would feel again, and that I had even looked at for years as a weakness.

I went home after that week and went shopping. I donated all my old, boring clothes made for conservative and practical ranch life and bought colorful, stylish dresses and cute outfits I could explore Denver in, reclaiming a life of curiosity and enjoyment I thought I had lost out on. I *was* only thirty, and that meant I wasn't nearly as old as I felt. It meant I still had a lot of life to live and enjoy and I didn't need to carry the weight of everyone else's happiness and approval on my shoulders.

Thirty didn't have to be only a time of desperately searching to find myself. It could also be the year I reclaimed myself. It could be the year that I found my joy again and finally learned that letting my guard down and loving people didn't have to be dangerous; having fun didn't mean I was being irresponsible. I deserved this life and wanted to reclaim the years I had remaining after losing so many already.

That next year, I shared my testimony with thirteen women, and during one of our women's ministry sessions, we discovered a woman living in severe domestic violence. We leveraged our privilege as outsiders to find her support from local law enforcement, convincing them to escort her to a community where her partner couldn't get to her and where she could get help from a women's shelter. The year after this, over eighty women arrived at a dinner, served by their husbands and sons at the encouragement of our men's team, and I spoke to them about not allowing circumstances of domestic abuse and oppression to define them, sharing my almost three-year recovery story from surviving my own cycle-induced trauma.

24

Memories

As my year of firsts slowly dragged by, I was constantly reminded of our family's wonderful times in the short months before Clay's death. I tried so hard to avoid looking at the pictures, fearing the pain would be unbearable. But one night in my grief recovery group, we were encouraged to bring photos of our loved ones to share, and I suddenly found myself flooded with those memories.

A photo from the Fourth of July weekend, just two weeks before Clay's death.

A picture from a beautiful June weekend—Clay's last birthday. We'd spent it at my softball tournament, playing ball, watching games, and enjoying the weather.

Then, a photo of Hunter. He was standing in a lake, water up to his little thighs, fishing pole in hand. The sun was setting in front of him, casting blues and purples across the water. When I'd taken this photo on Memorial Day, almost exactly a year ago, I hadn't known it would become a keepsake from the last trip we ever took as a family.

I had just flown in from South Carolina, where I had met Brad for the first time in a training course for work. After ten years of dating one of the biggest cynics I had ever met, I was not one to look for romance at every turn. But when I looked across the classroom at Brad's bearded, rustic face and frequently caught his crinkled, blue eyes for a smile throughout the week, I had butterflies in my stomach.

We went out for drinks with some of the other classmates from the training on our last night in town. I tried to play aloof, wearing a casual T-shirt and ordering loaded nachos and beer to blend in as one of the guys. After the group scattered, he asked me to meet him at another bar for drinks, and we sat across from each other talking about our similar educational paths, our goals and dreams, and our experiences in our field of work. We had so much in common that I was apprehensive but excited to think that maybe I had finally met someone who I could share a life with, someone who would appreciate my work and dreams and not hold me back with cynicism and doubt.

When I landed in Denver, I would be meeting Clay and Hunter to go camping, but I was so elated that I almost texted my girlfriends to tell them I was sure I had just met someone I could be with forever. After having experienced so much hurt and disappointment from loved ones throughout my life, though, I hesitated, thinking maybe I should just wait and see what happened.

I feel guilty now for not feeling guilty about the camping trip that ensued. Clay and I were barely speaking since his stunt in April that led to his second DUI and that, in hindsight, was his first attempt at stopping my life path. I was frustrated that as badly as he wanted to be in a relationship with me, he was still drinking so often, and if he had never wanted to accept it before, he now had hard evidence of how extreme his drunken behavior was getting.

I had asked the week before to take Hunter camping, just the two of us, but Clay had had the same plans. Since we couldn't agree on who should get him for the weekend, we chose to camp together. It would be easier that way, and I wouldn't have to plan it and figure out how to supply and fuel up with all my work travel the week prior and following, and Clay was happier having me there with them for the weekend.

The photo of the three of us in the canoe is one of my favorites because for whatever reason, I was sitting in the front of the boat, with Hunter in the middle and Clay in the back, steering. I had a brave moment and pulled my phone out to take a quick selfie of the three of us looking up at the camera. I found it humorous that I was in the front because Clay was never a strong canoer and didn't have the experience to steer the boat. Growing up so near the Ozarks, navigating a canoe was something I had been doing most of my life.

Still, Clay would sit in the back, Hunter would wiggle and lean all over the place while they were fishing, rocking the canoe and stressing me out because they wouldn't stay centered and I couldn't see what was going on. More than once I would feel the boat precariously and sharply tipping from one side to the other depending on which way they were leaning and would have to snap at them to sit still, and yet we all had so much fun being on the water together that here we were, canoeing.

Later that night, we all stood on the shore fishing, and Clay had allowed me to borrow one of his new, better lures. Without paying attention to what I was doing, I cast my line right into the weeds, about twenty feet out from the shore, getting his brand-new lure stuck just under the water's surface. In true Clay form, he wasn't just annoyed, he was pissed at my carelessness and that he hadn't had the chance to even use the lure himself before I tossed it out into the lake, possibly losing it for good.

I was familiar with the different kinds of his anger, and this was the kind of mad that says, "I'll forgive you later, but are you freaking kidding me, man?!" I laughed and offered to take the canoe out to get it, but being the prideful man that he was, he needed to prove he could canoe the boat out and successfully rescue the lure himself.

I followed him down the bank to where the canoe was sitting inside a small grove of trees and brush, inconveniently placed but closer to the camper so we could keep an eye on it. Knowing by his storming footsteps that he was already terribly frustrated with me, I still spoke up and suggested we either carry the canoe back to where the water was more open, or that he let me navigate it out of the brush and get the lure. Without speaking but with a glare in response to my suggestion, he got into the very back of the canoe and began furiously paddling.

Hunter's fishing pole was still in the boat from earlier in the day, sticking up in the air out of its holder. Almost immediately, it got caught in the tree branch hanging out above the canoe and Clay, already off-center from having all his weight in the back of the canoe (instead of the middle), twisted quickly to try to save it. He dumped straight over, flipping the whole canoe in three feet of water. I snort-laughed at him but helped him gather all the bobbers, water bottles, and poles that were now floating around him in the lake while he struggled to get his balance and stand in the shallow water.

We flipped the canoe back over, and even more angry with embarrassment than he was before, he returned to the back of the canoe without speaking. This time, he tried an even more awkward and ineffective "kick-off" and used his foot to push off hard from shore, like you might a skateboard, but not a canoe. This only caused more abrupt movement and misbalance and sent him rolling back into the lake, canoe still upright, but with Clay toppling in the water where he had been only moments before.

He didn't even look up at me this time since I was already doubled over, tears rolling down my face in laughter. Cursing at the canoe, he returned yet again and shoved the paddle into the shallow water to push off, angrily hitting the sandbank below him, sticking the paddle abruptly and vertically in the mud, bringing the canoe to yet another sudden, jerky stop in the water. He tried this a couple of times before realizing the water wasn't deep enough to leverage his paddle and exasperated, broke down laughing at himself from how ridiculous he felt. Meanwhile, I stood on the shore wondering if I might pass out because I was laughing so hard I couldn't even inhale a decent breath.

Finally, with tears rolling down my face, and still choking on my laughter, I managed to squeak out a recommendation that he sit in the canoe's middle seat. Once he awkwardly scooted his way up, I waded out to give him a push so he could navigate out of the brush and around to where his lure was stuck, no longer worth the effort he had just gone through. I don't know that his shoes or his pride ever dried out for the rest of the trip.

* * *

These memories are so incredibly dear to me. This moment was one of the greatest and funniest moments in our relationship. At the same time, with the wisdom of hindsight, I can see how Clay's anger controlled him. This time, he'd been able to shake it off and see the humor in the whole situation. But that wasn't always the case.

Perhaps my fear of coming up on this one-year anniversary was more about being afraid that the further I get from the memories, the more they may fade. I can never repeat them, and I won't ever be able to get them back. I will never again be able to camp with Clay, play softball with him, or enjoy his breakfast cooking. Camping was one of our favorite things to do, yet the depression that plagued him the years after leaving law enforcement prevented him from having the desire. My immediate reaction to seeing these photos of our family and reliving these moments is regret that I couldn't have been happy enough, that these times could not have been enough for me to just "stick it out" and stay.

I see the photos of him happy and doing something he loved so dearly, and I wonder if he could have gotten better if I had accepted that life as enough. I have to remind myself that of course these photos are all happy. Nobody takes selfies when things are bad. The fights, the abuse and depression, the drinking—none of this made the cut for the photos.

When I look back, I see how happy we were, but the real memories that fade are the bad ones that didn't get recorded. Yet those are just as important for me to hang onto because they are my voice of reason when I want to take the blame for his death. They reassure me that the camping trip should not have kept me from speaking to Brad again or have led me to rethink my dreams and goals so I could better accommodate Clay and my role as a mother. I have to remember that I tried that and it wasn't enough.

For years, I did sacrifice who I wanted to be, who it was that I was supposed to be, and I was repaid with anger and fear. I was given anxiety and verbal abuse in return. I lived in fear and had to constantly question Clay's health, his motivations, and even his faithfulness to our marriage. Camping didn't make this truth go away, and he wasn't using the tools he had to support his own recovery. His addiction to alcohol had nothing to do with me and he was the only one with the power to overcome it.

Those great weekends together were not enough of a motivator for him to find a healthier way of living and to stop drinking. How could I have expected they would be enough for me to willingly live the rest of my life without my safety and happiness? I had already sacrificed so much to try to force his sobriety and keep him stable, but I couldn't.

If nothing else, that decade of my life taught me that no matter what choices I make for myself, I don't have control over others' responses or actions. The good memories mean so much to me. But for my own sanity and stability, I can't allow them to take the place of the truth. My truth was that I was a victim of domestic abuse and that Clay was an alcoholic. A thousand photos of good memories cannot make that truth worth living through again.

MEMORIES

* * *

Coming into my first summer without these moments to share would be harder to bear than going into the holidays all alone. Maybe it's because I was better mentally prepared for the winter months, knowing my first Christmas was going to be hard, so I had planned an elaborate distraction and was ready to face it. My first Memorial Day though, driving by Little League games and smelling my neighbors' grill light up; just the thought of it had me in such a depressed state that I sometimes lost function all over again. Unexpectedly, the warm weather triggered me more than anything had so far on this entire journey.

To get myself through Clay's birthday weekend, I flew my then seventeen-year-old nephew out to stay with me for several days. The previous year, Clay, Hunter and I had run a 5k on this weekend, our last 5k together, and I was wanting to repeat the activity but was lacking the motivation to face it alone. He ran with me despite the abrupt shift in elevation from his Kansas hometown. In turn, I took him to a barbecue festival and went hiking, visited Denver candy shops, ice cream shops and the best restaurants I had been to, everything to expose him to a world I had no idea existed when I was his age. I took him paddleboarding, something neither of us had ever tried before (*check!*), and then rock climbing at a local gym.

I was so proud that he had none of the fears and apprehension I remembered from when he was younger and that he was so willing to experience these new things unafraid. On Clay's birthday, we took orange, black, and yellow balloons to the top of a nearby mountain overlook and tied suicide prevention cards to them, letting them off in the direction of the city and hoping they might reach people who needed them. Then we sat there on the outlook and ate birthday cupcakes.

It was a weekend of healing and adventure for both of us. Looking at my nephew and admiring all his maturity and open-mindedness, his kind heart and humor, realizing what a truly good young man he was growing to be, I thought back on his life as I had known it from my angle. I had been so young when he and his sister had been born, yet I had often played the role of caretaker for the two of them. I helped them to hold bake sales to pay for swim lessons and attending school meetings as a teenager while their mother was out living a completely separate life from theirs.

The trauma he had seen—the abandonment of both parents, abuse from their partners, not knowing food security, sometimes living without running water and utilities in his home—these were hardships I hoped Hunter would never know. And yet, here Alec was standing in front of me, a strong young man who had every intention of overcoming his own trauma even though he was still learning the language and gaining the resources to do so. I knew then, with huge relief and reassurance, that Hunter could do this too. That Hunter would be okay.

* * *

On the anniversary of Clay's death, I took several days off work. I had been on a flooding event in South Dakota, so I drove back across the state, down through Wyoming and back home to Denver, picking up Axel on my way to Buena Vista, Colorado. Buena Vista is a mountain town tucked in a valley of about fifteen 14,000-foot mountains and sits along the vast Arkansas River. I had rented a small villa-style cottage along the river, and my plan was to hike up Mount Belford, across the saddle to the peak of Mount Oxford, covering my two 14'ers goal, and then come back down in time to jump in a raft to whitewater down Brown's Canyon. Completing these two extreme activities was going to be a celebration of life and survival and check two more items off my Thirty in Thirty list.

I had been told that Mount Belford would be a reasonable mountain hike and shouldn't be too difficult, and with my experience running mountain obstacle course races, I agreed it couldn't be all that bad to get up and back in time to enjoy the rest of my day. All the math worked out for why reaching two peaks in one morning should not be anything I hadn't already trained for.

So, at three o'clock in the morning, Axel and I quietly left our cabin, got into the car, and drove thirty minutes to the trailhead. Walking through the thickly wooded trail in complete pitch dark with only my headlamp to guide us was probably the scariest part of the trip. I knew there were other people on the trail—their cars were already in the lot when I had pulled up—but I couldn't shake the eerie feeling that there was probably at least one mountain animal of some sort watching me nervously make my way along the trail praying for daylight.

As I climbed, Axel bounced along with me, darting around in the wildflowers and splashing in the creeks. We had one somewhat sketchy "bridge" of aspen trunks piled atop each other over a rapidly moving river that not even Axel would be able to navigate should he fall. Fortunately, he was as nervous as I was and made it across the makeshift crossing cautiously, both of us crawling on all fours to maintain our balance.

We continued hiking, and all morning people quickly passed us by, heading easily up the mountain. I started to peak down my watch more regularly, calculating our time and realizing we may not make it to the top of even one, and especially not two, peaks before afternoon storms, and I started to panic. The one part of the equation that I had not calculated for was the mental drain of the trauma. Climbing a mountain on the one-year anniversary of losing Clay was not enough to distract me from my reality—that it was still the one-year anniversary of his death and my near murder. As quickly as I imagined I was moving up that mountain, my body still felt like it was dragging through molasses from the thoughts that bogged me down.

When I looked at my watch again and saw that I had met the original time for getting to the first peak but I had only reached 13,000 feet, I broke down. Or at least, I tried to. I bent over and put my hands on my knees to begin crying before realizing that it would demand far more oxygen than what I had available to have a good cry. There wasn't enough air to even take in that first big breath, and losing myself now would mean I may not even make it off the mountain, let alone get to the top. I straightened up right away and pulled myself together and put one foot in front of the other again, moving even slower now but still going in the right direction—up the mountain. Falling apart now was only going to make things much, much worse. I continued climbing.

When I did, finally, get to the top of Belford, I collapsed on its rocky top and just sat. I took in the scenery around me. I was amazed not only at what I had just accomplished but how amazing the view could be from so high in the air, looking over all the other mountain tops in the Collegiate Peaks.

After a few minutes of rest, I looked over across the saddle where I needed to go next if I was to reach Oxford. It looked much farther and more complicated than what I had originally expected, and if I tried to hit the other peak, there was no way I would make it back down for my rafting trip. Not only that, but after reaching one mountain top, my body and mind had had enough for a long, long while.

I convinced Axel to take some selfies with me before heading back down. No longer bouncy and energized, he refused to cooperate, I'm sure feeling betrayed that our fun hike had turned out to be so strenuous. In the past he was always so good at taking pictures with me but now he wouldn't even acknowledge me when I called his name. We argued the entire time down the mountain, descending far quicker than what my legs could support, my knees buckling and numb, but I worried that

I would be too short on time to drop him off at the cottage and rush to my next stop to make the raft in time.

He really couldn't have cared less about my rush and took plenty of time stopping to lie down and rest on the way back. Every time we stopped, my knees shook uncontrollably, as if they would give out any second. I'd call to him to please keep moving, and he would glare at me for having this very terrible idea in the first place. As we made it to the tree line, down the trail's many switchbacks and back across the sketchy tree bridge, this time crawling even slower across on my hands and knees because I couldn't trust my legs to hold me, I mused dryly about having put myself in such a potentially dangerous situation again, and on the anniversary of the first time I had to fight for my survival.

We made it back to the car, and after a very fast snack and water break, I sped into town to drop Axel off, and then back again to the outskirts to throw on a wetsuit and jump into a raft. I made it! I didn't get to the second peak, but I could (and did) knock that out another time. As our group took off down the river, I quickly realized the strength I would need to find in my legs to wedge myself against the side of the raft to keep from getting bounced out and into the rapids. For the love. I hadn't planned for this!

* * *

As my year of firsts came to an end, I let out a great sigh of relief. I knew that my recovery was still years away and that my journey was not going to be an easy one. But I had made it farther than I initially feared I might. And if I could make it through one year of firsts, I could make it through the second. Eventually, one day, these days would get easier; they wouldn't hurt so badly, and I would form new memories. New reunions and celebrations would become commonplace, and just like the old memories, the pain would eventually fade, if even just a little.

Most importantly, the more I kept moving forward with grace for myself and in a mindset of post-traumatic growth, the more I came to know myself. The more I could release trying to control the actions of others and began relying only on the value I found in my life, the more I found freedom and self-love. And the more I would learn who it was I was meant to be all along, the more I could stop feeling the need to live my life for anyone else. When the dark days come, as they still do, and I am brought back to feelings of guilt, shame, and grief, I can find light in the journey by reflecting on my love for myself and my choice to choose me, over and over again.

25

Letter to Hunter

July 12, 2019

Dear Hunter,

    I miss you more than I could ever tell you. My heart breaks on every birthday, every first day of school, every day I know I am missing you growing into the wonderful young man that you are. I can only pray that you have found someone in your life to give you love and guidance, an adult who can champion you in this hard life. I hope with all my heart that the good character and values you were raised with will stick with you through your adolescence and you'll come out of this the man that your daddy and I were trying to raise you to be.

    I tried to shelter you for so long from what was going on around you. Even when you reached out to me after you lost your daddy, I didn't want to tell you all the horrible details, about how he died and how your mother and grandmother were treating me and keeping us apart.

    I wanted you to be safe from all the trauma these adults surrounding you were perpetrating onto your life. I know now that it wasn't something I could ever shelter you from. At some point, you were always going to know there is evil in the world. At some point, you were going to feel disappointment and betrayal from people you loved. I debate whether I should have been *more straightforward with you about all the chaos that was surrounding us all those years as a family, but you were so young. I just wanted you to grow up well-adjusted and to feel loved.*

Here is the truth now, the one I could never protect you from or control, no matter how desperately I tried: your biological mom and your dad grew up in their own traumatic and dysfunctional childhoods. Then as adults, they made a series of decisions to maintain that trauma instead of taking action to heal from it. When they did that, they guaranteed they would be passing it down to you. To be fair, I don't know if they ever had the resources or education to understand their childhoods were as painful as they were or to know they had a choice about who they would be as adults.

This is why I am telling you the truth now, so you grow up knowing your childhood has been filled with trauma and adults who have hurt you. But you will also have a choice one day. You will one day be old enough to make your own decisions and to seek out your own resources and education, and you will know that you have the choice about who you want to be and who you want your children to know you as. It doesn't have to always be this way.

I won't pretend I didn't have a role to play in all this. I enabled your daddy by helping him hide his actions. I covered up for him, and I made every effort in the world to raise you so he never had to step up in his responsibility. I did the same thing for your mother, making excuses for her, always being there for you so she wouldn't have to make the sacrifices. I won't act like I didn't make mistakes; I had no idea what I was doing, trying to raise you. I was still an adult in your life, so I am not trying to make excuses, but you will see in your twenties that none of us have any business raising babies and dealing with that level of adulthood trauma when we are still practically children ourselves. I wanted to be the perfect mommy, and I didn't have any of the tools to be that for you. I am sorry.

The truth is, by trying so hard, I let all of society, including your dad and biological mom, put all the shame and mommy-guilt on me to make sure you were taken care of. They took full advantage of me to be the sole parent responsible for your childcare when I was working, getting you to and from school, helping with homework in the evenings, and making sure you were eating nutritious food and performing in your sports. Don't get me wrong, I loved every second of being your mommy, and I would give up everything I have to have raised you myself these past years. But the shame they put on me to be good enough, while at the same time holding me on a leash, leveraging their roles as your biological parents every time we wanted something that they didn't, it put such pressure on me that sometimes I thought I would break.

Even worse, though, was the guilt they put on me whenever I tried to follow my own dreams and take you and your dad with me. They would tell me I didn't care about you by suggesting we move to a new town, a different school, and when I tried to leave your daddy's abuse, they all blamed me for not loving you enough to stay. That was never the case, buddy. I swear to you, it was never about you. I just wanted to be able to make choices to overcome my own trauma and childhood. I never wanted to settle for who they said I should be, and if I could have taken you with me, I would have, and we would have chased those dreams together.

Hunter, your daddy loved you more than anything in the world. He was haunted by the fear that he would ever hurt you the way his dad hurt him, and he drank to hide that fear. He drank to hide a lot of things from himself, but alcohol only amplified his fears and his hurts. When he died, it was for so many reasons but never because he wanted to leave you behind. Yes, he was drinking that night because of his broken heart but also because he had growing debt from his drinking and driving convictions and his attorney fees. He was weighed down by his fear that he was going to have to leave you and go to rehab again, or even jail, and he would have failed to be there for you as the daddy he so desperately wanted to be.

I don't know if anyone else knew about his struggles besides Phil and me. But the truth is that your daddy was facing jail time or rehab for a very long time for his drinking. He had been on probation for his second DUI and couldn't stay sober enough to pass his regular check-ins. His basement had flooded the week before his death, leaving him overwhelmed and ashamed of himself for being too drunk to remember to turn off the water spicket. He was experiencing retaliation at work for reporting an injury when he finally thought he had found his identity and pride in his job again.

His life had been spiraling out of control, buddy. It didn't have anything to do with you or anything you did. It was all about the consequences of his own choices, and by this point, he had decades of trauma and alcoholism that had been chipping away at his brain, effecting his ability to manage all of the stress.

What you need to know though is that even then, your daddy never made a good decision for his life that did not have you at the center of it. He, too, was trying to shield you and give you a life that would be filled with love and support. He loved you the best way he knew how, having never had a father to show him how to love a son. But he went without so much to make sure you always had what you needed. He had one or two pairs of shoes that he wore until they were falling apart because he wanted every penny to go to making sure you had a warm home, nice clothes, and healthy food so that you could grow.

You likely don't remember the details of who he really was, being so young. What child thinks to commit their parent's every detail to memory? You expect them to be there until you're old enough to think about those things. I have done my best to think of everything I can and have written it all down so I can answer all your questions about who he was as a person, as your father. I have boxes of photos from your childhood for us to go through so you never have to forget those memories of him. I will tell you every story behind every picture so you never forget his love for you and what a good person he really was.

For now, though, I can tell you that his favorite ice cream was vanilla, with peanuts and chocolate sauce over the top. His favorite breakfast was biscuits and gravy, but he was forever making the best pancakes for us, flipping the huge cake high in the air from the pan and then plating it with a fried egg on top. He drank his coffee with two packets of Sweet n Low, although he'd drink it black whenever he camped or hunted, and he always left the empty packets out on the counter.

He loved listening to 80s rock, especially the Eagles, but Chris Ledoux was his favorite artist. He donated blood whenever he had the chance and didn't like after-dinner mints or chickpeas. He loved old sports movies, Major League, Rudy, Field of Dreams and Bull Durham. He loved a good John Wayne movie too and watched westerns but the classic sports were more his thing. I do have to say, I miss you guys always picking the movies that we watched.

Your daddy loved being in law enforcement. It was so important to him to be trusted by the community, and he worked hard to build relationships with everyone, and it showed. He had so many awards and successes in his work from informants, people from the community wanting to talk to him about their fears and concerns, leading to some major drug and multi-state theft arrests. He was really good at what he did, and the people he served were his reason for the job.

But his favorite part of his job was working with the kids. He loved being in the schools so much, teaching the rhymes for crossing the street safely, introducing young children to Daren the DARE Lion, and building relationships with the teens in his middle school and high school. He loved announcing at the high school basketball games, and he knew every athlete by name. He attended school dances and prom, priding himself when students would come to him for advice and guidance. This was where he found his identity and value more than anything beyond being your daddy.

I know you are going to struggle with wanting to be just like him, honoring his memory while balancing the confusion with his struggles. I don't tell you all these things so you can grow up to follow in his footsteps. I want you to be able to remember every detail about him so you know who he was and why you should love him with all your heart despite his challenges in life. In fact, you are probably going to be faced with decisions on what you want to take from both parents, who you want to be based on who you think they might want you to become.

I want to tell you right now, you don't owe either one of them your future. You have your entire life ahead of you. They made their decisions and as a result, they both did you a huge injustice—they let you down.

When they both had the opportunities as adults to be better people, better parents, to do the work to heal, they both chose not to. It will be so hard to work through knowing that they both loved you so much, but they still chose their own comfort over the sacrifice it would have taken to get sober, be a present parent, show up for you when you needed it, and give you to a stepmother who could have intentionally raised you and found you the resources to heal after losing so much. In all those ways, they chose themselves instead. If you decide to be nothing like them, you should never feel guilty about that. In the end, they don't deserve for their legacy to keep cycling, and you deserve to be healthier than what they ever chose to be.

The best thing you can do is have empathy for them. Because somebody hurt them very much when they were young. Somebody taught them to be humans who respond to conflict and trauma in these ways, to hurt themselves and others. And while they did play a role in their acceptance of this behavior as adults, overcoming trauma is still very hard, especially in the societies that they lived in. By having empathy and realizing these things, you can break the cycle and choose to respond to life in a way that is yours and is healthy. It will help you overcome the confusion, the frustration, and the anger you feel as you go out into the world and try to adjust as an adult. You don't have to let them shape and hurt you by their past anymore; you get to choose how you see yourself and how you treat others in the future.

When your daddy's trauma started, he was too young to know how to manage it, or why it was even happening to him. He didn't have the resources surrounding him like you do. I understand you are still young and maybe the answers are not so apparent now, but that is why I wrote this book. So you can see you have options and choices for who you want to be. I wanted you to see that being depressed and angry doesn't make you a bad person, but also that grief and pain do not make you weak. Sadness, empathy, and kindness do not make you "less of a man"; they make you human. Your actions to this point do not have to define who you will be for the rest of your life. It is the decisions you make every day that will be your identity, and only you can control that. You alone get to choose the mindset you're going to have about how you are going to live the rest of your life with this trauma. It's never too late to choose growth and to do the work.

Hunter, I love you. For exactly who you are today. I want you to know that you don't ever have to be anyone besides your true self to be loved and accepted by me. It is a lot to process, I know. I don't even know what they've told you about your daddy's death or my role in it, or why I haven't been around these past few years.

While you take what I have said and work through it, know this before you know anything else—there is nothing wrong with you. You didn't cause any of this to happen. You don't dislike school because you aren't smart; you are so smart. You struggle in school because of the lack of value your dad put on it from the time you were such a little age, wanting to check out instead of helping you with homework. You are good at sports; you struggle in them because your mom never wanted to take the time to get you there or sit through games. You will struggle in a lot of areas of your life because of the influence they have had on you, but know that there is nothing wrong with you; what happened to you is the problem.

It's never too late to make a difference in the world. You are still right on track to do that in whatever way you see for yourself. You have your whole life ahead of you to do good and to make things right for yourself and your future children. Don't choose the cycle of trauma.

People ask about you all the time. Not just family, though Grandma Donna and Grandpa Steve do miss you intensely. But friends and coworkers ask about you too. They offer recommendations for your gifts every year because they think about you over the holidays. They check in and ask if I have heard from you yet, if I know anything. When we see you again, it will be a great reunion, and we will celebrate being together again. Then we will open five and a half years of gifts and cards and letters from the people who love you and miss you. We're all here, buddy. We're praying for you and cheering for you, we're missing you and can't wait to see the man you've grown into.

Until then, hang in there. You're going to get through this, and you're going to change lives.

I love you, buddy. With all my heart.

Unconditionally,
Mom

Notes

GUNFIGHTS ARE LOST IN MILLISECONDS

1. "Domestic Violence Statistics," National Domestic Violence Hotline, July 4, 2023, https://www.thehotline.org/stakeholders/domestic-violence-statistics/.
2. Ruth W. Leemis et al., "The National Intimate Partner and Sexual Violence Survey: 2016/2017 Report on Sexual Violence," Centers for Disease Control and Prevention, 2022, https://www.cdc.gov/nisvs/documentation/nisvsReportonSexualViolence.pdf.
3. Jacquelyn C Campbell et al., "Risk Factors for Femicide in Abusive Relationships: Results from a Multisite Case Control Study," American journal of public health, July 2003, https://pmc.ncbi.nlm.nih.gov/articles/PMC1447915/.
4. "Murder-Suicide and the Role of Guns," Violence Policy Center, May 28, 2024, https://vpc.org/revealing-the-impacts-of-gun-violence/murder-suicide/.
5. Marty Langley and Terra Wiens, "American Roulette: Murder-Suicide in the United States," *Violence Policy Center: 8th Edition*, October 2023, https://doi.org/https://vpc.org/studies/amroul2023.pdf.
6. Jacquelyn C Campbell et al., "Risk Factors for Femicide in Abusive Relationships: Results from a Multisite Case Control Study," American journal of public health, July 2003, https://pmc.ncbi.nlm.nih.gov/articles/PMC1447915/.
7. Ruth W. Leemis et al., "The National Intimate Partner and Sexual Violence Survey: 2016/2017 Report on Sexual Violence," Centers for Disease Control and Prevention, 2022, https://www.cdc.gov/nisvs/documentation/nisvsReportonSexualViolence.pdf.

DEAR TRAUMA

8. "Left behind after Suicide," Harvard Health Publishing, May 29, 2019, https://www.health.harvard.edu/mind-and-mood/left-behind-after-suicide.
9. "1 in 10 Suicide Attempt Risk among Friends and Relatives of People Who Die by Suicide," UCL News, January 17, 2016, https://www.ucl.ac.uk/news/2016/jan/1-10-suicide-attempt-risk-among-friends-and-relatives-people-who-die-suicide.
10. Margaret Stroebe, Wolfgang Stroebe, and Georgios Abakoumkin, "The Broken

Heart: Suicidal Ideation in Bereavement," *American Journal of Psychiatry* 162, no. 11 (November 1, 2005): 2178–80, https://doi.org/10.1176/appi.ajp.162.11.2178.

11 Holly Wilcox, "Children Who Lose a Parent to Suicide More Likely to Die the Same Way," The JHU Gazette , May 2010, https://gazette.jhu.edu/2010/05/24/children-who-lose-a-parent-to-suicide-likely-to-die-the-same-way/.

LETTER TO COLONEL PRITT

12 John M. Violanti et al., "Life Expectancy in Police Officers: A Comparison with the U.S. General Population," *Int J Emerg Ment Health*, 2013, https://doi.org/15(4):217-228.

13 Dr. Brian Kinnaird, "Preparing for Life after Law Enforcement," Police1, April 2019, https://www.police1.com/police-jobs-and-careers/articles/life-after-law-enforcement-ntEr8LbJlObY3QAy/.

LETTER TO PASSERSBY

14 "What You Need to Know about Willpower: The Psychological Science of Self-Control," American Psychological Association, January 2012, https://www.apa.org/topics/personality/willpower.

LEARNING TO SNOWBOARD AND OTHER LIFE LESSONS

15 "10th Mountain Division (Li)," U.S. Army Fort Drum, accessed January 3, 2026, https://home.army.mil/drum/index.php/units-tenants/10th-mountain-division-li.

LETTER TO MY BEST FRIENDS

16 Donna Rose Addis and Daniel L. Schacter, "The Hippocampus and Imagining the Future: Where Do We Stand?," *Frontiers in Human Neuroscience* 5 (2012), https://doi.org/10.3389/fnhum.2011.00173.

17 Stephanie M. Gorka et al., "Alcohol Attenuates Amygdala–Frontal Connectivity during Processing Social Signals in Heavy Social Drinkers," *Psychopharmacology* 229, no. 1 (April 13, 2013): 141–54, https://doi.org/10.1007/s00213-013-3090-0.

www.ingramcontent.com/pod-product-compliance
Lightning Source LLC
LaVergne TN
LVHW041906070526
838199LV00051BA/2519